Restorer of the World

The Roman Emperor Aurelian

The Emperor Aurelian

RESTORER
OF THE
WORLD

THE ROMAN EMPEROR AURELIAN

by

John F White

The ancient Sibylline Books had predicted that Rome would last one thousand years. The millennial celebrations had already been held (AD 248) and the anxious population of the empire, shaken by civil wars and battered by the Gothic incursions, fearfully awaited the worst. Then the barbarians poured across the frontiers.

SPELLMOUNT
Staplehurst

British Library Cataloguing in Publication Data:
A catalogue record for this book is available
from the British Library

Copyright © John White 2005
Maps copyright © Spellmount Ltd 2005
Photographs copyright © John White 2005
Coin photographs copyright © British Museums 2005

ISBN 1-86227-250-6

First published in the UK in 2005 by
Spellmount Limited
The Village Centre
Staplehurst
Kent TN12 0BJ

Tel: 01580 893730
Fax: 01580 893731
E-mail: enquiries@spellmount.com
Website: www.spellmount.com

1 3 5 7 9 8 6 4 2

Typeset in Palatino by MATS, Southend-on-Sea, Essex
Printed in Great Britain by
T.J. International Ltd
Padstow, Cornwall

Contents

List of Maps

Acknowledgements

I acknowledge gratefully the following aid and assistance, and permissions to quote extracts from copyright work:

Janet Larkin at the British Museum for her aid in providing examples of Roman coins for physical examination, and also photographs of the same coins.
The staff at the Joint Libraries of the Greek and Roman Society in Malet Street, London, for all their help and knowledge.
Sheila Longley who energetically worked her way through a preview manuscript, despite the fact that she had far better things to do.
Dr St John Stephens for showing me his collection of slides of the eastern city of Palmyra, and granting permission to reproduce them.
The Trustees of the British Museum, for permission to reproduce the photographs of Roman coins.

John White
Wokingham
December 2004.

Aurelian Epitaph

The following illustrates what might have appeared on Aurelian's tombstone, had it been preserved to recent times. It would have been located outside modern Istanbul and provides a convenient summary of this book.

AVRELIANVS RESTITVTOR ORBIS

HERE LIE THE MORTAL REMAINS OF THE GOD LVCIVS
DOMITIVS AVRELIANVS.
EMPEROR AND GENERAL OF THE ROMANS FOR FIVE YEARS.
CONSVL THREE TIMES.
RESTORER OF THE ARMY. HE REASSERTED DISCIPLINE SO THAT
ONCE AGAIN IT RECOVERED ITS ANCIENT SPLENDOVR.
DESTROYER OF BARBARIANS. HE VANQVISHED THE ALAMANNI AND
IVTHVNGI HORDES FROM GERMANY, THE VANDALS ON THE
DANVBE, THE CARPI IN ROMANIA, AND CREATED A GENERATION-
LONG TRVCE WITH THE POWERFVL GOTHIC TRIBE.
HE REVNITED WITH ROME THE STRONG BREAKAWAY EMPIRES OF
GAVL IN THE WEST AND PALMYRA IN THE EAST.
HE CRVSHED OTHER REBELS.
MASTER OF THE PERSIANS. HE RESTORED PEACE WITH
THE PERSIAN EMPIRE.
CHIEF PRIEST OF THE RELIGION OF SOL INVICTVS, WHICH
HE MADE DOMINANT IN THE ROMAN DOMAIN. YET STILL
HE TOLERATED ALL OTHER RELIGIONS.
RESTORER OF PVBLIC MORALITY. HE WAS FAIR AND
INCORRVPTIBLE, AND ENSVRED THAT HIS OFFICIALS WERE TOO.
HE VENERATED ANCIENT TRADITIONS.
RESTORER OF THE ECONOMY. HE REVERSED THE RELENTLESS
DECLINE OF THE CVRRENCY WITH THE ISSVE OF MVCH SVPERIOR
NEW COINS OF GOLD AND SILVER.
RESTORER OF THE WORLD.

NEAR THIS SPOT, HE WAS MVRDERED THROVGH THE
TREACHERY OF HIS CLERK.
HE WAS ACCLAIMED A GOD BY DECREE OF THE SENATE.

Introduction

About the emperor Aurelian

Ask any well-informed layman in Britain to name a few Roman emperors, and most will respond immediately with Julius Caesar (who was not, in fact, an emperor but a dictator), Augustus, Nero and Constantine. With a little more reflection, and depending on how much of the marvellous television adaptation of Robert Graves' semi-fictional work 'I, Claudius' that they can recall, they might also be able to name Claudius, Caligula and Tiberius. A few might have heard of that remarkable administrator, the emperor Diocletian, while the names of Marcus Aurelius and his son Commodus will be familiar to those who have seen the popular film *Gladiator*.

Not one of these laymen will know the name of the emperor Aurelian (AD 270–275), not to be equated with the philosopher-emperor Marcus Aurelius. Yet if it had not been for the actions of this one man – often justly acclaimed by modern historians of ancient Rome as a 'superman' – the Roman empire would probably have split asunder by the end of the 3rd century AD, leaving a very different heritage from that which so shapes our lives today, the Christian-Roman European culture that has for so long held sway.

The ancient Roman author of the biography of Aurelian found in the 'Augustan Histories' has this to say:

> When we had come to the Temple of the Sun consecrated by the emperor Aurelian, he [the prefect of the city of Rome] asked me who had written up the life of that man. When I replied none was known by me in Latin, but some in Greek, the revered man poured out the anguish of his groan through these words:
> 'Therefore Thersites, Sinon and such other monsters of antiquity both we know well and posterity will speak about; shall the divine Aurelian, most illustrious emperor, most stern general, through whom the whole world is restored to the Roman name, not be known to our descendants? May God avert this madness!'

And so, he informs us, the Latin biographer began his work (for its value, see below), yet posterity does indeed remain generally ignorant of Aurelian's achievements as 'Restorer of the World' and his acclamation as a god. His accomplishment is at least the equal of Augustus, who created the Roman empire as we know it, for Aurelian had to stitch the empire back together after the disruptions caused by endemic civil wars and seemingly interminable and unstoppable invasions from outside the Roman frontiers by barbarians seeking loot.

Modern scholarship is scarcely more informative. Archaeology has re-discovered remarkably few inscriptions or other lasting monuments from Aurelian's time, providing little new evidence, and a quick count in the indices of the prestigious *Journal of Roman Studies* of the number of references to Aurelian from the journal's beginnings in 1910 to 2003 scarcely reaches double figures.[1]

How is it that Aurelian's achievements are so poorly recognised? The answer can be found most readily in the lack of proper historians during the middle of the 3rd century. The fame of Julius Caesar and Augustus rests on the contributions of several outstanding historians of the early Roman empire, men such as Plutarch, Suetonius and Tacitus, who lived during a tranquil age in the course of which they could consult imperial records. Marcus Aurelius, the great philosopher-emperor, and the sterner Septimius Severus enjoyed the attentions of the historian Cassius Dio early in the 3rd century. Again, the reputations of Diocletian and Constantine depend heavily on the laudatory, and sometimes not so laudatory, biographies by pagan and Christian authors during the settled period towards the end of the 4th century, after Aurelian had put every-thing back together. However, in the chaos of the mid-3rd century, few could be found to write down the chronicle of the climactic events occurring around them, records were destroyed or falsified and few monuments or other enduring objects were left to be uncovered by modern archaeology.

Reasons for writing

My own interest in early Roman history arose when I was taught Latin at school. Part of the course involved the study and comprehension of Roman culture and history, for which I was fortunate enough to have an enthusiastic teacher. It was while reading Gibbon's celebrated *Decline and Fall* that I became awe-struck by Aurelian's spectacular accomplishments, something which Gibbon himself seems rather to have taken for granted as though empire fixing was all in a day's work.

After that I sought eagerly for more up-to-date texts on Aurelian, but could find none at all in English and now only century-old essays in German (1903) and in French (1904). Part of the reason for this omission is certainly the shortage of material from which to make a full-size history, but part, I think, can be attributed to the interminable debates about the accuracy of the sources that probably render any serious scholars reluctant to stick their necks out and say 'Here is Aurelian'. Two modern texts, Cizek's *L'Empereur Aurélien et son Temps* and Watson's *Aurelian and the Third Century*,[2] have sought to fill the gap with closely-argued critiques of the recent academic literature for classical scholars already familiar with the background, but there remains no readable popular account suitable for the layman who would wish to know more about the period.

This book is intended as a guide to some of history's most critical turning points, and it is derivative in the sense that I have not been out into the field to dig up any new artefacts. This book is based on the ancient literature, published academic papers, and published reviews and books summarising coins, papyri and inscriptions. I have spent many happy hours carrying out my own research in the library of the Society for the Promotion of Roman Studies based at the Senate House in Malet Street, London, and I wish to record my gratitude to the friendly and helpful staff there who gave me so much assistance. Modern scholars will look in vain for new facts about the mid-3rd century, but I hope they may yet discover some new insights from an account written from a fresh perspective. I have been careful to use the best-agreed modern dates for the events of the period, but have not hesitated to put my own interpretation upon them.

The literary sources

The only literary sources that survive, and which also cover the period in which we are interested, may be conveniently divided into two: the Latin and the Greek writers. Unfortunately, these are frequently in conflict, although the evidence of coins, inscriptions and archaeology has often enabled us to resolve some of the discrepancies. There are also contemporary Persian writers, whose accuracy concerning Roman events is very poor.

It is noticeable in any library that deals in ancient Rome that there are today many more commentaries about the surviving ancient histories than there are histories themselves. The harsh reality is that virtually no new discoveries of hidden ancient literature can be made, while by contrast the number of classical scholars keeps increasing. The interminable scholarly game of 'What did the writer really mean?' has indeed uncovered or highlighted some incongruities, but it has also led to the propagation of many theories about Roman history that can, most charitably, be said to be unlikely – I nearly said bizarre. Unlike many modern historians, I do not hold that those who live some 1,750 years after the events they describe must necessarily know more than those writing 50–100 years after the same events; quite the reverse. The ancient writers naturally assumed that their readers shared a common stock of culture and of knowledge, so that many details could be left unsaid. Hearsay alone would give the early historians an insight into the background of those whose lives they described and we cannot guess how many key elements colouring judgements – obvious to the writer and his audience – may be completely unknown to us today.

In ancient times the purpose of history was widely held to be to instruct, rather than to be strictly accurate, and therefore the modern obsession with trivial details would have been beyond the early writers' instincts or grasp. They shamelessly plagiarised each other's work and had no inhibitions about annotating or editing existing histories. The difficulty of mass production of written works also added to the problems, for the printing press would not be invented for more than another 1,000 years. Copies made by hand are likely to introduce anonymous errors, and therefore later scribes would insert corrections as they made their own copies. Thus it occurs that the original text may be 'corrected' with a false amendment, and the text loses its original accuracy. Those copies of the Latin and Greek historians that survived until the Renaissance, when most were printed and re-printed, had been copied by hand again and again, with all the scope for error and editorial 'improvement' that is implied. With this understanding, let us examine the surviving texts.

The principal Latin writers covering our period are Aurelius Victor (*De Caesaribus*), the anonymous epitomator who created a separate work also known as *De Caesaribus*, Eutropius (*Breviarium*) and the 'Augustan Histories' (*Scriptores Historiae Augustae*). An epitome is an abbreviated form of the original with annotations added, created by a copyist.

Victor's work was written by a provincial governor in 360. It covers all the emperors from Augustus to Constantius II in a fairly condensed manner, and adopts a highly moral tone. Unfortunately, there is a large gap in surviving manuscripts omitting a significant part of Aurelian's life. The epitomator who wrote *De Caesaribus* describes the period from Augustus to Theodosius (end 4th century). The *Breviarium* of Eutropius was written very close to 369 at the request of the emperor Valens, as a short, summarised history for the emperor himself and for others in the eastern half of the Roman empire who lacked knowledge, but not curiosity, about Rome's background. It was intended to be short, and covers the period from the foundation of Rome to the emperor Jovian (363–364) in only some seventy pages of modern typescript, but was evidently still too lengthy for Valens, who commissioned an even shorter summary from the historian Festus of which only the second half survives. Eutropius, who was a high-ranking civilian and would later become proconsul of Roman Asia, had a hidden agenda: he seems to have been pressing for a Roman attack on Persia and biases his history favourably towards previous exploits in that direction – perhaps at the instigation of the emperor himself. The *Breviarium* has proved to be an exceedingly popular introduction to the Roman era ever since it was first published. It was copied early into Greek, while the Latin version served as a text book for schools during many hundreds of years, well into the 19th century.

German scholars who examined the original texts, or rather – let us be clear about this – the earliest texts still surviving, which had themselves been copied many times and perhaps edited away from the originals, noted that the histories of Victor and Eutropius shared many details, as well as many errors. Those parts of the histories that covered common ground, i.e. from the first emperors onwards, contained little information that was unique to either history. Enmann proposed in 1883 that both Victor and Eutropius had relied for information on a common source, now lost, that he named *Kaisergeschichte* (*History of Emperors*). Internal evidence suggests that the *Kaisergeschichte* may have covered the years from about 30 BC to AD 357 and appears to have comprised little more than names of emperors, their place and date of accession, and their principal achievements; probably it also contained many errors.

The contention that the *Kaisergeschichte* provided the primary source to Victor and to Eutropius, at any rate for the later Roman emperors, has been disputed, but seems at least reasonable and now represents the majority view among modern historians. If one theorises further that the *Kaisergeschichte* is just a fancy name for a short list of written facts and speculations about the emperors that was widely available to the well-educated in the 4th century, then there can be little room for dissent. Multiple copying and recopying of the list by scribes or slaves is certain to have introduced errors of transcription that would slowly multiply with each fresh copy.

The *Kaisergeschichte* may have been the only extant source of information in Latin for the period of the mid-3rd century to a historian writing in the 4th century. Victor and Eutropius (according to the modern hypothesis) then mined it for basic information to which Victor added other recollections – and a great deal of moralising – while Eutropius, whose needs were simpler, did little more than summarise the *Kaisergeschichte* so thoroughly that the original source fell out of use and thus failed to survive to modern times.

Much more curious are the series of short biographies of emperors known collectively as the 'Augustan Histories'. The entries purport to have been written by six authors during the period 285–335, allegedly at the request of the emperors Diocletian and Constantine, or of other eminent Romans. The authors of the period that concerns this book are 'Trebellius Pollio' (The Two Gallieni, Thirty Tyrants, Claudius) and 'Flavius Vopiscus of Syracuse' (Aurelian, Tacitus, Probus, Four Tyrants, Carus and sons). Vopiscus informs us that, for Aurelian, he made use of 'the written journals of that hero' and also of 'his wars arranged as a history'. He admits openly that his work may contain errors. The biography of Aurelian is the second longest in the entire 'Augustan Histories'.

It was recognised long ago – by the great Edward Gibbon, among others – that the 'Augustan Histories' contain many peculiarities. In discussing these below, let us remind ourselves of one key feature: *all* the extant texts derive ultimately from just one 9th-century codex (parchment arranged as a book), which appears to be incomplete. Thus all subsequent commentators are at the mercy of this truth: we have no way of knowing the extent of tampering with the original text. It is entirely possible that an editor has been at work in the five to six centuries that preceded the version that survives. In this context, we must note that a medieval scholar definitely *did* tamper with the 'Editio Princeps' of the 'Augustan Histories', which had been re-discovered by the Renaissance in 1475, by adding interpolations. We can be sure of this, since the original edition remains intact.

The first major problem with the text is the remarkable fact that it attempts to cover every emperor from Hadrian up to, but not including, Diocletian. Yet the six authors have not overlapped at all; no emperor is covered by more than one biography. It is puzzling to note that the text jumps straight into the life of Hadrian without any preamble, and it is believed that an introduction and the biographies of two preceding emperors, Nerva and Trajan, may have been lost. There are other gaps apparent in the text too.

The second problem lies with the use of anachronistic terms. For example, some military titles are employed before, so far as we know, they had been invented. The authors of the 'Augustan Histories' claim to have consulted the Ulpian Library at Rome for sources and copies of letters, but many of the examples again contain anachronisms. Thus, in one letter an emperor addresses a Persian king who had yet to ascend the throne. Another difficulty lies with the appallingly sloppy nature of the histories. The accounts jump backwards and forwards between events within each biography without there having been any subsequent attempt at tidying or revision to make the narrative coherent. Some passages in the biographies bear a striking similarity to those found in Victor and Eutropius when describing the same emperor. The overall effect is of an absent-minded lecturer dictating notes and, indeed, at one point the author confides to the reader that he *is* dictating to his secretary.

In the case of Aurelian, the narrative proceeds uniformly from the birth to the death and achievements of the emperor – and then starts all over again, as though the narrator has just discovered a major new source of information and has tacked it in the form of notes onto the end of the existing biography without any attempt at combining the two sections.

The second section bears many similarities to information also found in Victor and Eutropius, and implies a common source – perhaps added at a much later date, but by whom?

Taken individually, these problems do not add up to very much. Do the biographies not overlap? Perhaps the authors were commissioned to write different sections. Trouble with anachronisms? A later editor took a hand. I can remember how baffled I was to read, as a child, a fictional story *Biggles Flies Again* that had supposedly been written in 1932, but in which a central character describes shooting down a German 'Heinkel' aircraft over France. Heinkel became a famous aircraft manufacturer during the Second World War (1939–1945) and could not have been relevant for the First World War. The explanation, I learned many years later, was that the original version had accurately stated a 'Rumpler' biplane, but a later editor had gratuitously updated the aircraft type for the edition published in the 1950s. Do the 'Augustan Histories' contain close similarities to Victor/Eutropius, and share the same errors? They must have copied the Histories, or the latter copied an early version of the *Kaisergeschichte* while Victor and Eutropius copied the later, extended version. Another explanation might be that an editor patched gaps in the 'Augustan Histories' with sections taken from the later works.

All these difficulties, then, can be explained, but coincidence gets stretched further with every added explanation. In 1889 the German historian Dessau produced the startling hypothesis that *all* the biographies in the 'Augustan Histories' were written by just one author, and that he wrote near the end of the 4th century, not the beginning. Another German scholar postulated, by comparison of grammatical and literary styles, that nearly all the documents and letters quoted in the 'Augustan Histories' were written by the same original hand, and that these common documents were all fabricated. Further evidence of this was provided by a computer study in 1979, which demonstrated that sentence lengths in all the biographies of the 'Augustan History' were very similar, but unlike those of control Latin texts.

This controversy has raged for over a century now, and only future discoveries will resolve the problem definitively. It would certainly be desirable to find another manuscript of the 'Augustan Histories' that predates (say) the 7th century. We may note in passing that to check the authorship of ancient documents by analysis of style is a dangerous game, and the computer study mentioned above has been criticised on technical grounds. Recently one sceptic subjected the publications of one of the computer-critics of the authorship of certain letters to a similar analysis, and deduced that the critic had written only half of his own research papers! However, most modern historians accept the basic tenet of Dessau's thesis: the 'Augustan Histories' were written by one author, later than generally supposed, and fictional documents were used to augment the text. We can never know why the Histories were so written. One might guess that a bored aristocrat wrote, or dictated, a Roman history for the amusement of his friends. A common view is that the Histories were actually written as a joke, or hoax.[3]

There remain some sceptics of the concept of one author for the 'Augustan Histories'. As I have described above, it is possible to assign all of its inconsistencies to later editing and to the use of defective sources, such as the Kaisergeschichte, for the period that concerns this work. As already related, the ancient writers were more concerned to draw the correct moral judgements from history than to worry about its accuracy. The fictitious documents within the 'Augustan Histories' would be simply a device to convey a sentiment. There was already a well-established practice of quoting for posterity a general's exhortation to his troops before a battle, although no one could possibly have recorded the speech at the time.

In the light of this information, of what value are the 'Augustan Histories' to a modern writer? Some say that nothing in the Histories should be regarded as true, unless confirmed by other sources, but I beg to differ. My view is that an amateur Roman historian took the most convenient contemporary sources, which varied from emperor to emperor but for the period covered in this book appears to have been the Kaisergeschichte, and provided a lot of colourful gossip or hearsay to fill out the accounts. Others have observed that the author(s) of the Histories has/have attempted to emulate the similar style of that well-known gossipmonger Suetonius. Given these constraints, the 'Augustan Histories' may well be as accurate as contemporary memory permitted. Any other form of history would have invited ridicule, rather than laughter, from the author's readers or listeners, since public readings were common in Roman times.

If the 'Augustan Histories' really were written at the time they profess (285–335), then the events described within the biographies that concern this book would have occurred well within the living memories of the authors' contemporaries. Classical scholars today are not accustomed to interviewing eye-witnesses, and therefore can have no concept of how unreliable the memory of such witnesses can be. I found this out the hard way, trying to rationalise the accounts of several U-boat survivors, interviewed fifty years after the events, for a study on U-tankers. It is not the case that the accounts were intended to deceive, simply that the passage of time distorts the human memory, particularly if the witness has an idée fixe about some particular event. Many modern historians will not accept the validity of eye-witness accounts at all, if they were written down decades after the events they purport to describe. The defects of the biography of the emperor Aurelian could easily be explained away by a combination of reliance on one or two master sources, themselves perhaps unreliable, a handful of documents of doubtful provenance such as official Roman government propaganda, and the testimony of defective eye-witnesses. There is a lamentable modern tendency to write 'history' by assembling the recollections of a bunch of senile old men and then publishing them without any documentary checks whatsoever. The result is very similar to that provided by the 'Augustan Histories'.

If a later date is accepted for authorship, the same events would be as remote to the author as Queen Victoria is to us. Sayings about Queen Victoria are still widely circulated even if their precise accuracy may be questioned. Her phrase 'We are not amused' is a well-known example. If there were no proper history of the Victorian age in the 19th century, I could write a modern history of Queen Victoria through use of a children's history book for key dates and by dredging my memory, and that of my neighbours, for other information. The result would be very much like the 'Augustan Histories'; a lazy, but honest, history where important events were muddled, anachronistic titles were used, but the substance of the work would be correct. The cultural and technological background would be pretty accurate. It is true that I would not cite fictional documents, but then I would not quote imaginary speeches to her generals either; my cultural heritage is different from that of the Romans. And certainly I would not make the error of having Victoria address her Viceroy of India by e-mail.

To illustrate my point further, I have no idea whether the title 'Viceroy of India' that I cited above was known in the mid 19th century, although certainly it was in the 20th century. Yet I am quite sure that Victoria was Empress of India – the title appeared on coins that survived into my pocket in the 1950s – and that she described India as her 'Jewel in the Crown'. Thus my previous paragraph may have contained an anachronism, and I have quoted her description of India from a modern work of fiction, but the substance is all correct. It is in this context that I have felt able to trawl the 'Augustan Histories' for biographical information. The biographies contain many valuable details that simply are not available elsewhere, and I believe that their substance is also correct. At least this view enables me to avoid the common scholarly trap: first of declaring the 'Augustan Histories' to be worthless, and then of quoting extensively from them whenever their argument supports the scholar's pet hypothesis, or when he has a book chapter that needs filling.

It is likely that the *Kaisergeschichte* was strongly pro-senatorial in its tone, and the emperors were judged by their attitude towards the Roman Senate. In consequence, or perhaps as independent judgements, all three of the major Latin writers, Victor, Eutropius and the 'Augustan Histories', show similar partiality. The emperor Gallienus (253–268) is particularly harshly criticised by all. He presided over the near disintegration of the Roman empire, although it is unlikely that the blame was his even in part.

The 'Chronicler of 354' created an illustrated calendar, listing the pagan holidays including those 'good' emperors whose birthdays were still celebrated, the zodiac, consuls, urban prefects of Rome, Christian bishops and martyrs. Appended are a tourist map of contemporary Rome, a world history starting with Adam and a chronicle of the city of Rome. The original calendar, which was evidently given to a well-off Roman Christian, disappeared in medieval times, but fragments of several copies survive, enabling cross-checking for accuracy. The list of consuls starts in the time of the Roman kings and continues to the year AD 354; it is the most complete tabulation known. The city chronicle provides a chronological list of all the rulers of Rome, again starting with the kings, together with the length of their rule and any noteworthy events that occurred during their reign. The source of the information remains in dispute, and does not appear to be related to the *Kaisergeschichte*, which reinforces the idea that there may have been several contemporary lists of events in circulation with differing degrees of accuracy. Other Roman calendars have survived in very fragmentary form, but that of Polemius Silvius (449) is complete.

The principal Greek sources are Zosimus, who wrote early in the 5th century, Syncellus and Zonaras, two Byzantine historians who provided additional information, apparently from sources now lost, in the 9th and 12th centuries long after the events they describe. Syncellus compiled an annotated catalogue of history up to his time; for our period he relied heavily on Eusebius (see below). Zonaras compiled a world history. All three Greek writers offer a considerable check, in both senses, on the Latin writers, since they provide both independent confirmation of events and sometimes ameliorate the reputations of emperors, such as Gallienus, who showed less enthusiasm for the Senate.

There exist a few other literary sources covering our period. The Greek historian Dexippus wrote two outstanding eye-witness accounts (*Scythia* and *Chronicle*) of the wars against the Goths in the middle of the 3rd century, but only fragments survive. Zosimus and the authors of the 'Augustan Histories' appear to have used it. Similarly, the early 5th-century Greek author Eunapius has also been plundered by Zosimus; again, little of the original work survives but it is believed to have been a continuation of the history of Dexippus and covers the period 270–404. Petrus Patricius and the 'Anonymous Continuator of Dio Cassius' are also fragmentary offerings that once described the emperors from Augustus to Constantius II (361). Some believe that the last two authors are one and the same. The loss of all these histories is particularly frustrating, since the surviving fragments indicate that they were of much detail and high reliability.

The 'Panegyrici Latini' – laudatory speeches made to assorted 4th-century emperors – contain brief references to our period. Cassiodorus was a 6th-century Italian who wrote a highly coloured account of Gothic history for his Gothic masters; little survives, but Jordanes summarised his story and created a Roman history a few years later. Ammianus Marcellinus, the outstanding historian of the late 4th century, makes passing mention of some of the events of the preceding century. The 4th-century pagan ruler Julian, one of the most prolific of the emperors, has left a few references to Aurelian in his surviving material. The emperor Justinian in the 6th century authorised the creation of a huge summary of all existing Roman Law, including pronouncements by previous emperors that were still current. A handful of Aurelian's edicts have survived into Justinian's Codex.

There are also brief mentions of the 3rd-century emperors by the early Christian authors, such as Lactantius, who was a near-contemporary of Aurelian and prepared early in the 4th century his chronicle *On the Deaths of the Persecutors*, and Eusebius, who composed the *Church History* during the 4th century. Jerome, also known as Hieronymus (a Latin version of the lost *Chronicle* of Eusebius) and Orosius (*History against the Pagans*) wrote in the 5th century, and Orosius' work would later be translated into Anglo-Saxon on the orders of King Alfred, whence it became the standard medieval textbook on world history. The accounts are generally slanted by the emperor's treatment of the Christians. However, the early Church was particularly concerned with accuracy in all its sources – anything less might have been construed as blasphemy – and was also one of the chief instigators of the best methods for preserving and re-copying ancient texts. Thus the Christian writers are exceptionally reliable, in the sense that they were writing honestly, even if they are not always the most accurate. Eusebius makes it clear that he is often quoting from official records. Further, it was the early Church that first popularised the binding of parchment together to make the 'codex', a book-like collection of parchments which would better withstand heavy use than the older scroll. The Byzantine Malalas wrote a world history in Greek from the Creation that is so unreliable that I have not used it. Malalas has not attracted the same degree of censure as the better-informed 'Augustan Histories', probably because he is assumed to have been as honest as the other Christian writers.

The literary deficiencies of the middle of the 3rd century have to some extent been made good by the continuing discoveries of coins,[4] inscriptions and monuments,[5] and papyri,[6] although the supply is inevitably slow and unpredictable. The extent of monumentary evidence concerning Aurelian is depressingly small. There is no known statue, so that we know his appearance only from his coins, and the number of unique surviving inscriptions is probably little more than 100; the 19th-century compilers of Latin inscriptions scatter only a handful relating to Aurelian through their voluminous archives, while more recent dis-coveries bring the total to eighty-two unique inscriptions in the Frankfurt

University electronic database. There appear to be no Greek inscriptions from Greece[7] (a handful are known from elsewhere), while only a few papyri survive that mention Aurelian. However, the turbulence and uncertainty of the times ensured that coin hoards, where the owners buried their coins in the ground for safety, were abundant. Unfortunately, the debasement of the same coins by the issuing mint has the result that most of the detail has often seriously deteriorated by the time the hoard is excavated in modern times. Inscriptions sometimes supply dates, although never in the modern BC/AD style that had yet to be invented.

Most of our knowledge from papyri comes from excavations at Oxyrhynchus, a region in Egypt five days' journey to the south of Alexandria, so that delays might occur in reporting events. The records are frequently dated, always according to the Egyptian system where a year runs from 28 August, rather than the Latin system where the year starts on 1 January. The extent of literacy within the Roman world is one of the most remarkable features attested by the papyri, and confirmed by the number of graffiti found in the ruins of Pompeii. It is evident that official meetings and legal matters were minuted, and that government proclamations were widely distributed in the form of hand-written copies.

The records of history were everywhere for the Romans. It is, perhaps, worth emphasising here how reliable Roman historians are in general. Modern archaeology may sometimes amend the details of what we read in the ancient texts, but it is unusual indeed to have to make substantial changes to the historical record on the basis of recent discoveries. This observation may be applied, in particular, to the 'Augustan Histories', despite their supposed fictional nature. For example, my 1932 edition of these histories has a footnote that three of six titles allegedly claimed by Aurelian, including 'Sarmaticus Maximus', had not been verified. Yet Sarmaticus Maximus has been found on one inscription, although its authenticity has been disputed. To take another example, the government position entitled 'Corrector', which was once thought to be an anachronism in the 'Augustan Histories', is now known from new inscriptions to have been extant when the Histories cite it.

Finally, no mention of classical Roman history would be complete without an acknowledgement of Gibbon's masterly *The Decline and Fall of the Roman Empire*,[8] published in several volumes of which the first appeared in 1776. Gibbon was the earliest historian to provide a complete account in English of the later part of the Roman empire using all available sources in Latin, Greek, French, German, Arabic and Syrian, including many re-discovered during the Renaissance two to three centuries previously. He produced his narrative with such total command of his native language that the *Decline and Fall* was recognised within his lifetime as a classic, not only of history but also of literature, a position that it has never forfeited. Further, although inevitably later discoveries have rendered some of his historical details inaccurate, the broad sweep of his story remains substantially correct. Only his treatment, as a self-confessed non-believer, of the rise of Christianity, and his unenthusiastic account of Rome's successor, the Byzantine Empire, is criticised today. Gibbon's *Decline and Fall* continues to be arguably the single most readable narrative of later Roman history for the layman today.

Translations

All the translations from Latin into English for quotations were made by the author. Translations from Greek are attributed in footnotes for each chapter.

Dates

All dates mentioned here and in the main text are AD unless otherwise specified.

Nomenclature

It is easy to use modern names for geographical features, such as countries, rivers and mountains, which will have altered little over the centuries, but the naming of Roman towns presents a problem. Some have disappeared in the last 2,000 years, and have no modern equivalent. I have followed convention in generally naming Roman provinces, cities and towns with their original Latin names, with the modern name added in brackets where appropriate.[9] The names of emperors also follow conventional usage, for example 'Aurelian' and not 'Aurelianus', 'Caracalla' and not 'Caracallus' or 'Bassianus' or 'Marcus Aurelius Antoninus'.

NOTES

This book is intended to popularise the emperor Aurelian for a non-academic readership. Therefore we do not feel it necessary to provide a long list of references in the notes for each event in the narrative. References are instead limited generally to 'further reading' for the interested reader, particularly sources available in English translation. Some sources are available only in their original language (especially Latin), and these will be indicated. A few citations to the modern academic literature have been provided where the text refers to an extraordinary event directly concerning Aurelian.

1   *Journal of Roman Studies* (1910–2003). All indexed references found in the *JRS* to Aurelian or Palmyra or the wall round Rome.
2   (i) Watson, A, *Aurelian and the Third Century* (Routledge, 1999) provides a long overdue survey of the 20th-century academic literature concerning

Aurelian, for those already familiar with the background; (ii) Cizek, E, *L'Empereur Aurélian et son Temps* (Les Belles Lettres, 1994) fulfils much the same requirement for French speakers; (iii) Kienast, D, *Römische Kaiser – Tabelle* (Wissenchaftliche Buchgesellschaft, 1992) offers a modern German view of the 3rd-century emperors, as well as those of other periods. Interestingly, the consensus among French, German and Swiss writers regarding disputed texts often differs from the Anglo-Saxon view.

3 Syme, R, *Emperors and Biography* (Oxford University Press, 1971). The peculiarities of the 'Augustan Histories' (*Scriptores Historiae Augustae*) have been widely discussed since before Gibbon's time, and there is even a bi-annual colloquium now dedicated to the subject. The most comprehensive single account of the 'Histories' and the modern academic viewpoint can be found in Syme.

4 Pictures of Roman coins are available on the Internet, e.g. the 'Virtual Catalog of Roman Coins': http://vcrc.austincollege.edu. Coin dealers also provide many excellent pictures with a narrative.

5 For inscriptions, (i) the huge volumes of the 19th-century 'Corpus Inscriptionum Latinarum (CIL; Prussian Academy). Several attempts have been made to update these volumes with more recently discovered inscriptions, but today the emphasis is on making the inscriptions available electronically; (ii) 'Epigraphische Datenbank Heidelberg': www.uni-heidelberg.de/institute/sonst/adw/edh/; 'Frankfurt Latin inscriptions': www.rz.uni-frankfurt.de/~clauss/index-e.html.

6 Rea, J P (ed.), *The Oxyrhynchus Papyri*, for the papyri discovered at Oxyrhynchus in Egypt published in the volumes of the periodical.

7 The general absence of Greek inscriptions concerning Aurelian can be discerned from the indices of the 'Inscriptiones Graecae', which mention several other Roman emperors. However, at least three genuine Greek inscriptions are known, e.g. CIG II:2349n, AE 1927:81.

8 Gibbon, E, *The Decline and Fall of the Roman Empire*, Vols I–III (Everyman's Library, 1910; 1980 reprint). Gibbon's famous work has been justly admired, discussed and criticised since it was first published towards the end of the 18th century.

9 (i) Smith, W (ed.), *Dictionary of Greek and Roman Geography*, Vols I & II, John Murray, 1854; (ii) Talbert, R J A (ed.), *Barrington Atlas of the Greek and Roman World* (Princeton University Press, 2000).

CHAPTER I
The Roman Republic

Early Rome[1]

A principal feature of the fertile soils that surround the Mediterranean Sea is that they are strips of land separated on the one side by the ocean and on the other by high land or marshes. This happy circumstance forces peoples to live in close proximity, while the temperate climate allows the inhabitants to farm well and to mingle freely during most of the year. Conversation is easy, societies are readily constructed, famine is not a constant worry and ideas are rapidly disseminated. The benefit of the invention of the wheel is greatly enhanced if there are neighbours to use it, to improve it and to propagate the idea.[2]

It is no coincidence, then, that most of the world's first civilisations can be found scattered around the Mediterranean: the Egyptians, Babylonians, Israelites, Phoenicians (who invented a recognisable alphabet) and more recently the Greeks and Romans. While these peoples were founding the early states through the medium of smelted metals, sculptures, writings and great buildings, the inhabitants in the dreary drizzle and fog of the forests of northern climes had to devote all their energies to the struggle for existence. They painted themselves in woad and squatted in mud huts. Warfare also followed quickly. The earliest weapons used by farmers were developed from sharpened farming implements and their bearers fought as infantry; the hunter-gatherers of other areas tended to prefer missiles fired from horseback.

The earliest inhabitants of Italy with a distinctive culture, i.e. excluding Neolithic wanderers, were a motley selection of hunter-gatherers who, having ascended the icy natural passes of the Alps, must have looked in wonder at the lush, green terrain, mostly wooded, spread out below them in northern Italy. These early bronze-age tribesmen descended and scattered throughout Italy (ca. 1000–800 BC). They are known collectively as 'Villanovan' peoples, a name used to indicate a common cultural heritage rather than any particular racial type. Iron working followed quickly.

The Etruscans were probably a group of culturally advanced settlers from the eastern part of the Mediterranean, although this has been hotly

1

disputed by ancient and modern writers. Their arrival in Etruria on the north-western coast of Italy around 800–700 BC served as a 'seed' around which the Villanovan culture began to coalesce. The result was an elaborate, wealthy civilisation with clear roots in the east. Greek traders also left many traces of their wares, but little of Greek civilisation, at this time; however, the Greeks did introduce the art of cultivation of the wild vines and olives in Italy.

Another external seed caused coalescence of villages in Latium, the fertile area around the Tiber river with its rich, arable land. Latium was bounded on all sides by natural defences – the river, the sea and mountains and marshes. One site with seven hills, ideal for defence, and set one day's march inland so that it was well sheltered from pirates and sea raiders, attracted the new settlers. Modern archaeology has discovered that there had been few signs of occupation, probably due to local volcanic activity, until about 800 BC when a large settlement suddenly sprang up as a collection of huts on the tops of the different hills. The style of these huts is still known, as some clay models have been discovered on the original sites, where they had been used as crematorial urns. The early settlers were Latin-speaking farmers dealing in cultivation and cattle. The dwellers on the heights slowly began to mingle in the marshes between the hills. They called the area Rome.

The later Romans did not themselves know their own history accurately, as it long predated the use of writing in their culture. Centuries later, the famous story of Romulus and Remus, abandoned as babies, suckled by a she-wolf and subsequently the founders of Rome, gained wide circulation. The Greeks also claimed part of the credit. They had already a wandering hero, Odysseus, who was supposed to have landed in Italy albeit probably centuries before Romulus and Remus arrived. The final 'official' story accepted by Greeks and Romans was that the Greek hero Aeneas had abandoned a sacked Troy (in modern Turkey) and had wandered the Mediterranean looking for a new home. He had landed in Latium where he was welcomed by King Latinus, took the king's daughter in marriage, their son founded the Latin city of Alba Longa and there were twelve kings. The last king was the father of Ilia, who became the mother of Romulus and Remus. This story neatly filled the lost centuries between the fall of Troy and the founding of Rome, whose foundation date had been fixed precisely by later Roman historians to 753 BC in modern parlance. The Romans did not use the Christian method of reckoning dates, which was not invented until ca. AD 700–730 by a monk, Bede, in Britain.

Archaeological evidence at Rome shows that the powerful Etruscans arrived in Rome around 650 BC. They encouraged trade, land reclamation and new technologies, some of which appear to have originated in Greece. The Phoenician alphabet was probably introduced at this time by the new arrivals, although the poor farmers retained their native Latin language. Nevertheless, the isolated area of Latium was now irretrievably linked to the wider world that lay outside.

The Roman literary tradition suggests that their first established rulers were Etruscan kings. It is quite certain that at some stage the Etruscans did indeed rule Rome. The Romans acknowledged a series of kings with typical Etruscan names in their mythology, and the literary tradition, supported by archaeology, places the first such ruler in 616 BC. Rome rapidly flourished as an Etruscan city with many new building works including a magnificent, large temple placed on top of the Capitoline Hill.

The last of the Etruscan kings behaved in a manner so tyrannical and licentious to the Romans that there was an uprising, dated to 510 BC. Thereafter Rome became a republic, ruled by a Senate (a committee of the leading aristocracy) and two consuls, who were changed every year. The annual consular system provided the earliest Roman writers with a method of dating the years; each successive year was marked by the names of its two consuls. Inevitably, loss of contact with the Etruscan mainstream resulted in an economic decline. Yet the Roman memory of regal rule was so abominable that never again would a Roman ruler be called a king, although the later emperors might act in a way that was certainly indistinguishable from that of a monarch.

The Roman peoples at this time were a dour, stolid farm-working race, small in stature, and with physical and mental attributes substantially different from those of the quick-witted peoples who populated most of the Mediterranean. It is indeed ironic that we use the phrase 'Latin temperament' for the latter when the original example was so different. Yet these very mental qualities, which also included a strong sense of fair play and a dogged tenacity to gain their objective at any cost, clearly set the Romans apart from the inhabitants of neighbouring towns. The actions which would so distinguish this infant city state that it would become master of the Mediterranean could already be discerned: the obsession with law and the wisdom of its statecraft, or public relations, with other peoples.

Technically all the Roman citizens had a vote, but the votes of the higher classes counted for much more than those of the classes below them. In practice, the aristocratic, land-owning senators made virtually all the decisions, occasionally aided by the 'Equites', the next lower order commonly known as knights. This need not have been so unfair as it sounds, as it was the wealthiest Romans who had most to lose in the event of warfare, and who therefore were expected personally to provide the best-equipped soldiers and cavalry; the poorest classes, with nothing to lose, were often exempted from fighting altogether. However, as is so often the case, unaccountable power led to abuses by the aristocracy and this, coupled with economic decline, led to the common people physically

3

seceding from Rome. That is, the peasants actually walked out of the city on several occasions. As a result, the laws were published as 'The Twelve Tables' (ca. 450 BC) to protect the ordinary people from arbitrary abuses. The laws emphasised natural justice and applied to all; they were so well formulated that some survived, unaltered, to the end of the Roman empire. The concept that citizens had 'rights' was thus accepted early in Rome's development. The willingness of Rome to extend those rights to other peoples would become one of the secrets of her great empire building.

Rome's freedoms were so highly regarded that the city sucked in many of the local populations, creating a need for more farming land. The attempts to grab extra territory precipitated many minor wars with the surrounding towns and city-states, probably mostly boundary disputes although the early Roman writers tend to favour more heroic explanations. Many of the neighbouring towns grouped together against the new upstart, but it was here that Roman tenacity paid off. Defeats were always avenged. Yet the Romans also revealed imaginative statesmanship. They gave unusually merciful treatment, by the standards of the time, to those whom they conquered – coupled with savage repression of those who cheated or rebelled against the terms agreed – and were quick to extend Roman rights to their victims. Rome also pushed her surplus population out into new colonies that all retained allegiance to their mother-state. A feature of this expansion was that Rome as an entity rapidly reached 'critical mass', a fact that was not well recognised in ancient times. The larger Rome grew, the greater her prosperity and the larger the armies that she could raise relative to her smaller rivals, who had little to gain by standing up against Roman might and much to benefit by joining in an alliance.

This slow expansion, fuelled by the offer of stick or carrot to her neighbours, coupled with cities changing sides to join Rome, meant that the area once controlled by the Etruscans was slowly pushed northwards over a period of decades. The Etruscans in turn developed towards Gaul (modern France), but fierce attacks by Gallic barbarians around 350 BC rapidly whittled away Etruscan influence.

It was not only the Etruscans who felt the weight of Gallic tribesmen, who were seeking plunder rather than migrating in search of new homes. In 390 BC a group of wandering Gauls found their way as far south as Rome, having defeated Roman legions en route. The city was sacked, and the barbarians departed. This event had a profound influence on all later Roman military thinking, even though a Roman general would later exact terrible retribution as the slow-moving Gauls, burdened with plunder, headed northwards towards their homes. At all costs Rome had to be defended against another such incursion, although two and a half centuries would elapse before Roman armies annexed Trans-alpine Gaul just north of Italy as a precaution to contain the movements of wandering tribesmen.

The survivors at Rome elected to stay on in their shattered city, rather than build a new town, and it is likely that it was shortly afterwards that the wall attributed to the ancient king Servius Tullius was really built. It surrounded all the built-up area of Rome and had a circumference of five miles, providing a clear indication of the size of Rome at this time. There was also a major reform of military tactics. Hitherto the main stratagem by the organised states had been for waves of poorly armoured spearmen to advance as a solid phalanx, providing an early example of shock tactics in warfare. The barbarians just ran around in a semi-naked rabble, relying on numbers or individual courage to win the day. However the Romans had discovered that both types of enemy could be readily dealt with by armoured swordsmen with room to fence and to use shields. The legion comprised thirty maniples, each of 120 shielded swordsmen carrying a deadly double-bladed short sword that was handy and principally intended for stabbing, ensuring a mortal wound. The maniples stood in three lines, with gaps in each being covered by the next line. This innovation created a tremendously effective and mobile army. It was at about this time that pay was introduced for military service, to compensate for the lengthy periods that agricultural workers were having to neglect their farms while on active service. If the Latin historian Livy's account is to be believed, the question of who was going to provide the pay nonplussed the senators, until several wealthy individuals volunteered to start things rolling by paying their share of a new tax.

Meanwhile, Rome's weakness in the face of the Gauls had caused some of her neighbours, who were jealous of Rome's ascendancy, to rebel and this took some time to quell. There followed three hard-fought wars against the Samnites in 343–342, 326–304 and 298–290 BC. The first had ended with a major defeat for the Romans, while the dates show their tenacity in getting their revenge in two later campaigns. Another salutary lesson for the Romans occurred in their first brush with a Greek city, the colony of Tarentum in the heel of Italy. The wealthy city rulers hired a Greek mercenary, King Pyrrhus, to come and fight for them (280 BC), which he managed successfully with the aid of highly trained soldiers and a number of elephants. Although Pyrrhus won several victories, he lost the war of attrition and the phrase 'pyrrhic victory' has entered our language for a victory that is so costly that it cannot be followed up. In 275 BC the Romans finally managed to defeat Pyrrhus in open battle and the king decided that other fields of opportunity would be more profitable for his private army. Tarentum itself surrendered in 272. Now Rome expanded north and south throughout Italy, and she ruled all of Italy and the Mediterranean islands of Sicily, Corsica and Sardinia by 218 BC.

Rome as a Mediterranean power

An agricultural economy like that of Rome had always been able to make do with barter – the Latin word for money (pecunia) derives from cattle (pecus) – but this changed with the expansion of Rome's interests. It was, and is, unrealistic to expect tradesmen and farmers to walk around with their pockets stuffed full of chickens, pigs and cows, and with hand luggage loaded with bales of hay, on the off-chance that they might meet someone who happened to need whatever they had at hand to offer. The Romans, like many other civilisations at an equal stage of development, started to use chunks of bronze, copper or iron as a medium of exchange. The metal had an intrinsic value; some future owner would convert it into a sword or plough. However, now the expansion of trade with her neighbours meant that Rome required a more formal contract, by coinage and by writing.

It was not until 300 BC that the first Roman copper coins appeared, followed by silver coins in 268 BC. The non-tarnishing metals silver and gold were recognised throughout the Mediterranean as stores of value. The usefulness of coins for carrying images and messages of a more-or-less heroic nature was immediately appreciated, the issuers always stamped some kind of information on them, and ancient coins remain one of the most objective means of dating historical events. Even their metallic content conveys important knowledge about trading patterns and general prosperity.

Writing was also introduced late, being used mostly for religious and administrative records, and the first Roman history was not written down until about 200 BC.

It was in the course of this expansion that Rome first encountered the sea-trading empire of Carthage, a city on the north-east coast of Tunisia, in Sicily in 263 BC. Rival claims between Carthage and some mercenaries led the latter to appeal to Rome for support. The Senate was unenthusiastic about a collision with Carthage, which must by now have been a trading partner, but allowed essentially a free vote by the people. The peasantry were seduced by promises of easy booty from the overthrow of Carthaginian forces in Sicily and the war began. This casual opening of hostilities culminated in three increasingly bitter and global wars, during the second of which Hannibal made his legendary assault on Italy with troops and elephants led through Spain and across the Alps. When Carthage was finally destroyed, in 146 BC, Rome found herself mistress of the western Mediterranean with new provinces in Africa and Spain. The Romans had also been compelled to build several fleets to combat the sea-going Carthaginians. These gave her control of the seas and enabled the perennial menace of pirates to be checked, greatly facilitating overseas trade.

As the Romans became the predominant Mediterranean power, other foreign states increasingly sought her alliance or even her military aid. Such was the reputation of good Roman foreign policy, and the fear of Rome's military prowess, that several monarchs bequeathed their kingdoms to Roman rule, notably in Greece, Turkey (Asia Minor) and North Africa. Rome appears never to have possessed a policy of deliberate expansion into non-Italian soil for any systematic purpose, commercial or imperial, but kept getting dug into deeper and deeper difficulties in increasingly remote lands, requiring annexation of whole territories to repress rebellion against Rome herself or against friendly allies.

The Romans had initially been reluctant to extend full Roman citizenship outside the city-states of the middle of Italy. However the disastrous Social Wars of 91–88 BC changed their minds. Insurrections by whole swathes of Italy in protest at their inferior status led to the most appalling devastation, utter ruthlessness on all sides (Rome's attitude to rebels has already been remarked), massive depopulation due to slaughter and, finally, a Roman military victory combined with the concession of virtually all the rights that had been demanded in the first place. Some modern historians have asserted that Rome never really recovered from the Social Wars and the loss of so many of her troops, leading to the increasing conscription first of Italian soldiers and later of legionaries from all round the empire. Unlike the truly Roman soldiers, few had much allegiance to Rome herself.

These horrors led into an equally disastrous series of Rome's first civil wars (88–82 BC), battles for supremacy between Roman generals such as Sulla and Marius to see who would rule the Roman State. It was to establish a terrible precedent that would plague the Roman empire for the remainder of its existence.

Marius completely reorganised the Roman legions during his ascendancy. Hitherto composed of conscripts dragged from their farms, the Roman army found that its core troops were either dead or bankrupted after serving so long away from their small-holdings. Marius recruited a professional army of volunteers drawn from the poorest ranks of society, a beguiling prospect to the dispossessed with the promise of regular pay, booty taken from vanquished enemies and, on retirement after twenty-five years' service, their own farm. Thus was created a permanent, well-trained, highly professional and heavily armoured army of the poor, that looked to its generals for success in warfare to provide the promised plunder and land. No hastily created militia or marauding band of savages could possibly hope to withstand such an army. And thus, too, the generals rapidly acquired enormous power to dictate events to the Senate, rather than the other way round. The legion now numbered 6,000 in maniples each of 200 men.

Augustus and empire

By the middle of the first century BC Roman adventurers were jostling with each other and with the Senate-appointed consuls for supreme power at Rome. Each sought to justify his prowess, and at the same time to pay his armies, with gratuitous annexation of foreign lands. Thus Julius Caesar conquered Gaul and explored Britain, all of Spain was annexed, Octavian seized the fabulously wealthy state of Egypt and Pompey and Crassus grabbed, or attempted to grab, territory in the Middle East. Finally, another catastrophic series of civil wars was enacted as each tried to secure for himself control of the expanded army, while the Republicans tried to wrest it back. The wars between professional Roman armies led in turn to successes for Caesar and then, after his assassination, for his appointed heir, Octavian, who finally overthrew all his enemies in bloody conflicts. Octavian now appointed himself 'Princeps' (leading man of the state) and 'Augustus', the name by which he is better remembered. Octavian/Augustus is today recognised as Rome's first emperor (31 BC). If Princeps was the title tactfully claimed by the new emperor of the Roman State, then the fiction was extended to his empire, called the Principate.

It has often been claimed that Rome needed a single strong man to end the interminable civil wars of the first century BC, but we must never forget that most of the protagonist generals were motivated solely by a desire for personal power. In an era when life was short, due to famine, sickness or strife, and there was as yet little concept of an after-life, the best to which a man could aspire was either or both of self-indulgence during life and immortality through fame after death. The ability of a Roman general to gratify both desires by using his loyal personal army to seize the empire created a permanent instability.

However, Octavian's rule was marked by the extreme clemency that he showed to defeated opponents and he was always careful to pay at least lip service to the power of the Senate. His reign was exceptionally prosperous due to the new wealth of the east, especially of Egypt which had made the error of backing one of his opponents in the civil war. Taxes, fines and tribute from the eastern part of the empire financed the rebuilding of Rome and put an end to direct taxes on Italians, while the protracted freedom from civil wars ushered in a golden age of art, literature and building works. Moreover, so strong were the Roman armies perceived to be by her external enemies that the 'Roman Peace' (Pax Romana) would endure for some 250 years, an achievement unparalleled in history. It was into this world that Christ was born, and the prolonged period of peace and the excellent communications between towns favoured the spread of His message.

Consistent with his policy of pretence that he was only the leading man of the state, Augustus continued with the fiction of maintaining the Senate – which actually served an important administrative role in the first two centuries of the imperial era – and maintained the ancient practice of two Roman consuls. Augustus, and subsequently later emperors, would frequently take one of the consulships while a worthy senator or a member of the emperor's family would take the other. It was quite common for an emperor to take several successive consulships, notwithstanding the prohibition under the old Republic of this practice. An important advantage of maintaining the system of consulships was that it continued to preserve the dating system favoured by the Romans, reckoning years from one pair of consuls to another.

In order to prevent abuse by the formerly aristocrat-elected consuls, and other senior magistrates, the Roman people were represented in Republican times by 'tribunes of the people', elected annually, who had legal authority to check the excesses of the principal officials. An early equivalent of the trade union official, perhaps. Because the new emperor wished to exert his authority by fictions that were apparently legal, he took the title 'Tribunicia Potestas', which may be translated as 'executive tribune'. Later emperors would take the same title as soon as they came to power, and thereafter on either 10 December or the anniversary of their accession. By contrast, the consulships had to begin on 1 January of each year regardless of when the new ruler began his rule. Any other system would have wrecked the Roman method for dating years.

The emperor was distinguished from the senators by his special toga, which had a border of purple requiring, in those days, a very costly dye. Thus new emperors attaining power would be said to have 'ascended to the purple', while pretenders or usurpers had 'taken the purple'. In later years, the simple act of wearing clothing containing the purple dye would itself become a treasonable offence.

Generals who had been victorious over foreign foes had in Republican days been allowed the honour of a 'Triumph'. The general and his army were permitted to march through the streets of Rome – normally prohibited – to the cheers of the population, while representatives of their conquered enemies were led in front of the general's chariot together with examples of the spoils of conquest. The imperial system attributed all such victories to the emperor, regardless of which general had achieved the victory, doubtless to prevent too much enthusiasm from turning the victor's thoughts to one of rebellion. Doubtless, too, there was a public relations aspect, in that the emperor received all the reflected glory. A successful general might once have been named 'Imperator' (loosely, 'Conqueror'), but now only the emperor could hold the title.

An agricultural economy

Even at its zenith, the Roman empire was always an agricultural, not industrial, economy. There is archaeological evidence that the seasons in Roman times were warmer than they are today in modern Italy; evidence has been found of crop cultivation at higher altitudes in the mountains than is today practicable. Farming was the major preoccupation of all, land was the principal source of wealth, whilst the few industries supplied the military, earthenware or luxury goods (e.g. glass) trades. The Romans never discovered the art of printing, although they made inked seal impresses and even put two or three seals together onto a single strip of wood to print several seals at once. The flimsy writing medium of papyrus was replaced in the 3rd century AD by the much sturdier parchment, largely at the instigation of the newly emergent Christian Church that was anxious to record its origins for posterity.

A side effect of the import of vast quantities of grain, distributed at no charge to much of the population of Rome, was that agriculture in Italy declined. The rural population began to migrate to the cities and Rome's population reached a peak of about one million at this time, by far the largest city ever supported by the food surpluses of a purely agricultural economy. The city dwellers were deemed to make inferior recruits for the army, which preferred the hardier farming peasants from outlying parts of the empire. Recruits from the harsh Balkan lands adjoining the Danube were particularly favoured for service in the legions. The neighbouring provinces of this area, Noricum, Pannonia, Dalmatia, Dacia and Moesia, are traditionally known as 'Illyricum'; technically the area encompasses only Pannonia and Dalmatia. During the 3rd century AD, some of Rome's finest generals, and their best legions, were recruited from the Illyrian area. I have followed the modern trend to call these emperors and their legions 'Danubians'.

The Roman domain

Rome now ruled almost all the world known to the Mediterranean peoples, with the notable exceptions of the east, where the highly civilised Parthian empire held sway, and in the north, east of the banks of the Rhine river, where savages populated a wooded territory of unknown extent. Yet, consistent with the haphazard manner in which the empire had been put together, Roman administration of the provinces comprised little more than a governor, a local garrison of troops deployed predominantly along the frontier, and a substantial civil service recruited from the local nobility. The provinces had been established as convenient units for government, taxation and/or collection of tribute, and the larger provinces were divided into two described as 'Superior' and 'Inferior', which mean Upper and Lower and are not an imputation of their status. One important innovation was the introduction of auxiliary troops from other parts of the empire. The auxiliary troops filled specialist niches in the Roman army, particularly of cavalry and archers, and the volunteers were granted Roman citizenship at the end of their lengthy period of active service.

Roman religion

The Romans, both aristocracy and peasantry, had a strictly formal contractual arrangement with a variety of gods, who were but dimly recognised and often addressed as the local 'unknown god'. The Roman gave the god a sacrifice, usually of a burnt animal, but it might be a monetary offering or even a promise of a new temple, and the god was expected to give something back – otherwise, forget the new temple. It was understood that the god had occasionally initiated some helpful deed and a sacrifice would be offered up in return. It was not until the Romans came into contact with the Greeks that there was formal identification between the well characterised Greek gods and the hazy Roman deities. Thus 'Jupiter' was identified with the Greek 'Zeus', and became the most important of the gods with a temple dedicated to 'Jupiter, Best and Greatest' on the top of the Capitoline Hill. The contractual relationship between Roman and god persisted until the end of the pagan empire.

In order to reinforce his position as absolute ruler, Octavian introduced the concept of worship of the 'genius' (roughly, the soul) of the emperor as a god. Shrines were placed for this purpose throughout the empire and, in the case of Octavian and of a majority of his successors, the Senate would decree that the emperor should be deified after his death. This led to the celebrated death-bed joke by the emperor Vespasian: 'Dear me, I must be turning into a god!'. Exceptions were made in the case of emperors deemed to be unworthy, usually those hated by Senate and population alike. The privilege of granting divine honours to a deceased emperor remained exclusive to the Senate throughout the imperial period. Remarkably, the senators would even grant pagan divine honours to those Christian emperors whom they thought sufficiently worthy, presumably for the benefit of the large number of remaining pagan worshippers. Constantine the Great, who made Christianity the formal religion of the Roman empire, was thus deified.

The pagan rituals were very highly formalised, and portents of all kinds were sought and taken seriously by the highly superstitious Roman people. The most prominent oracles were held in the Sibylline Books, which were of uncertain origin but had appeared towards the end of the rule of the Roman kings. According to Roman legend, the Sibyl of Cumae (south-west Italy), reputedly of fabulous old age, had come to the ancient king Tarquin Superbus of Rome and had offered to him nine books of prophecies at a huge price. Tarquin had declined to buy the books, whereupon the Sibyl had burned three and offered the remaining six to Tarquin at the same price. Again he refused, again three books were burned. Tarquin now bought the last three books of prophecies at the original price.[3] They were stored for safekeeping in the Temple of Jupiter on the Capitoline Hill.

The Sibylline Books could only be consulted formally at the instigation of the Senate, usually in times of national emergency. We still have descriptions of the ceremony that was practised when the sacred books were opened. First, the Senate had to pass a decree requiring that they be consulted. Then the appointed pontiffs, a special group of priests dedicated to this purpose, clothed in white, purified, cleansed and holy, ascended to the Temple of Jupiter and decked the benches with laurel, while boys 'with both parents living' sang ritual songs. There followed sacrifices, sacred meals and ceremonies before, finally, a priest, with gloved hands, unrolled the scrolls to inquire the fate of the State.

The surviving Sibylline Books had been lost during the burning of the Capitol in the course of the civil wars of 83 BC, but copies had been passed on to other temples in other parts of the empire. The prophecies, which were apparently poems, were again collected and a body of priests was charged with the authentication of the fragments as they were received.

By Augustus' time the writing had faded and the books were re-copied and moved to the temple of Apollo on the Palatine Hill. There were various forgeries circulating by now and Augustus believed that dissemination of the oracles into the public domain would result in widespread disturbances. He set a date by which all existing Sibylline fragments – or forgeries – in private and public hands had to be handed in to the authorities; a wise decision as even today Nostradamus' vague and mystical portents cause periodic panic among the gullible.

Most notable of the predictions by the Sibyl was that the Roman empire would last one thousand years.

NOTES

1   The condensed narrative of early Roman history outlined in this and the next chapter has been biased to provide the reader with a relevant grasp of both the historical background and contemporary Roman culture and customs necessary for a proper understanding of Aurelian and his achievements. Numerous excellent sources cover these periods in greater detail. We need cite here only: (i) Carey, M and Scullard, H H, *A History of Rome*, 3rd edn (Macmillan, 1979, reprinted 1986) gives a detailed overview; (ii) Grant, M, *A Guide to the Ancient World* (H W Wilson, 1986); (iii) Overy, R (ed.), *The Times History of the World* (Ted Smart, 1999); (iv) Livy, *The Early History of Rome*, translated by A de Sélincourt (Penguin Classics, 1960), for the Romans' own view.

2   The benefits to humanity of accidents of nature (restricted local terrain, good
     farming land, good weather) that allow peoples to cluster together had been
     recognised by Gibbon's time. As recently as December 2000, newly
     discovered rock art in the Egyptian desert confirmed that the drying up of
     once fertile savannah forced nomadic peoples to cluster around the Nile river
     in 6000 BC – and to create Egyptian civilisation.
3   Pliny the Elder, *Natural History*, various translations (e.g. the Loeb edn).

CHAPTER II
The Principate and its Enemies

Consolidation of empire

Augustus continued to expand the limits of the Roman empire until it had reached natural frontiers that were easy to defend. These were the oceans to the west and, less obviously, the wide banks of the Rhine in Germany, on the north-eastern frontier of the empire, and the Danube, on the mid-eastern frontier. The Sahara Desert protected the southern flank of the African provinces that were, in those days, far more fertile for agriculture than they are today. To the east, Asia Minor was guarded by the Black Sea, but the defence of Syria posed something of a problem. The Arabian Desert afforded some protection, but on the other side resided the formidable Parthian empire in Persia. This eastern frontier tended to fluctuate, with both empires operating through client buffer states that tended to change sides; nevertheless, simple diplomacy usually afforded security here too.

Britain was added to the Roman empire under the emperor Claudius (AD 43), but its economic advantage was always somewhat doubtful. It was unique among Roman possessions in that it shared a border with barbarians while being wholly separated from friendly provinces by a sea, and the positioning of its frontier to separate the Britons from the Picts in Scotland was never wholly resolved. The Romans could see no purpose at all in annexing the whole of Scotland, and therefore never did so.

The general-emperor Trajan began a new series of acquisitions in the east during the first part of the 2nd century AD, and the province of Dacia (modern Romania) north of the Danube was annexed while Mesopotamia, Armenia and other provinces in the east were seized from the Parthians whose power was waning. However, the new provinces proved to be difficult to retain and the next emperor, Hadrian, discarded most (although not Britain and Dacia) when he came to power. Hadrian personally supervised the construction of strong defences around the Roman frontiers that he retained. The famous wall that bears his name in the north of Britain was the most enduring of his legacies to that country, and was designed to restrain a sudden incursion by the warlike Picts. Less

15

well known are the more extensive walls and fortifications ('Limes') that Hadrian built to defend the weak spot in the Roman defences between the upper reaches of the Rhine and Danube rivers, and also along the Euphrates to defend the eastern provinces. Generally speaking, Hadrian's successors were content to maintain the frontiers that he had bequeathed them, although there was some expansion at the end of the 2nd century under a new general-emperor Septimius Severus.

The great difficulty from which the Roman imperial system always suffered was that of ensuring the safe succession after the death of each emperor. Since the first emperors had seized power by the force of arms, they had set a dangerous, and ultimately disastrous, precedent. The emperors owed their positions to the loyalty of their legions – and the legions knew it. It became necessary to hand out constant bounties to the troops to ensure their fidelity, and this expedient gradually caused a rise in general taxation. Taxes were commonly levied on land in the provinces, while customs duties provided the other main source of revenue.

The first dynasty of emperors, the Julio–Claudian, had originated, loosely speaking, by the seizure of supreme power by Julius Caesar, who called himself a dictator, a Roman legal description for an absolute ruler which did not have the pejorative connotation that the title has in modern times. After the civil wars that followed as the Senate tried to regain control, Caesar's adopted son Octavian had, as we have seen, ushered in a new era of peace. Adopted sons were treated in all respects as the equal of natural sons in Roman Law, probably due to the poor life expectancy of all, requiring the nobility to be always able to create a line of succession. This fortunate expediency ensured a recognised line of emperors from Augustus to Nero. Unfortunately for Rome, the later emperors lacked the wisdom, modesty and statesmanship of Augustus, and when self-indulgence and cruelty reached a new peak with the last of the line, Nero, there was a rebellion that spread rapidly round the empire. Nero killed himself and the rebellious general appointed himself emperor (AD 68). However the generals of three of the other Roman armies thought that they would make better rulers and thus it was that later Romans could look back incredulously on the 'Year of Four Emperors' (AD 69) when Galba, Otho, Vitellius and Vespasian ruled in turn. Each overthrew his predecessor and Vespasian was left as the last man standing.

Vespasian created a new dynasty with his two sons, but the second, Domitian, proved to be so vicious towards the existing nobility and to his own household that he was assassinated by a member of the latter. 'What makes emperors evil?' asks Vopiscus in the 'Augustan Histories',[1] and he then answers his own question:
1. Freedom from restraint
2. Abundance of wealth
3. Unscrupulous friends and hangers-on.

16

An emperor of a much later age (Diocletian, 284–305) added:

> Nothing is more difficult than to rule well. Four or five men collect
> themselves together and form a single counsel to cheat the emperor.
> The emperor, who is enclosed in his palace, does not know the truth.
> He is forced to know what they speak, he makes judges who should
> not be made, he withdraws from the State those who should be
> retained. The good, cautious, even excellent emperor is sold.

The Senate now appointed one of its own order, Nerva, as emperor.
Although Nerva survived only two years, he initiated a series of adop-
tions that resulted in the golden age (96–180) of Roman history, when five
consecutive good emperors, Nerva, Trajan, Hadrian, Antoninus Pius and
Marcus Aurelius, ruled for the benefit of their subjects and not for
personal gratification. It was of this period that the 18th-century historian
Gibbon[2] made his celebrated judgement:

> If a man were called to fix the period in the history of the world,
> during which the condition of the human race was most happy and
> prosperous, he would, without hesitation, name that which elapsed
> from the death of Domitian to the accession of Commodus.

That is, during the lives of Nerva to Aurelius. It is possible that the slaves
might have expressed a different view. The sequence of deserving adop-
tions fell apart when the philosopher-emperor Marcus Aurelius died,
leaving as successor his unworthy natural son Commodus. Commodus
was endured for the memory of his father for twelve years; then he was
assassinated to the relief, especially, of the sorely tried Senate, many of
whose members had themselves been murdered on the orders of
Commodus.

So far it may be said that the Roman armies had remained loyal to the
empire and that it was their highly distinguished Senatorial generals who
had rebelled against predecessors whom they deemed unworthy of ruling
the Roman state. Nevertheless, the seeds of the idea that it was the Roman
soldiers themselves who could make or unmake the emperors must have
been sown in the civil wars of 69. Augustus had stationed a large garrison
of troops, the Praetorian Guard commanded by the praetorian prefect, just
outside Rome for the purpose of protecting the emperor. After the
assassination of Commodus, which had occurred unexpectedly through
the agency of one of the members of his own household, the Praetorian
Guard saw their chance and auctioned the empire to the highest bidder in
Rome, having first taken the precaution of murdering the Senate's new
appointee, the emperor Pertinax.

The winner of the auction did not survive for long. The frontier Roman generals, still men of nobility, would not countenance rule by such an unworthy individual, while their armies had received no benefit from the auction. Again in 193 the Roman empire was plunged into civil war as Severus marched on Rome, avenged Pertinax by destroying the pretender and then overcame his two fellow usurpers in separate campaigns. The Severan dynasty lasted, with interruptions, until 235.

The Roman historian Dio Cassius summarised the Severan age with an oft-quoted maxim: 'The history of Rome fell from a reign of gold to one of rust and iron.' The civil wars had caused high military expenditure, and the Roman mints had increased the output of silver coinage by the simple expedient of reducing the amount of silver that they contained. The process had, we must acknowledge, already begun during the reign of Antoninus Pius (138–161) and slowly become worse. The silver content of the standard coin, the denarius that had been roughly equivalent to one day's pay, was reduced to under 50%, with the inevitable result that tradesmen now required more of them in exchange for their wares. The Romans seem never to have quite grasped what causes inflation, although they certainly appreciated its consequences well enough. Severus himself recognised only too clearly the part that his legions had had to play in his accession to the emperor's throne. He raised their basic pay from 300 to 450 denarii, although a large part of this may have been simply to compensate for the rising prices caused by the debasement of the coinage.

Severus proved to be a good administrator and during his reign (193–211) slightly extended the limits of the old empire bequeathed by Hadrian, again annexing parts of Mesopotamia, and he considerably consolidated the existing frontiers. The adjoining map (pages 20–1) shows the limits of the Roman empire around about 211. He raised three new legions, to create a total of thirty-three (there had been thirty under Trajan, twenty-five under Augustus) but increasingly the latter became a purely frontier defence rather than, as previously, a highly mobile rapid reaction force. The process was accelerated by grants of land to some military units for farming purposes. One legion was placed in northern Italy to create a central reserve. At the same time the number of auxiliary troops from the provinces was greatly increased. Severus also abandoned virtually any pretence that the Senate had any say in the rule of the empire. According to the historian Herodian, 'Rome was wherever the emperor was'. And the Roman state was becoming increasingly an aggregation of equals, comprising not only Italians but the citizens of all the other far-flung provinces.

When Severus died in 211 his son, Caracalla, gratuitously increased the legionaries' pay to 675 denarii, but this had to be paid for. Caracalla extended Roman citizenship in 212 (or 213) to all free men within the Roman empire, thus increasing the tax base, and he deliberately debased the silver coinage with a new silver piece, the antoninianus (see next chapter). Hitherto, soldiers who had served in the Roman army received full citizenship when they were discharged at the end of twenty or twenty-five years. One effect of Caracalla's extension of citizenship was to remove the incentive for ambitious provincials to join the army, and it is likely that the standard of recruits from the provinces declined. The distinction between regular legionaries and auxiliary troops was marked now by their standards of training and equipment.

Severus and Caracalla together reinforced the eastern frontiers of the empire along the Rhine and also beat off barbarian attacks by Gothic and Alamanni tribesmen. The Goths were east Germans who had moved from the area of the upper Vistula river to the Black Sea. The Alamanni comprised various tribal groupings in southern Germany.

The monstrous personal behaviour of Caracalla, who had murdered his own brother in front of their mother among other abominations, soon saw him assassinated. After the now usual civil wars, and the murder of Elagabalus, a latter-day Nero, the last emperor of the Severan dynasty was the virtuous Severus Alexander, who donned the purple toga of the emperor in 222 at the age of 14. He was ably assisted by first his grandmother and then his mother. Alexander's biggest problem remained that of his troops. Unlike his Severan predecessors he had not raised their pay, excepting the customary donation whenever a new emperor came to the throne, and he now sought to curb their excesses by increasing the power of the Senate. These reforms were only partially successful and ultimately Alexander was murdered in 235 (see below) by an insurrection among the Rhine Army that he was visiting with a view to dealing with barbarian attacks. The peace and civilisation of Alexander's reign would appear in later years to be a haven of tranquillity separating the 'iron' rule of Severus and the catastrophes that would follow after the death of Alexander.

The barbarian menace

The Romans never understood the extent of the menace posed to their frontiers by the barbarians beyond it. Early emperors had hoped that they might in due course conquer all of Germany with its wild tribes, but for various reasons this was never done. Probably the conquest and maintenance of Roman rule appeared far to exceed any likely benefits from such distant and inhospitable lands; Britain had previously set an unpromising example. Moreover, usurpers tended to rebel against long-absent incumbent emperors. Yet strangely the Romans appear to have made little effort to send teams of explorers into Germany to find out what lay beyond, although we know of expeditions to find the source of the Egyptian river Nile and even into India.

Upheavals in distant China, with which the Romans had no direct contact, were forcing tribes of barbarian hunter-gatherers to drift

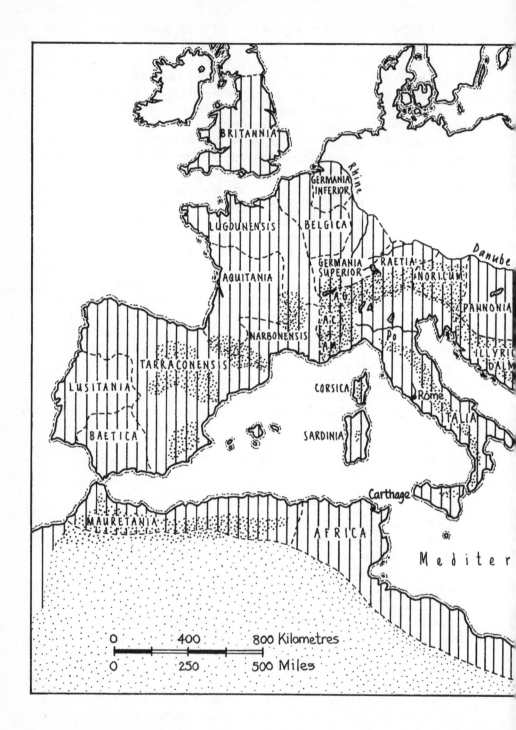

·ROMAN·PROVINCES·IN·211·

- Water (sea, river or lake)
- Steeply rising land
- Desert
- Roman Provinces
- Barbarians or Persians

A.G. Alpes Graiae
A.C. Alpes Cottiae
A.M. Alpes Maritimae

Caspian Sea

DACIA

Danube

MOESIA

Black Sea

THRACE

CEDONIA

Kura

ARMENIA

BITHYNIA·AND·PONTUS

Euphrates

ASSYRIA

CAPPADOCIA

ASIA

GALATIA

MESOPOTAMIA

Tigris

LYCIA
PAMPHYLIA

CILICIA

Antioch
SYRIA

Euphrates

Ctesiphon

CRETA

Palmyra

nean   Sea

Persian Gulf

SYRIA
PALAESTINA

Alexandria

ARABIA

CYRENE

EGYPT

westwards across Russia. The conditions in the Russian steppes induced each tribe to continue to migrate westwards, until finally they emerged in Germany and southern Russia where they encountered the eastern and northern frontiers of the Roman empire. There, they could only marvel at its civilisation and envy its wealth – which was there for the taking. Gibbon[3] devotes several pages to a vicious attack on the vices of the barbarians: too lazy to farm or create wealth, too devoid of distractions to treasure peace, too ignorant of the alphabet, too willing to get drunk and too willing to embrace war as a means of providing purpose, excitement and the fruits of other peoples' labours. Attacking neighbouring tribes offered few opportunities to acquire riches. However the civilised Roman world contained fabulous quantities of gold, silver, iron and gems, as well as textiles, pottery and herds of livestock.

The biggest menace was the Gothic tribe, which settled north of the Black Sea round about 170–230. Soon after, some of the Goths migrated to the lands north of the Danube river and began to send raiding parties into the Balkans. The withdrawal of Roman subsidies in the 240s (see next chapter) precipitated massive invasions of plunder-seeking barbarians in the following decade. At some point towards the end of the 3rd century the Goths split, for reasons unknown, into two separate groups: the Visi-Goths moved to the west where they threatened the Rhine defences, while the Ostro-Goths remained north of the Danube. We should mention in passing that the illiterate savages knew little of their own histories and their tribal names are irretrievably tangled in the ancient literature so that one writer will describe an invasion by the Scythians or the Goths while another attributes the same event to the Marcomanni or the Juthungi and yet another describes the Alamanni or the Vandals or the Franks. The names seem to reflect different groupings of tribes of barbarians, with little other significance. Broadly speaking, the Goths/Scythians dwelt around the Black Sea and east Danube, the Vandals on the middle Danube, the Franks along the Rhine and the remainder along the upper Rhine or western Danube.

There were, however, other wandering bands of nomads that had clearly established identities. One such was the tribe of Sarmatians, who dwelled in south-west Russia, north of the Danube, after migrating from Persia. The Sarmatians were characterised by their use of distinctive helmets and of cavalry, and had waged intermittent raids against Roman territory for at least a hundred years previously. We will meet them again as they took advantage of the opportunities afforded by the Gothic incursions to renew their own plundering attacks across the Danube.

An empire that has fixed frontiers that are menaced by external barbarians can protect itself in one of three ways:[4] 'Preclusive Security' means that the perimeter is heavily patrolled, and no enemy can get in. There is no central reserve of troops. This was the system created by

22

Augustus and solidified by Hadrian. 'Defence in Depth' requires multiple lines of defence backed by a central reserve, and is the most costly option. If the perimeter defence is over-run, then isolated outposts remain to harass the enemy rear, while the enemy advance is checked by reinforcements arriving from other areas or from the reserve. 'Elastic Defence' intends that no particular area is defended. Potential invaders are deterred only by the knowledge that the mobile, main Roman army will smash them when they are encountered. This is the cheapest form of defence but is also the least desirable for those whom it is intended to protect, the civilians living close to the frontiers.

All these defensive systems were tried at one time or another by various Roman emperors, but there was never a systematic policy. The Roman army could never police the vast boundaries of the empire tightly; there would always be gaps through which raiders could slip despite the partial security afforded by stone walls such as those of Britain and the Rhine, and the fast-flowing rivers of the Rhine, Danube and Euphrates. The Romans could only hope to discourage such raids by a vigorous policy of crushing the invaders as they departed homewards burdened with loot, or by the occasional punitive expedition deep into the barbarians' own heartland beyond the Roman frontiers. The large number of independent kings meant that the Romans could not hope to stamp out the menace with a single decisive battle, nor would any treaty be held to bind all of the barbarian rulers.

The third option was often the only one available to a weak ruler or a usurper pressing his claims against the central authority, and is the type of defence that we shall encounter most frequently when considering the emperors of the 3rd century. The standard formation of Roman troops had to be modified to provide rapid, mobile detachments ('vexillations') drawn from legions and auxiliary troops which could rush to a threatened area. However, walled cities provided a good temporary defence against opponents too ignorant, or too impatient, of the techniques of siege warfare. The local citizens would retire behind the walls with all their farm animals in the face of a barbarian attack while sending messengers for legionary help.

Contact with the civilising influence of the Romans slowly made the barbarian tribes more appreciative of the softer side of life. The Romans had earlier found that their knowledge of the secret for producing wines was a powerful trade weapon. The barbarians' only previous knowledge of alcohol was through the tedious and erratic process of dumping sugars, such as honey, and yeast-bearing fruits into holes in the ground, where the ingredients fermented to produce a type of mead or beer. They appreciated particularly a goblet of red wine. Ultimately many would choose to settle within the Roman frontier where they must have maintained close contact with their kinsmen on the opposite side. Roman emperors therefore began a policy of settling defeated barbarians within the frontier Roman provinces, partly so they could make good the devastation that they had caused and partly to soften up their neighbours on the other side. Still the mass migrations of barbarians from the east continued and each successive tribe appeared to be more savage than the one adjacent to the Roman frontier, with the result that the nearest barbarians preferred always to flood into Roman provinces – and loot them – rather than face the tribes to their east.

It is difficult to say today at what point the barbarians from the east changed from being simple plunderers, who would return home after their forays for loot, to being predatory migrants who feared Rome less than the tribes behind them. The ancient writers were, however, quite clear that the barbarians who attacked Rome during the 3rd century AD were motivated by nothing more than simple greed. When those who returned home with their loot told tales of the fabulous wealth to be had for the picking within the Roman provinces, the lust of their neighbours was raised precipitating new waves of pillaging. The 6th-century Gothic apologist Jordanes uses the feeblest excuses to 'justify' all the plundering and mayhem wrought by his rapacious ancestors.[5]

The Persians

Centuries previously, the Greek general Alexander the Great had conquered the Persian empire of Darius. The successors to whom he had bequeathed his empire fought numerous internecine wars, until finally a Parthian, Arsaces, had rebelled and set up the so-called Parthian empire that gained dominion over the other lands in the general area of what is now Iraq and Iran (Persia). The long established Parthian monarchy, on Rome's eastern front, represented a formidable opponent but was also a civilisation with which sensible negotiations could be conducted. The last war between the two empires had been fought in 165.

Some Persian nobles remained dissatisfied with their position under Parthian dominion and one of them, Artaxerxes, fostered a rebellion around 208, that spread at first almost unnoticed by the Roman world. Artaxerxes overthrew the last of the Parthian kings, Artabanus V, in three battles in 224. These actions initiated the new Persian 'Sassanid' dynasty under King Artaxerxes I (also known as Ardashir, 227–241) who subjugated the old Parthian dominions. A later Roman historian would remark on the new king's mild temper that encouraged all his new subjects to support him. Artaxerxes placed the Sassanid capital at Ctesiphon, far to the south-east on the Tigris river and on the opposite east bank to the old capital of Seleucia that the Romans had destroyed in 165. He built the new city of Coche in 230–240 on the west bank of the Tigris, opposite Ctesiphon, to replace Seleucia. Artaxerxes claimed sovereignty over all the former realms of Darius – and this meant he laid claim to the Roman-controlled eastern empire as far west as Greece. All the former peace treaties and agreements between Romans and Parthians were null and void and the Persians invaded the Roman province of Mesopotamia in 230 where they tried to seize the Roman client-city of Hatra and also the client state of Armenia, both semi-independent realms that acknowledged Rome's authority.

Severus Alexander first tried diplomacy. He sent letters to the Persian upstarts pointing out that it was one thing to overcome a disorganised rabble in civil wars, but another to tangle with the might of Rome. When the warnings went unheeded, Alexander took an army to relieve the siege of Nisibis in Mesopotamia in 231, which was ultimately successful (232) but with heavy losses to the Roman army – some said that the emperor had failed to bring his main relief force in time to the aid of one of the two flanking assaults that had suddenly become encircled. Yet Artaxerxes had also been discomfited and he disbanded his army for the winter season; unlike the Romans, he did not pay for a standing army. The emperor might have avenged the defeat, but reports came of a barbarian invasion of Europe so Alexander led his disgruntled legions back.

When Alexander led a new army against the resurgent Alamanni tribe near the Rhine in 234 his troops became mutinous. Alexander spent a year trying to reorganise the army but one of his own staff, C Julius Maximinus, started a riot that resulted in the death of Alexander and his mother (235). Maximinus then declared himself emperor.

NOTES

1   'Vopiscus of Syracuse' in *Scriptores Historiae Augustae*, Vol. III, 'The Deified Aurelian', translated by D Magie (Loeb, Harvard University Press, 1932; reprinted 1982).
2   Gibbon, E, *The Decline and Fall of the Roman Empire*, Vol. I, Chapter III (Everyman's Library, 1910; 1980 reprint).
3   Gibbon, op. cit., Chapter IX.
4   Ferrill, A, *The Fall of the Roman Empire* (Thames & Hudson, 1986) gives a good account of the means by which the Roman army could secure its frontiers. Ferrill is a military, rather than a Roman, historian.
5   Jordanes, *On the Origins and Deeds of the Goths*, translated by C C Mierow (widely distributed on the Internet, e.g. www.romansonline.com/sources/).

CHAPTER III

The Armies Choose the Emperors

Revolt of the legions[1]

The death of the popular Alexander in 235 was widely acknowledged by the Latin historians as the end of a golden era and the beginning of the age of crisis. In the next fifty years more than sixty army generals would claim the imperial purple, backed by their armies. Virtually all would be murdered by their successors or during their uprisings. The seizure of imperial power would remain a regular occurrence even thereafter, despite attempted reforms by Diocletian, who tried to set up a formal line of succession, until later Christian emperors could claim their divine right to rule. Modern scholars, too, have traditionally accepted the same watershed date, while acknowledging that the upheavals that followed owed their origins to Augustus, who had first seized power violently and never formally acknowledged his own position as an imperial ruler.

Maximinus had hitherto been an unknown provincial, from Thrace in Greece, who had made a purely military career. He was renowned for his gigantic size and physical strength – he was also only semi-literate. Almost all the previous emperors, or usurpers, had been able to claim a distinguished senatorial background. The inability of Maximinus to do so ensured that he was an outsider from the start of his rule. Immediately he had to quell two mutinies in his fellow Rhine legions, then he returned to the original, unfinished business and quashed the Alamanni before pacifying the Danube frontier (236–237). However, the Persians resumed their attacks on the eastern perimeter and finally captured the important cities of Nisibis and Carrhae in Mesopotamia during 237–238.

Maximinus had also promised to double the pay of the legionaries in order to secure their allegiance. This led to oppressive taxation and some African landowners revolted. Then they tried to protect themselves from retribution by the appointment of the elderly African proconsul (Gordian I) and his more active son (Gordian II) as new emperors in 238, elevations that were recognised by the Senate which was still resentful of Maximinus. The two new emperors were killed within a month in a hopeless battle with the governor of Numidia, who was loyal to Maximinus.

The elite African legions at once put to flight the poorly armed rabble of the Gordians, who both died, but the Senate remained resolute, re-appointed two of its own number as new emperors, mobilised the Praetorian Guard in Rome and adopted a scorched-earth policy against Maximinus as the tyrant marched towards Rome. Maximinus was murdered by his own famished army. Within one more month the Praetorians had disposed of the Senate's emperors in favour of their own candidate, Gordian III (238), a 13-year-old related closely to the earlier Gordians. The Senate deployed young recruits and gladiators against the Praetorian Guard, which took heavy losses in savage street fighting, and the battles resulted in the conflagration of a large part of the city of Rome.

The new Gordian, or his advisor, tried to behave as a good emperor and was fortunate to have the talented praetorian prefect Timesitheus effectively as his guardian and father-in-law from 241. In the east, Shapur I (241–272) had become the Persian king, and proclaimed himself at once as 'King of Kings. King of all Persia and non-Persia'. He had initiated fresh attacks on the Roman eastern provinces and seized Hatra, while still co-regent in 240, and it became clear that he was more interested in plunder than in empire building. Shapur relied on a policy of savage terrorism to force the luckless local inhabitants to yield to him at the first onslaught. The Greek historian Agathias informs us that Shapur was 'very wicked and bloodthirsty, quick to anger and cruelty, slow to mercy and forgiveness'.

Gordian and Timesitheus led a huge Roman army and fleet against Shapur and the skilled prefect rapidly rolled up the Persian forces, finally inflicting a severe defeat on them near Rhesaena in 243. However Timesitheus fell ill, or was poisoned, and died before the victory could be consolidated. His successor as praetorian prefect was Philip 'The Arab', who demanded of the army whether they wanted to be ruled by a child or by himself, previously the understudy of Timesitheus. The soldiers backed Philip, and Gordian was murdered in February 244; the Senate was told that he had died a natural death. Philip then ended the Persian war on fairly favourable terms, retaining most of Armenia and Mesopotamia but paying a large ransom to the avaricious Persian king, then rushed back to Rome to secure his position against any other would-be pretenders. Shapur carved a rock monument to preserve for posterity his claim to have inflicted a defeat on Gordian and to have sent away Philip in humiliation.

Now emperor, Philip celebrated the thousandth anniversary of the foundation of Rome in 248 with the most magnificent celebrations that had been seen for centuries. Although the Romans did not use our modern method of counting years BC and AD, they were perfectly capable of reckoning time in years backwards and forwards, predominantly relying on the dates of the annual consular appointments. In the same year there followed a succession of usurper emperors, little more than names, who

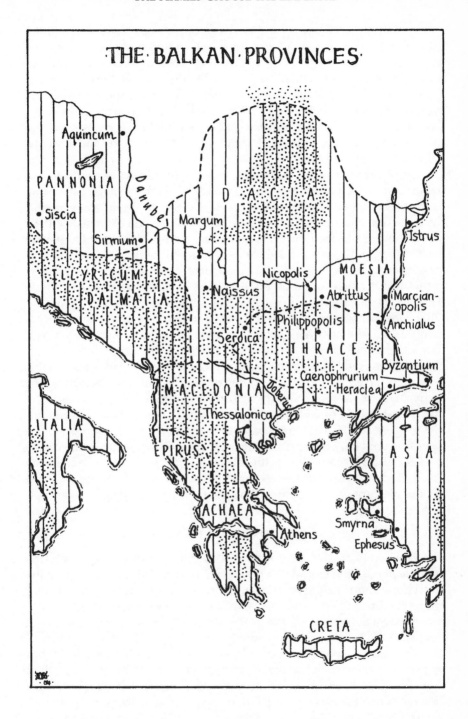

THE·BALKAN·PROVINCES·

were put up by their legions and were murdered one after another. Philip himself, who was already ill, lost his nerve and offered to resign but his military advisors kept their heads and took appropriate counter-measures. It was only when the general Decius, sent as 'Dux Moesiae et Pannoniae' (C-in-C, Moesia and Pannonia) to recover the Balkans from pretenders, also rebelled that Philip had to head an army personally. Decius won the ensuing battle easily (249), killing Philip and his son, but the new emperor in turn had to face revolts in Thrace, Syria and at Rome. All were quickly put down.

Most of the short-lived emperors had sought to stabilise the frontiers before removing border troops in pursuit of their own ambitions but, probably taking advantage of the preoccupation of the Roman generals, the barbarians suddenly pressed hard on the Rhine and Danube frontiers. Decius had abandoned the Balkans to a massive incursion of Goths and other tribes, who ravaged Thrace as far as Philippopolis, and the new emperor was forced to rush back to the defence of the area. He won one battle, lost another and was finally killed in action with the Goths at Abrittus, in the province of Lower Moesia, after being lured into a swamp (251). Decius had already inflicted heavy losses on the Goths before his own death and that of his appointed successor, his son. Rumours spread that his general Gallus, who had taken no part in the battle despite being close, had enticed Decius into the marsh where a hail of barbarian javelins destroyed the entire army stuck in the mud. Certainly Gallus then let the badly mauled Goths depart with all their plunder and a promise of a yearly cash payment, before rushing back to Rome as the new emperor. The promise of subsidies to the barbarians set a dangerous precedent. The bribes secured only peace from one tribe of Goths, while tempting others to seek similar largesse. It was the later withdrawal of these payments by firmer emperors that precipitated fresh incursions by those originally paid off, but blackmailers always tend to raise their price anyway.

Onset of the plague (250–270)

The Romans had previously experienced bouts of plague (possibly the bubonic plague that would wreak such havoc in the Middle Ages) and the last serious outbreak had been brought back from the east by the returning armies of Lucius Verus in 167. However a new, more virulent form, described by the ancient writers as the worst of historical times, had arisen from Ethiopia and was spreading throughout the Roman empire. Contemporary accounts state that the effect was worst in north Africa but by the reign of Gallus it had reached Rome where up to 7,000 citizens died each day. Gallus earned popularity by ensuring that even the poorest victims were scrupulously buried to try to prevent further contagion.

The Christian writer Eusebius quotes a letter from the bishop of

Alexandria in Egypt, revealing that the recipients of all ages (14–80 years) of free corn at Alexandria after cessation of the plague were only equal to middle-aged recipients (40–70 years) before the plague. Gibbon[2] used 18th-century mortality tables to demonstrate that this meant that some half of the population of the major city of Alexandria had died from all causes. If this figure can be applied across all of Roman Europe, then the plague must have exceeded the terrible Black Death of medieval times when 'only' one third of the population of Europe died. The effects on agriculture, trade and Roman military capability must have been devastating, quite apart from the human tragedy.

Indirect persecution of the Church

Decius' brief reign had marked two unexpected events. Firstly, he himself was the first Roman emperor ever to die in battle with barbarians. Secondly, he had instigated – indirectly – a persecution of the expanding Christian Church. There had previously been short-lived attacks on Christians, beginning with Nero's persecution when he sought scapegoats for the burning of Rome, but most had been initiated by over-zealous local governors.

The principal objection to Christianity, and to Judaism, from the Romans' point of view was that both religions denied the existence of any other gods; neither would their adherents offer sacrifices to the 'genius' of the emperor. At a time when barbarians were pressing on every Roman boundary and civil wars seemed to have become endemic, Decius decided that everyone in the Roman empire must offer a sacrifice to the Roman gods and an oath to his 'genius' in order to show their loyalty. Those who did so could walk free.

A particular feature of Decius' decree was that the Christians were *not* required to give up their faith, only to sacrifice to show that they acknowledged the emperor as ruler, and modern historians have rejected the Christian tradition that this was really a systematic persecution of the Church, but was rather merely an attempt to force at least some kind of common cohesion on the disintegrating Roman empire. The persecution caused tremendous difficulty within the early Church, with whole communities making the sacrifice, while thousands of individuals were martyred for not so doing. The persecution ended with the death of Decius.

Valerian and Gallienus as joint emperors

The reputation of Gallus – supposed disloyalty to Decius, luxurious living and lethargy against the barbarians, coupled with plague and famine – ensured that he did not survive the first usurper put into the field against him. The Goths had invaded Illyricum and plundered every object stored outside a walled town, and even many that were within fortified cities. Aemilian, commander of the Pannonian legions, heartened his dispirited troops to tackle the invaders. Somewhat to their own surprise, the legions managed a surprise attack upon a large force of barbarians and routed them. The victorious soldiers gladly saluted their general as the new emperor and all marched into Italy to confront Gallus. The latter's army counted its inferior numbers and the warlike spirit of the Pannonian troops, then murdered their own emperor. Aemilian's army in turn deserted him when one of Gallus' loyal generals, Valerian, arrived on the scene with a yet larger army from the upper Rhine. Thus it was that the patrician P Licinius Valerianus (Valerian) succeeded to the purple in the year 253 backed by all the armies and the Senate. He would be the last emperor who had been simultaneously a senator and a general.

The ancient Sibylline Books had predicted that Rome would last one thousand years. The millennial celebrations had already been held (248) and the anxious population of the empire, shaken by civil wars and battered by the Gothic incursions, fearfully awaited the worst. Then the barbarians poured across the frontiers.

Weakened by years of civil war, the few remaining frontier troops were in no position to withstand the onslaught of barbarian bands, exploiting the opportunity and fuelled by the expectations of the Goths whom Gallus had allowed to return home. There had always been pressure from across the Rhine, but now Rome was faced with the following invasions:

- Across the western Danube: Alamanni;
- Across the middle Danube: Marcomanni;
- Across the eastern Danube: Goths and Sarmatians;
- Across the northern Rhine and Britain: Saxons (including sea pirates);
- Across the southern Rhine: Franks;
- Across the Black Sea: Borani and Heruli tribes
- Across the Euphrates: Shapur with the Sassanid Persian hordes.

The resurgent Persians again invaded Mesopotamia in 252, ejected the Roman army on the Euphrates and besieged Nisibis in 254. They occupied all of Armenia, over-ran Syria and captured the great city of Antioch through treachery, perhaps in 252–253. Shapur gave the traitor the usual reward: death. The Romans were faced with that most awful of problems for military forces: simultaneous war on several fronts.

Recent events had shown the dangers to an incumbent emperor of allowing his generals to command large forces. Yet large forces had to be provided if the barbarian invasions were to be checked. Valerian tried a dynastic solution, appointing members of his own family both as principal army commanders and as successors-designate. With fire breaking out on every border, the elderly emperor appeared briefly in Rome in 253, where he appointed his son Gallienus as 'Augustus' (joint emperor) with command of the northern armies, and tarried awhile to organise his forces to meet the most dangerous threat, the Persian forces of Shapur. Meanwhile Gallienus, who was clearly no poltroon, moved at once in person to the area at which the Rhine and Danube overlap where he defeated the Alamanni in five campaigns (254–258). For this he was granted the title 'Ruler of the Western Empire', and several coins commemorate the victories: 'Germanicus Max. V(ictor)' and 'Restitutor Galliarum'. Coins also suggest that Gallienus additionally overcame the Carpi tribe in Dacia, north of the Danube. The eldest son of Gallienus, Valerian II, was appointed caesar (junior emperor) in the mid 250s, and remained as commander south of the Danube while his father was in Gaul. Valerian II died around 258 from unknown causes.

In the Balkans, the Goths had devastated all of the province of Thrace as far south as Thessalonika by 254 or 255 (dates uncertain). This encouraged other raiders to try their luck. At some point the town of Panticapeum in the Crimea was sacked, affecting the Roman grain supply. The Heruli and Borani tribes then made a sea-borne attack, using flat-bottomed boats with poor seaworthiness and carrying perhaps twenty-five occupants each, from the Crimea to the Roman town of Pityus on the far east coast of the Black Sea. The defenders, under a vigorous Roman governor, stoutly repelled the attack (ca. 256), but in the following year the Borani returned with a new fleet, seized Pityus, then moved to the undefended southern coast of the Black Sea. The provincials had supposed that the Black Sea provided a bulwark against intruders, rather than a convenient access, and the wealthy town of Trapezus was taken by surprise, plundered and burned to the ground before the victorious Borani sailed home again.

The empire divided for defence

The Roman literature is curiously reticent about the movements of Valerian at this time, although we know that he had undertaken to defend Rome's eastern provinces. Persian attacks there in 253 were checked by the priest-king of the large Syrian city of Emesa, an hereditary ruler who promptly declared himself emperor. He was murdered by his own men as soon as Valerian arrived in 254. The real emperor must have moved next to Asia Minor in response to the Gothic harassments. Valerian and Gallienus split control of the empire in 256 or 257 so that each could concentrate on handling local incursions.

In the west, other invaders had burst in and Gallienus could not be everywhere at once. Franks descended upon Gaul and Spain in raiding parties of up to 30,000 men, during which a little-known military tribune called Aurelian would first establish his reputation. Some of the Franks even reached north Africa; others devastated the Spanish city of Tarraco so effectively that the Spanish priest Orosius could discern the marks of the passage two hundred years later. The key defence area of the Agri Decumantes, the land between the upper Rhine and the upper Danube, was also overrun by the Alamanni peoples, and would later be abandoned by the Romans.

Combined Alamanni and Juthungi tribesmen swept into Italy across the Brenner Pass in 258. Gallienus was at this time quartered north of the Alps so that Rome herself lay undefended. With praiseworthy energy, the Senate armed all the troops present in the city, recruited civilians and mobilised gladiators from the training schools. The insurgent barbarians found themselves faced with a larger army than their own outside Rome, and decided to content themselves with plunder from northern Italy. The threat was so serious that Valerian felt moved to send reinforcements to his son. However the intruders were bashed by Gallienus, hastening back to aid Rome, near Mediolanum (Milan) in 258 or 259.

The Senate's action had a sting in its tail. Gallienus was less than enthusiastic about its vigorous defence of Rome, perhaps fearing that one day the senators might mobilise a similar force against him. He therefore passed laws forbidding senators to command armies, or so we are told, although it is also likely that Gallienus simply intended to ensure that capable military commanders should command legions (see next chapter). Unfortunately, the dating and sequence of events by the ancient writers is so erratic that it is hard to tie together cause and effect.

When the Marcomanni threatened to re-invade Upper Pannonia at about the same time, Gallienus allowed some of them to settle within the province and he 'married' the king's daughter to ensure their loyalty. He was already married under Roman Law. Gallienus may have hoped by this means to acquire a buffer through which other marauding barbarians would have to pass before threatening Roman lives. It would appear that it was at about this time that Gallienus also abandoned the defence of Upper Dacia, although the more southerly Lower Dacia was retained. The province of Dacia lay at this time entirely north of the Danube river. By now, the eldest son of Gallienus, caesar Valerian II, had died, and Gallienus appointed his second son, Saloninus, as the replacement caesar currently based on the Rhine.

Valerian and his main armies had moved into the Danube area. He had initially been very friendly with Christians, many of whom could be found in his own palace at Rome, but, in the middle of this nightmare, he felt moved to follow the precedent of Decius and issued an edict against the senior Christian clergy stating that they must sacrifice to the Roman gods. Unlike the persecution of Decius, the edict was aimed explicitly at the new religion. The Christian literature for this period is much better

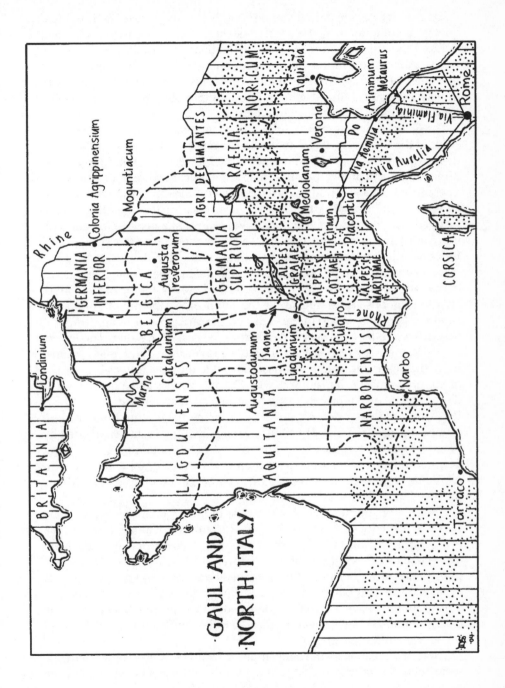

GAUL · AND ·
NORTH · ITALY ·

dated than the pagan; the edict was promulgated in August 257. Eusebius[3] quotes a contemporary belief that jealous 'Egyptian magicians' had induced the mild emperor to kill the Christians, whom they perceived as rivals. Valerian extended the persecution against all Christians in 258. Penalties of slavery in the mines or confiscation of property were threatened against those who refused to sacrifice, with death as the punishment for recalcitrant clergymen.

The Goths now mounted a full-scale naval invasion down the western coast of the Black Sea, while foot soldiers ran as fast as they could down the western shore (ca. 257–258). They seized the city of Chalcedon in Asia Minor and many other cities. Nicomedia and Nicaea were put to the torch. These tribal advances into Greece threatened Valerian's communications, as well as the Roman cities, and a recurrence of the dreadful plague ravaged citizens and the army alike. Valerian sent a general to deal with the Goths, while moving east himself into the threatened province of Bithynia still suffering from the attentions of the Borani.

It had always been the Roman custom to defend the provincials against barbarians as a priority over attacks elsewhere by the armies of more civilised nations. After regaining the town of Nisibis in Mesopotamia from the Persians, Valerian had ignored the latter. Yet now the emperor was distracted by even worse news from the eastern frontier. The failure of the Romans to respond to Shapur's provocations and raids against individual cities induced the Persian despot to mount a full-scale invasion of Mesopotamia, perhaps in 260, when Nisibis was sacked again. News of the savagery of Shapur, who had renounced the civilised ways of his Parthian predecessors, seems to have precipitated the Romans into immediate action in that direction. Despite having an army weakened by plague, Valerian marched from Bithynia into Mesopotamia, probably lost a battle, and asked for a truce with Shapur, for which a monetary payment would be handed over. News of a fresh barbarian invasion of Asia Minor may well have distracted the emperor.

However Shapur insisted that progress of the negotiations required the personal presence of Valerian himself. The latter went alone, apart from a few guards, to the talks and was promptly seized by Shapur's men. Valerian was held captive until his natural death in 260. Rock reliefs and inscriptions near Persepolis (Iran), created by Shapur and rediscovered in 1936, show the emperor on his knees before the mounted Persian king who claims to have personally defeated and captured his enemy; the inscription also shows several other victories by Shapur against thirty-seven walled Roman cities.

This left Gallienus as the sole emperor (260). However, other generals were reluctant to acknowledge the cultured intellectual who ruled the devastated provinces and commanded Rome's shattered armies. They began to rebel.

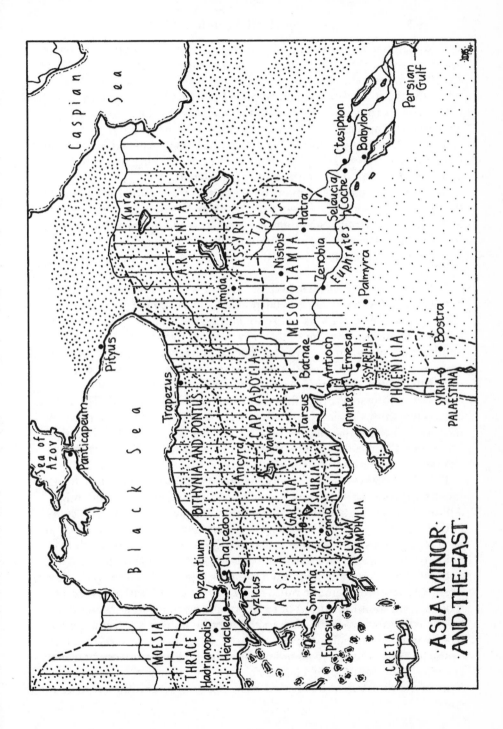

ASIA·MINOR·
AND·THE·EAST·

The Thirty Tyrants

The Romans never really developed the principle of a strong strategic army reserve, notwithstanding Severus' attempts fifty years earlier. Available troops would be deployed at the frontier of threatened areas, while the Praetorian Guard looked after Rome. In sixty to seventy years' time the emperor Constantine would formally create a frontier army and a mobile field army to dash around to threatened areas, but there was no concept of 'defence in depth'. When any area was threatened, troops had to be rushed in from a neighbouring frontier, weakening that province's defences. But what if all frontiers were threatened?

By now, as we have seen, many of the Roman soldiers had strong ties to the areas in which they served. This was abetted by the military authorities as it would encourage the local forces to fight harder for their own families. The old idea of automatically shuffling soldiers from their own lands, to create a mobile army with no local ties, was largely disappearing.

With the frontiers threatened on all sides, the soldiers were very reluctant to allow themselves to be moved to other combat areas. Since the allegiance of the troops was sworn to their generals and to their emperor, and not to the Roman State, the easy way to avoid a forced move to another part of the empire was to appoint your own general as the new emperor. He, in turn, would authorise the soldiers to stay at home to guard their own territories. And in the terrible crises and panics of the 'end of the Roman World', this was exactly what happened. The Latin chroniclers of this period tried to explain the phenomenon by a different means: Gallienus, they agree, had started his reign well but had then 'abandoned himself to wantonness and loosened the reins of rule with shameful idleness and despair' (Eutropius).

The 'Augustan Histories' source claims that thirty pretenders to the imperial throne arose during the confused period of Gallienus' reign.[4] Although this is certainly an exaggeration and even the Histories count two usurpers from irrelevant times, modern historians have identified at least nine serious rebellions, and that was quite enough with which to be going on. The pretenders of lesser armies faced a terrible dilemma when appointed emperor by their own soldiers, for the honour was often unsought: to decline and be murdered by one's own army in favour of a more accommodating officer; or to accept and be murdered by one's own troops when they were offered an amnesty by a more powerful general nearby who had remained loyal to the official emperor. In these blighted years, few had time to create official histories and the sequence of events becomes confused. However, archaeology has managed to unscramble most of the disasters of this period from inscriptions and the evidence of coins.

First Ingenuus, the governor of Pannonia on the Danube, rebelled probably in 260, although some would place the revolt before the capture of Valerian earlier that year. Gallienus and his general Aureolus put him down. The recalcitrant army in Pannonia promptly installed another new emperor, but the local population arranged for his murder too, fearing that even the mildest of emperors was likely to exact bloody vengeance on a second rebellion in the same area within a year. Gallienus was severely wounded in the fighting.

Gallienus' young son, Saloninus, had been appointed as caesar at Colonia Agrippinensium (Cologne) in the middle-Rhine area, protected by the praetorian prefect Silvanus. When Silvanus asked the commander of the Rhine armies, Postumus, to hand over booty recovered from a Frankish raid, Postumus claimed that it had all been distributed to his own men. Silvanus unwisely persisted, and the Rhine army rebelled and besieged him at Colonia Agrippinensium. Gallienus had been wounded in the fighting with Ingenuus, so could not give aid and the garrison finally surrendered, handing over Silvanus and Saloninus. Postumus ordered both killed, and set himself up as the emperor of the Gallic–Roman empire (260), issuing coins from the Rhine army mint at Augusta Treverorum (Trier).

All the western provinces of Gaul, Britain and Spain seceded to join Postumus, as well as, briefly, the Danubian province of Raetia. Postumus guaranteed to protect their lands from barbarian incursions and also that he would not permit the spillage of a single drop of Roman blood against fellow Romans. The latter statement was probably intended to head off a counter-attack by the recuperating Gallienus, who still had numerous barbarian invasions with which to contend; a diversionary attack on Italy by Postumus would have been the last straw. It is unclear today to what extent Postumus' assurances – that he would not initiate a civil war against Rome – were trustworthy. However, he never did commence such a war, and he did honour his promise to defend the eastern frontier of Gaul against the barbarians. Nevertheless, Gallienus had lost the income from taxes, and also the armies, of the western empire as he struggled to deal with the other invasions. According to the 'Continuator of Dio', Gallienus challenged Postumus to single combat but the offer was declined.

The Agri Decumantes, the land between the upper Rhine and the upper Danube which now formed a buffer zone between Postumus, Gallienus and the barbarians, had been occupied earlier by the Alamanni. Faced with a potential three-way tussle to dislodge intruders, neither Postumus nor Gallienus felt inclined to make the attempt with the result that this important weakness in Rome's frontier defences, the gap between the Rhine and Danube rivers, was abandoned forever to the Alamanni around 261 or 263.

Rebellion in the east

It is not clear to what extent the Roman armies in the east had been defeated by Shapur, but the Persians were able to plunder at will in the eastern Roman provinces of Syria, Cilicia and Cappadocia. The elderly general Macrianus and his deputy Callistus rallied the Roman soldiers, reorganised the Roman eastern fleet and checked Shapur's advance on the Cilician coast with a major battle which recovered much booty. The Romans then pushed the Persians all the way back to the Euphrates. Macrianus, who was old and lame, appointed his two sons as joint emperors and was joined by the provinces of Syria, Asia Minor and Egypt. At a stroke, then, Gallienus had lost the wealth and the armies of the east to Macrianus and his sons, as well as the defections to Postumus from the west (260).

Economic collapse

The wars of conquest fought in earlier centuries by the Romans had resulted in massive inflows of gold, silver, precious gems and other booty that had combined to keep the armies sweet, general taxation low and economic confidence high. By the middle of the 3rd century, the conquests had ended and the armies were used primarily to defend the frontiers – when they were not engaged in emperor-making. However the armies still had to be paid, and they still expected their share of booty.

Wars were now being fought on Roman territory, and the spoils were those that had once belonged to the Roman people. The most common source of such treasure was to recapture it from barbarians who had previously seized it from the provincials, and we may assume that little was returned to the original victims. Some was used to pay subsidies to buy off, or even recruit, those same barbarians who had taken it in the first place. The wretched provincials were then heavily taxed to provide the pay for the legions. Their lands had been ravaged resulting in loss of homes, crops and possessions; their routes to market were disrupted, the markets themselves deserted. The principal taxes of the Roman empire at the beginning of the 3rd century comprised a customs levy of 2–2.5%, a tax on slave releases and on inheritances of 5%, a capitation levy rather like a poll tax and a tax on land, which varied according to its quality and location. Somewhat surprisingly, the fixed-rate taxes were generally not increased in line with the inflation caused by the deterioration of the currency. Instead they were increasingly replaced by levies on goods-in-kind (the 'annona'). The Roman treasury even used surpluses from such levies to pay for other goods, effectively reverting to barter.[5]

Weighing most heavily upon the rural peasants were the capitation and land taxes, both of which varied from area to area. In addition, the farmer had also to pay a rent to his landlord. The collection of taxes is known to have been inefficient, being irregular and often targeted at those who could not pay and thus placing a larger burden on those contributing. As taxation rose to support the army, and markets collapsed, the poorer farmers found it increasingly difficult to pay their taxes. The easy solution was to abandon the farms, as there would be few willing purchasers of land with a crippling tax burden. There is ample evidence of the decreasing usage of farm land, especially that of marginal quality, during periods of disturbances. It is not surprising that brigands and pirates arose as a new menace from some of those newly displaced.

Debasement of the coinage

The coinage of the later Roman empire provides a lot of information that would otherwise be unavailable.[6] Chemical analysis tells us something about the issuing mint and the type of metal content gives a close assessment of the date when it was manufactured. The coin provides information about the emperor and from his portraiture we can see his physical appearance. The standard of engravature of images remained excellent throughout the later Roman period. The text on the coins tells us of the titles that the emperors assumed, and what values they judged to be important; often idealised, or simply wishful thinking, such as 'Happy the City of Rome' during a period of barbarian invasions.

The coins were pieces of metal stamped on both sides, generally of uneven size although attempts were made to standardise the weight of the piece. Unlike the modern flat currency, the Roman coins were convex in shape, particularly noticeable with the gold pieces. The metals comprised either gold, silver with a varying amount of base metal, bronze or copper. The gold coins were almost invariably of high metal quality and were called aurei, singular aureus. Initially the silver coin was also of high purity, and was called a denarius. Under Augustus one Roman pound of gold was pressed to give 40 aurei and one pound of silver produced 84 denarii, but the emperor Nero (54–68) changed the output to provide 45 aurei and 96 denarii, a ratio between gold and silver coins that remained unchanged, nominally, for over 200 years. Although the ratio of gold to silver content of coins remained more or less as a constant throughout the imperial period, the values of brass and copper coins were linked to the denarius by a ratio that could be fixed by decree of the emperor. The base metal coins were essentially employed as tokens, rather like modern coinage, and were used for small change.

The Roman gold and silver coins were given the full monetary value of their metal content and relied on continuous production of gold and silver from mines scattered throughout the empire. Silver always possessed the lower value; consequently silver coins circulated more widely, putting strain on the ability of the mines to keep up with demand. An early fear was that the export of silver coins to India in exchange for perishable silks would ultimately bankrupt the empire, but the silver mines kept going until the end. It was unlikely, however, that production could ever be greatly increased to meet sudden demand.

Gold coins are much scarcer to find than those of silver and it is often asserted that the reason is due to their high value and the fact that loss of a gold coin would result in a very careful search by its owner. However, handling the gold coins (courtesy of the British Museum, London) shows that they are small and not actually very heavy, and their loss from a Roman purse would scarcely be more noticed than the loss of a valuable, latter-day £50 note from a modern purse. Who today, however poor, would waste time searching for a missing £50 note that had vanished who-knows-where? The shortage of re-discoveries of Roman gold coins can best be explained by their comparative uselessness in daily shopping. To buy a glass of wine or a pound of bacon with a gold coin would be rather like making the same purchases today with a £250 note, if such existed. It is likely that comparatively few gold coins ever circulated in the Roman world, relative to the silver currency. Since they were of high gold purity, surviving examples would have been melted down in medieval times to create new gold coinage.

The metal currency lacked the milled edges that we see on modern coins. Because they were larger than the stamp and comprised valuable metals, 'clippage' became a problem. Unscrupulous coin owners would shave off a small sliver of metal from the gold and silver coins before returning them to circulation. Repeated clippage caused the coins to shrink in size and thereby drop in value. Naturally clippage was illegal, and subject to severe punishment when detected, but usually it would be impossible to place the blame on the guilty party.

Roman smelting for lead, copper and silver in Spain was on such a scale that it has left characteristic traces in the frozen ice cores of Greenland, to an extent not re-encountered until the Industrial Revolution. Yet the same evidence indicates a decline in the scale of smelting in each century after the first BC until the end of the Roman era. In addition, the north Dacian mines that were the major non-Spanish source of silver were lost in AD 258/9.

Thus the supply of silver was in decline throughout the imperial age and this alone may explain the debasement of the coinage. At the beginning of the imperial era, under Augustus, the silver denarius had a silver content of around 97%. However shortages of silver led the mints to mingle in increasing quantities of base metals, so that by the time of Septimius Severus (193–211) the silver content had declined to some 75%. By now the emperors had learned that, by deliberately reducing the silver content of the coin, they could keep the silver saved and insist that their subjects value the debased coinage as though it retained its original value – except for the payment of taxes. The emperors were not so foolish as to accept their own devalued coinage back in settlement of taxation unless at a steep discount.

The Roman rulers therefore discovered inflation the hard way. If the silver content of a denarius was one quarter of its original content, tradesmen demanded four times as many denarii for their goods. Equally, as the 97% silver coins of Augustus had the same face value as the new debased coins, people hoarded the early coins, and buried coin hoards rediscovered in recent years show clearly the preference for retention of earlier, better quality issues. A curious feature of this debasement was that, as the silver content of the denarius fell, the weight of the gold aureus declined proportionately to maintain the gold:silver value ratio, although the gold content remained very high. The fiscal ratio of gold to silver in coins finally collapsed, when the 'silver' coins contained virtually no silver.

Inflation induced by the debasement of the currency did not matter to the Roman population as much as it would today. Very few people of the Roman empire received salaries for their work. In an agricultural economy, most people received agricultural products – vegetables, milk, cattle and the like. Money was only used as a convenient medium of exchange. Where a farm labourer might once have sold some of his surplus produce for one good denarius, and then buy his requirements with the same coin, now he simply shuffled four denarii for the same series of transactions.

The army, however, was paid with debased money, so it was customary for emperors to provide gold coins and silver bullion as extras to keep the soldiers content. The interminable civil wars of the 3rd century must have greatly accelerated the debasement of the silver coinage, as usurper emperors with limited or no access to the silver mines must have had to reduce the silver in the coinage in order to pay their troops the increased bounties promised for their support. Ironically, it was the demands of the armies for more pay that led them to receive decreasingly valuable money, a self-perpetuating cycle. A papyrus has survived from Egypt from one of the 3rd-century pretenders, telling reluctant local bankers that they must accept the tyrant's new, and virtually worthless, coinage at full value – or else.

It was the emperor Caracalla (211–217) who deliberately started the downward process when he increased the legionaries' pay from 450 to 675 denarii. He now introduced his 'antoninianus', a coin with a face value of two denarii but a silver content roughly equal to one and two-thirds of the denarius (215). By the reign of Severus Alexander, the silver content had fallen to about 50%. Thereafter there was a speedy collapse in quality. As later emperors reduced the silver content of both denarius and antoninianus, the former simply dropped out of the financial system during the reign of Gallienus. The antoninianus was now struck over the face of the surviving denarii. The shortage of silver is sometimes attributed to exhaustion of the silver mines, but Gallienus had in any case lost the output of many of the empire's mines with the defection of Britain and Spain to Postumus, although he retained those of Pannonia and Dalmatia. Up to this point the debased 'silver' coinage had at any rate retained a satisfactory appearance, but now even this degenerated. By the reign of his successor, Claudius, the antoninianus had shrunk to a weight of just three grams, of which only 2% was silver in the form of a wash over the surface of the coin that rapidly wore off.

There had been a number of civil mints that produced the lesser-value bronze coinage, but they had mostly ceased production by the reign of Gallienus. The coins they produced had become worthless, when even the 'silver' coins were of such little value. The inevitable result was a large increase in the production of fakes – sometimes even from the official mints! – today referred to as 'barbarous radiates'.

The disruption of routes by barbarian incursions and by brigands meant that the government mints had to be placed close to those who most required the coins, namely the armies. The process of moving the mints began under Valerian and was never fully reversed, although later emperors might move mints a little farther away from troops whose loyalty was suspect.

NOTES

1   As well as continuing to use a general distillation of Roman history, the following Roman sources of Latin history are being worked in: (i) Eutropius, *Breviarium*, translated by H W Bird (Liverpool University Press, 1993); (ii) Orosius, Paulus, *Seven Books of History Against the Pagans*, translated by R J Defarrari (Catholic University of America Press, 1992); (iii) Victor, Aurelius, *De Caesaribus*, translated by H W Bird (Liverpool University Press, 1994). In Latin only: Anon., *Epitome de Caesaribus*, Appendix to Aurelius Victor (Teubner, 1911). General sources: Grant, M, *The Roman Emperors* (Phoenix-Giant, 1997); Brauer, G C, *The Age of the Soldier Emperors* (Noyes Press, 1975); Dodgeon, M H, *The Roman Eastern Frontier and the Persian Wars, AD 226–363: A Documentary History* (ed. S N C Lieu, Routledge, 1993).
2   Gibbon, E, *The Decline and Fall of the Roman Empire*, Vol. I, Chapter X (Everyman's Library, 1910; 1980 reprint).
3   Eusebius, *The History of the Church*, translated by G A Williamson, Chapter 7 (Penguin, 1965, reprinted 1989).
4   (i) *Scriptores Historiae Augustae*, Vol. III, 'The Thirty Pretenders', translated by D Magie (Loeb, Harvard University Press, 1932, reprinted 1982); (ii) Drinkwater, J F, *The Gallic Empire*, Historia-Einzelschriften, 52:13–276 (1987).

5   For taxation generally: Jones, A H M, *The Later Roman Empire*, Vols 1 & 2 (Blackwell & Mott, 1964, reprinted Johns Hopkins paperbacks, 1986).

6   The debasement of coins: (i) Casey, P J, *Roman Coinage in Britain* (Shire Archaeology Press, 1980); (ii) Green, K, *The Archaeology of the Roman Economy* (Batsford, 1986); (iii) coins held at the British Museum.

CHAPTER IV

The Start of Recovery

Reaction of Gallienus[1]

The year 260 represented the nadir in Roman fortunes. Valerian had been captured and was now dead. His son Gallienus ruled alone, and was widely reviled for not having come to the rescue of his father. Macrianus and his sons controlled the eastern empire, while Postumus had defected with the empire of the west. In the year 261 there were three pairs of Roman consuls, those of Gallienus, of Macrianus and of Postumus. Shapur was still brooding on his defeats. Two pretenders had revolted within the limited area (Italy, Africa and the Danube provinces) over which Gallienus' writ still ran and all the time barbarians roamed freely over the provinces, plundering, killing and burning.

However, desperate situations require desperate remedies, and Gallienus decided to appoint all his military commanders on the basis of their abilities, rather than of their civilian rank. This meant that Roman senators, who were accustomed to receiving key military posts, no longer were considered; indeed it appears that Gallienus showed scant sympathy for the Senate, a policy which did not endear him to later writers of Latin history, who were mostly themselves drawn from the senatorial classes.

His energy and courage could hardly be disputed, yet the author(s) of the 'Augustan Histories' can scarcely pen a word about Gallienus without spitting at his name. However, the same source is willing to acknowledge the emperor as a talented orator, poet and artist, and that he was 'very clever'. Clearly Gallienus, a highly cultured man, was held personally responsible for all the disasters that had befallen the State.

Yet Gallienus did not despair, and we may observe that he simply did what he could, reacting to each emergency according to its priority. Christian writers of this and succeeding periods were noticeably kinder to Gallienus than the pagan Latin writers, while Gallienus favoured the new religion without going so far as to become a convert himself. Valerian's persecution of the Christians had been rescinded by Gallienus as soon as he possessed sole authority and Christians were now permitted to join the army and were not required to worship the 'genius' of the emperor. The

Church had often previously declared that it was willing to offer up prayers *for* the emperor, but not *to* the emperor. One might guess that, whereas Decius and Valerian had sought to unite the empire by causing everyone to swear allegiance to the Roman gods, Gallienus tried to achieve the same objective by not wantonly antagonising an important section of the community. Eusebius quotes the relevant edict and it is interesting to note that Gallienus claims never to have intended to interfere with Christian worship:

> The Emperor Caesar Publius Licinius Gallienus Pius Felix Augustus to (the Pope and named Christian bishops). I have ordered the bounty of my gift to be declared through all the world, that they may depart from the places of religious worship. And for this purpose you may use this copy of my rescript, that no one may molest you. And this which you are now enabled lawfully to do, has already for a long time been conceded by me. Therefore Aurelius Cyrenius, who is the chief administrator of affairs, will observe this ordinance which I have given.[2]

Gallienus drove back an invasion of Upper Pannonia around 260 or 261. However, the year 261 began poorly when his general Aureolus rebelled against Gallienus. He was besieged and, extraordinarily, pardoned. Now Gallienus took steps to control the rot in the east. Macrianus and one of his sons had advanced as far as the Balkans, but both were stopped and killed by one of Gallienus' generals, Domitianus, a subordinate of the cavalry commander Aureolus. Another general Theodotus may have put down a revolt by one Aemulinus in Egypt. Gallienus then appointed Septimius Odaenathus, the energetic, hereditary ruler of the desert town of Palmyra, as the supreme commander (Dux Orientis) of all Roman troops in the east, a position with no clearly defined responsibilities to the legitimate emperor. Later Latin writers seem to be unanimous that this was the emperor's most significant achievement.

Palmyra[3]

Palmyra was a trading city placed on an oasis in the middle of the Arabian desert to control the most southerly camel route trading between the Roman empire and the exotica, such as perfumes and spices, of the east, principally from Persia and India. It was situated some ninety miles south-east of Antioch and about sixty miles from the Euphrates river. The city had been a trading post since the time of Alexander the Great, and it had been raided in 41 BC by Mark Anthony's cavalry seeking plunder. Under the emperor Tiberius, Palmyra had become a Roman subject state. Septimius Severus had made the city a Roman colony, although the emperor was willing to concede that the local king ruled in his name. This was a common arrangement in the eastern provinces; Herod the Great provides a better known example. By exacting tolls on the caravans that passed, the city had reached a high degree of wealth and even supplied archers and heavy cavalry as auxiliaries for the Roman legions.

The size of Palmyra, now in ruins, measures ten square kilometres. This makes no allowance for the nearby oasis, which still exists, and the fertile, irrigated land that once surrounded the city. The buildings were protected by strong walls that could certainly withstand a siege by a professional army, although the main threat was probably from nomadic desert tribes. Although much of the stone of Palmyra has survived, unfortunately the same cannot be said of the brick that once created the buildings within the stone skeleton. The city was oriental in style and was at that time populated predominantly by Bedouin Arabs although, as a key trading outpost, it must have contained many foreigners. Its culture was certainly very cosmopolitan. Private houses were filled with a mixture of Roman mosaics and Persian carpets; its inhabitants wore Roman-style robes or Persian-style trousers. There was a variety of religions practised.

The most important structure was, and is, the fabulous Temple of Bel (not a Sun god, contrary to most accounts) with its classical facade of Greek columns and sloping roof. The temple was built on an earlier religious site, and was surrounded by a huge courtyard measuring 210 metres by 205 metres. It was dedicated in AD 32. Next to the courtyard ran the 'Great Colonnade', 1,200 metres long in the direction west to east, and lined with 1,500 Corinthian columns. The colonnade passed through the official quarter of the city, with its public baths and theatres, before reaching the 'Tetrapylon', a magnificent monumental arch comprising four groups of four massive columns, on which some of the original pink granite can still be seen. After reaching the arch, the avenue then changed direction fifteen degrees to the north, apparently for aesthetic purposes, and ran another 500 metres to the city gate.

Outside, the Valley of the Tombs still remains nearby, with its unique tomb towers (some over five storeys high) and crypts. The tombs were used to bury generations of wealthy Palmyrenes who, while alive, came to feast with their ancestors before being interred when their own times had come. Much of our knowledge of Palmyrene life derives from the sculptures and artwork that decorate the tombs.

P Septimius Odaenathus had been the ruler of Palmyra since the 240s, as we now know from the evidence of a recently discovered inscription. He was a member of the Roman Senate and had been awarded the honorary 'Ornamenta Consularia' by Valerian in 257 or 258. Although described in the literature as the 'Dux Orientis', the name never appears in inscriptions, where he appears initially as the 'Ruler of Palmyra' or as 'Corrector', a Roman title for the ruler of certain provinces. Awkwardly poised between a great Roman empire to their west, that seemed to be falling into decay, and a resurgent great empire to their east, the Persian, the Palmyrenes had to play their cards carefully so as not to antagonise their imperial trading partners. Odaenathus had cautiously sent camel-loads of gifts to Shapur on the pretext that the Persian had 'greatly surpassed the Romans', but was rocked by the reply of the self-styled 'King of Kings', who unceremoniously dumped all the gifts into the Euphrates:

> Who is this Odaenathus that he thus dares to write to his lord? If he hopes to reduce his punishment, let him fall prostrate before the foot of my throne with his hands tied behind his back. If he hesitates, rapid destruction shall be poured on him, his people and his country.[4]

The contrasting actions of Shapur and Gallienus set the seal on Odaenathus' loyalty. It is hard not to imagine that Rome would have been his preferred choice anyway, considering Shapur's reputation as a bloodthirsty, merciless and cruel despot. Besides, Palmyra's economic interests lay with the Romans, as Shapur had blocked the caravan routes trading from east to west. Thus encouraged by self-interest and by Gallienus, Odaenathus quickly suppressed Macrianus' surviving son and his general Callistus at Emesa, and thereby restored nominal Roman rule over all the east. Yet only nominal rule. In practicality, Odaenathus was able to rule the east as his personal fiefdom, although there is no evidence that he and Gallienus ever quarrelled. Indeed, remarkably among these years of pretenders and usurpers, Odaenathus always acknowledged Gallienus as the true emperor, a fact attested by his coins. The Palmyrene's success – indeed, his survival – shows remarkable political skill in these turbulent times.

In autumn 262 Gallienus was able to celebrate his decennalia (ten years of rule) at Rome with appropriate celebrations. There is no doubt that Gallienus intended to deal with the usurper, Postumus, in the western Gallic empire. Gallienus won a battle against Postumus in Gaul in 263 but Aureolus failed to follow it up, although it is probably at this time that the defected province of Raetia returned indefinitely to the central authority. Postumus sent for reinforcements from his frontier troops on the Rhine, and even employed German mercenaries, but suffered a second defeat. He retired to a town (unknown) where he was besieged, but Gallienus was wounded by an arrow and had to be taken back to Rome. Once again he was distracted by barbarian invasions, and there seems now to have been an unwritten agreement that Gallienus and Postumus would leave each other alone.

The Goths were again overrunning most of Asia Minor in 262–264, and Gallienus and his armies hastened to the rescue. The fabulous Temple of

Artemis (Diana) at Ephesus, which was at least five centuries old and had been accidentally destroyed, then rebuilt, on several occasions in the past, contained the riches of generations of worshippers and had always been respected by previous invaders. This was the temple visited by St Paul in the 'Acts of the Apostles'. The Goths sacked the temple, which was ruined and never restored. The remains can still be seen in Turkey, and are quite surprisingly small to those accustomed to the giant size of Christian cathedrals. There has been considerable dispute about the precise date of its destruction, some favouring the date given here, others preferring to place the destruction during the Gothic invasions of 257–258, when Valerian took the necessary counter-measures; yet others prefer to place the date during the third great Gothic onslaught of 267–268.

Gallienus personally led the armies that threw out encroaching Goths from Cappadocia, an eastern province north of Syria, in perhaps 262 or 264. Gallienus recaptured various cities and then moved to the neighbouring province of Bithynia where a rebellion of troops who had been seeking a strong local emperor to deal with the marauding Goths was itself squashed. The 'Augustan Histories' record that Gallienus faced a rebellion at Byzantium, later better known as Constantinople, and suppressed it by offering an amnesty and then breaking the terms of the surrender and massacring all the nobles and many of the population. However, the Greek historians remark on the clemency that Gallienus always showed to his enemies, so this may be another example of the blackening of the emperor's name by Latin writers. The 'Augustan Histories' claim that another rebellion in Isauria was put down by his generals. No other source supports this claim.

The ruler of Palmyra, Odaenathus, conducted a series of campaigns during 262–264 against the Persians, starting by hitting their forces retreating along the Euphrates after their earlier defeat by Macrianus. The Palmyrenes recaptured north Mesopotamia and perhaps Armenia too. While Odaenathus was doubtless following a personal agenda, reducing the Persian threat to his own realm, he had clearly also done the Roman State signal service. Even if he had only kept the Persians at bay it would have been enough and Gallienus was glad to award his 'subject' the title of 'Imperator', ambiguously indicating a successful general in Rome's foreign wars – or an emperor. Gallienus took the opportunity to display a magnificent Triumph in 264 to celebrate Odaenathus' early victories over the Persians. The event was marred by a number of Roman jokers who examined the face of each Persian captive in the triumphal procession, to discover whether they could find the unavenged emperor Valerian.

Again Odaenathus punched into the Persians (ca. 267) taking Mesopotamia up to, but not including, the Persian capital city, Ctesiphon. However Odaenathus, despite having appropriated for himself the title of 'King of Kings', did not live to enjoy his successes. A palace intrigue, doubtless concerning which side he was really taking (although it may have risen over a trivial dispute during a wild beast hunt), resulted in Odaenathus and his successor, his eldest son, being murdered by court officials at Palmyra in 267 or 268. This brought the widow and second wife of Odaenathus, a talented and aggressive woman named Septimia Zenobia, into power. Since rule by women was never a very agreeable state for ancient populations, Zenobia appointed a respected team of counsellors to provide advice; even so, she continued to rule through her infant son Vaballathus. Gallienus seized the opportunity to try to overthrow the new dynasty through his new praetorian prefect Heraclianus, but the attempt failed; the 'Augustan Histories' provide the sole evidence that Zenobia's army defeated Heraclianus. We may guess that this piece of opportunism soured relations between Rome and Zenobia, who built for herself a new city, also named 'Zenobia', on the Euphrates river, north-east of Palmyra.

Gallienus improves the Roman army

Gallienus improved the officer classes and between 264 and 268 he created a heavy cavalry force organised in squadrons each of 500 men. The Roman army had hitherto comprised predominantly infantry, although light cavalry had been recruited from the provinces as attachments to the legions. The latter, however, had proved to be inadequate against well-armoured opposition. The new unit consisted of heavily armoured cavalry to counter similar attire worn by Persian horsemen – not only the rider but also the horse bore the armour, as a protection against the proficient archers who could be found in the east. There were also light mounted troops drawn chiefly from the eastern provinces, as well as a body of Dalmatian cavalry. The formations were intended to serve both as a strike force and as a central reserve, reintroducing Severus' concept of a defence in depth. They were accordingly based initially at Mediolanum (Milan) that now served as a pivotal point in a key defence line connecting the towns of Aquileia, Verona, Mediolanum and Ticinum. After the loss of the Agri Decumantes, the new bulwark provided the only strong hindrance to a barbarian attack on Rome herself.

The new mobile army, totalling some 30,000 men, was very powerful; therefore it had to be headed by the best and most loyal officers. The initial command was delegated to the general Aureolus, who was expected to guard Italy against both barbarians and any sortie by the deeply distrusted Postumus over the Alps. Some of the cavalry were used as Gallienus' personal bodyguard, and coins struck at this time honour the new, elite force. Most thought-provoking are the large gold medallions offered to the unit's officers and inscribed 'Because you have remained loyal'.

Details of the organisation of the heavy cavalry are unknown. There would be no formal separation of infantry and cavalry units until the reorganisation by the emperor Constantine in the 4th century. The late Roman military historian Vegetius[5] hints that legions of the late 3rd century incorporated 726 cavalrymen, less than one eighth of the total legionary manpower. He also states that the purpose of the armoured cavalry was to be used in close conjunction with the armoured infantry, where they would be effective against enemy soldiers advancing in loose order towards, or running away from, the Roman infantry. The mobile army was however very costly, for horses are expensive to maintain. It resulted in an increase in the financial burden, already enormous, borne by the citizens. As coins were virtually valueless, payments had to be made in kind.

The worst barbarian invasion[6]

In 267–268 Gallienus had to face the worst incursions of all by barbarian invaders. The Goths had previously made a land and sea assault from the Dniester river in the north of the Black Sea in ca. 258 (see last chapter).

Now the Goths made a renewed raid to the west with sea transport provided by the Heruli tribesmen. Five hundred ships carried barbarian pirates from the Sea of Azov towards Asia Minor and Greece; thousands of other barbarians ran on foot on the northern shores of the Black Sea until they entered the Balkans. Ravaging and looting all the Roman provinces in the area, apparently they seized many cities. The general/ historian Dexippus tried unsuccessfully to check them when they attempted to seize Athens, probably in 267. Unfortunately only fragments of Dexippus' chronicle have survived, but we learn that the historian himself held out on a series of fortified hills, managed to rally some of the troops fleeing from Athens and made a sudden swoop on the poorly guarded pirate fleet at Piraeus, destroying it completely.[7]

The Goths had now lost many of their unseaworthy 'ships', little better than barges, through the actions of Dexippus and through accidents. Because they were poor sailors anyway, they had little enthusiasm for the homeward passage across the choppy waters of the Black Sea as winter approached. The Goths resolved to trek back home northwards through Thrace and across the Danube river. This gave the Romans their chance.

The sequence of events is again unclear from the sources. Some say that Gallienus was at this time engaged in a battle with Postumus, but he sent generals such as Marcianus to deal with the invasion in his name and they won many hard-fought battles by land and by sea. The modern belief is that subsequently Gallienus in person, hastening from north Italy with his armies and his heavy cavalry, caught the Goths in spring 268 as they trudged northwards laden with their booty and heavily defeated them near the Nestus river on the Macedonian–Thracian boundary, a victory more often attributed to Gallienus' successor, Claudius. At long last, the grasping barbarians had been given a decisive thrashing. Gallienus tried to negotiate with the survivors, offering them safe conduct out of Roman territory and awarding 'Ornamenta Consularia' to one of their chieftains.

Gallienus could not stay to savour his victory. He had left the cavalry commander Aureolus as commander in Raetia, but the news now reached Gallienus that the treacherous Aureolus, who had already revolted and been pardoned once, had declared himself for Postumus at Mediolanum. It is not clear whether he expected aid from the latter who in any case did not give it. Aureolus actually issued coins in the name of Postumus in Mediolanum, which was one of the most important mint cities. Back went Gallienus with most of his forces to northern Italy. He left behind two generals to mop up any straggling Gothic parties returning from their looting expeditions. Gallienus' army defeated the forces of the traitor north-east of Mediolanum in the summer, and Aureolus retired to that town, his base, where he was bottled up and besieged by Gallienus.

Deaths of Gallienus and Postumus

Several officers of the besieging force now entered into conspiracy against Gallienus. Heraclianus, the praetorian prefect, Marcianus, his general against the Goths, and Cecropius, the commander of the Dalmatian cavalry, decided to murder their emperor and to replace him with another general, Claudius. Aurelius Victor claims that the plot was that of Aurelian, already a highly respected general, while Zonaras, apparently citing a different source, acknowledges that the plot was hatched after the arrival of Aurelian and his heavy cavalry, but that the principal architect was Heraclianus. It is possible, just possible, that the future emperor Claudius was himself involved. Although Claudius was not physically present with the other conspirators, it has been surmised that he was sent away to a safe distance so that he could not become a suspect party.

The reasons for the conspiracy are unclear to us today, although the ancient Latin writers moralise at great length about Gallienus' (alleged) personal vices and weaknesses. Was it because he was too cultured for the military requirements of the time? Not sufficiently Danubian? All the conspirators were themselves of Danubian origin, as was Claudius, and this Balkan area continued to produce the best generals and the hardiest troops. Was it inspired by the Senate, still smarting from its deprival of its accustomed military commands? Was the problem economic chaos, for the currency was reaching new lows of value, or highs of debasement depending on your point of view? We may never know, unless archaeology makes new finds. What *is* clear is that Gallienus was to be murdered by a group of his own, hand-picked officers, who must have owed him many favours, and this fact alone has caused very recently a certain amount of reconsideration as to whether the ancient writers understood him better than we think we do.

The assassination was worked somewhat elaborately. One of the conspirators rushed into the emperor's tent late at night, shouting that Aureolus and his forces had made a sortie from their city and were approaching. Gallienus at once jumped onto his horse, without armour, and charged towards the supposed scene of action, shouting behind him for his personal bodyguard to follow as quickly as they could. In the darkness, a prearranged assassin waited; he rode up and stabbed the unprotected Gallienus to death. Whatever the opinion of the Latin writers, it is clear that the conspirators had correctly assessed their emperor's courage. The evidence of papyri, which usually salute the reigning emperor, places the death around August 268, although some historians favour dates as early as March.

Gallienus had been joint emperor from 253 to 260, and sole emperor from 260 to 268. He had been detested by the Senate who flatly refused to make him a god according to the usual custom. Further, rejoicing at his death, they then went on to arrange the murders of all the friends and relatives of Gallienus at Rome, including his widow, his younger brother (consul in 265) and his last surviving son. However, the reputation of Gallienus with his own troops was far higher. After his death the legionaries of his army mutinied and had to be quietened by the time-honoured expedient of a donation to each man of twenty gold pieces. The new emperor, Claudius, countermanded the orders to kill those supporters of Gallienus who still survived, insisted to the Senate that it was necessary to deify Gallienus to placate the army, and eventually he got his way. Nevertheless, we may note that Gallienus' name was erased from all monuments at this time.

Gallienus managed to save the disintegration of the entire Roman world through his tenacity. The judgement of posterity has been far kinder to Gallienus than that accorded by his fellow countrymen.

The guardian of the Gallic–Roman empire lasted scarcely longer than the official emperor. While Gallienus fought usurpers and barbarians, the pretensions of the western empire under Postumus had continued to ape those of Rome herself. Postumus, who may have been a Gaul, manu-factured his own Senate and two consuls, and created a Praetorian Guard of his own to defend his capital at Augusta Treverorum (modern Trier). Archaeology suggests that the economic efficiency of his empire, and the levels of its culture, were at least the equal of those at Rome, and coins were produced with Postumus' image from his own mints. His government was described as restrained with its citizens and conducted with great vigour against its enemies. Postumus defeated the Alamanni and Franks on the Rhine frontier in 261, and awarded himself the titles of

'Germanicus Maximus', 'Restitutor Galliarum' and, provocatively and inaccurately, 'Restitutor Orbis' (Restorer of the World). Interestingly, his coins also display the legend 'Roma Aeterna'. The Gallic–Roman empire might have a new ruler, but it had not seceded from Rome. Although the uneasy peace between Gallienus and Postumus had resulted in the loss of the Agri Decumantes to barbarians, Postumus was able to re-establish forts in that territory.

Postumus himself, although much admired by the Latin writers in preference to Gallienus, could never march on Rome without facing a rebellion in his rear centred on the powerful Rhine armies. When Aureolus mutinied against Gallienus and called on Postumus for aid, the latter was even then engaged in putting down a major revolt. After he refused to let his victorious troops plunder the defeated city (Moguntiacum; modern Mainz) of the rebel, his own troops put Postumus to death, probably in late 268 or spring 269.

Postumus had ruled for eight-nine years, a length of time far in excess of that achieved by any previous pretender, and the military commanders of the Gallic empire can have had little enthusiasm for a return to rule by the legitimate emperor. The original prime reason for their defection – fears about barbarians crossing the Rhine if the garrisons were depleted for use in other parts of the empire – remained valid, and they must also have feared punishment for their desertion. These considerations did not apply to Spain, which reverted to central rule shortly after the death of Postumus. Thus Postumus' successors ruled only over Gaul and Britain.

Claudius II 'Gothicus' (268–270)

M Aurelius Claudius was born on 10 May around the year 214 in the Roman province of Upper Moesia. Later Roman historians believed him to have been a descendant of the young emperor Gordian III. By 268 he was the training commander for senior officers at Ticinum, twenty miles from Mediolanum, and was clearly highly regarded by preceding emperors as a capable general. He was one of the Danubians, commanding some of the toughest troops of the Roman army. His accession as emperor was arranged by the murderers of Gallienus, who claimed that with his dying breath Gallienus had appointed Claudius as his successor. This was wholly improbable, as Gallienus had already appointed two sons, Valerian II and the Saloninus murdered by Postumus, as caesars, and there remained a third son at Rome who would have been the natural successor. Moreover, the circumstances surrounding the death of Gallienus hardly favoured the opportunity for any genuine expression of dying wishes. However, with the loyalty of the troops secured with a bribe, Claudius' first action was to settle the siege of Aureolus at Mediolanum. The isolated pretender tried to negotiate with the new emperor, but Claudius rejected his overtures. Aureolus then surrendered, presumably on terms that he judged favourable, but was at once put to death by the angry soldiers of Gallienus' army.

It was at this time that the Alamanni festering in Germany made a disastrous misjudgement. They noted that the Roman frontier defences had been weakened by the withdrawal of troops by Gallienus and Aureolus, and poured into the province of Raetia, where many settled, before surging over the Brenner pass through the Alps into northern Italy. Happily for the Romans, Claudius had arrived to take command of the huge, combined armies of Gallienus and Aureolus that were conveniently on the spot just as the Alamanni burst into the area around Lake Garda. There nemesis overtook the marauders; Claudius utterly smashed them and only half of the barbarians survived to return to their homelands with tales of the might of Rome. Another important battle was fought near Ariminum in north-east Italy.

Claudius was now able to hurry down to Rome, where he tried to check the attacks on Gallienus' supporters, and was also recognised as emperor by the Senate in 268. The grateful senators also conferred the title 'Germanicus Maximus' on Claudius for his victory over the Alamanni. His coins show another of the stern-faced, bearded Danubian generals, but it seems that he made a real attempt to restore good relationships between emperor and Senate, after his predecessor's disregard of that institution.

After the death of Postumus, the time must have seemed right to try to re-take the Gallic–Roman empire. Claudius sent an expeditionary force under Julius Placidianus to harry the rebels during spring 269, and the mere arrival of the army west of the Alps, at Cularo (modern Grenoble), was sufficient to induce Spain to revert to the central Roman rule, as previously mentioned. Furthermore, the town of Augustodunum (Autun), which was within central Gaul and far to the north of Cularo, and was the centre of the Aedui tribe, declared for Claudius.[8] The townspeople waited eagerly for the arrival of reinforcements from the new emperor, but Claudius himself could not tarry; the Goths in the Balkans were again causing trouble. Claudius announced: 'the quarrel with the Gallic emperor is my quarrel, but the barbarian invasion is the State's quarrel. The latter must have priority.' The expeditionary force was withdrawn to its barracks, and the new rebel emperor, Victorinus, recaptured and plundered the unfortunate Augustodunum after a seven-month siege had wreaked famine and ended the town's ability to man the gates. The ruins of the city would not be restored for another three decades.

Having looted all the Roman provinces, it appears that the new Gothic invaders had now resolved to settle as permanent bandits within Roman territory. A huge migration of tribes, with baggage trains bearing possessions and families, moved across the poorly guarded Danube into

Thrace and Macedonia and across the Bosporus and thence spread their violent activities around Asia Minor (269). It may be recalled that Gallienus had earlier inflicted a severe defeat on the first invaders, before being summoned away to deal with Aureolus. In his absence, his general Marcianus had continued to harass the Goths, but the barbarians were now reinforced by the new arrivals and again besieged many cities in the area. The most important siege was that of Thessalonika.

Claudius ordered the consultation of the Sibylline Books before setting out against the Goths. When the oracle announced that 'the leading man of the most elevated order had to be sacrificed to victory', the leader of the Senate, T Pomponius Bassus, twice consul and prefect of the City of Rome, offered himself, but Claudius declared that it was for the emperor to make the sacrifice. Claudius left his brother, Quintillus, in charge of the north Italian garrisons, then hastened to join Marcianus. The sieges were lifted as Claudius arrived on the spot in person with many legions under their commander Aurelian, a fellow Danubian general, together with the Roman heavy cavalry.

The Goths were driven north by Aurelian and his cavalry. Fresh bands of Goths came down across the Danube to aid the first wave. All were crushed by Claudius in a pitched battle at Naissus in 269, separate from that won by Gallienus in 268, which also resulted in heavy Roman losses. Inscriptions dated to 269/270 show that Claudius overcame the Goths at Doberus in Macedonia and at Naissus in Moesia.

The barbarian survivors wandered in large bands around Thrace, harassed all the time by the deadly Roman cavalry. Finally they were driven into the 'Great Balkan Range' of mountains, principally Mt Haemus, in Moesia. The Roman strategy was to place a ring of steel around the hills and then to draw it tight. The Goths had to endure an evil winter (269/270) on the mountain tops, wracked by famine and plague. When their provisions ran out, the barbarians came down in small groups in search of food. They were hit in turn by the Roman cavalry and then by the slower infantry; thousands of barbarians were massacred near Marcianopolis, a walled city that they had previously tried unsuccessfully to capture. The barbarian survivors in the Balkans tried to flee north, but they had already ravaged the lands and could find no food. Famished, and stricken by plague, they were chopped down piecemeal by the pursuing Roman cavalry. Some of the desperate pursued made a stand and managed to make a surprise attack killing 2,000 Roman infantrymen, but again the Roman heavy cavalry turned the tide.

The Roman navy operating out of Egypt had destroyed the barbarian ships, manned by Heruli tribesmen, in the Aegean. Some of the pirates had reached as far as Cyprus and Crete but had achieved little. Those remnants of the Goths that survived the land war were conscripted into the Roman army or settled as colonists in the areas near the Danube that they had devastated (270); the original population had largely fled or been killed. The 'Augustan Histories' tell us that many, many slaves were also taken from the Goths and huge amounts of booty were seized – one should say, recovered. For these comprehensive victories Claudius was awarded the title 'Gothicus Maximus' and his coins commemorate 'Victoria Gothica' (Victory over the Goths).

The idea of settling former enemies within Roman territory was not a new one and had a practical intent: the newcomers provided a welcome source of hardy recruits for the army and also acted as a buffer between other barbarians outside the frontier and the more civilised parts of the Roman empire. However, the loyalty of such subjects was always uncertain. One hundred years later, a rebellion by other Gothic tribes settled within the frontier would lead to the destruction of the entire Roman army sent to tame them, and set in motion the sequence of events that effectively brought down the Roman empire. Moreover, the import of barbarians into what had once been a Roman, then an Italian, then an imperial army resulted in the increasing barbarisation of that army. However, all these difficulties lay far in the future.

While he was still mopping up the Goths, a task that would take all summer, Claudius learned of yet more barbarian invasions: by the Juthungi tribes into Raetia and of Vandals into Pannonia. Claudius delegated command of the legions against the Goths to Aurelian and then marched to Sirmium. However the devastating plague had already afflicted his army, and Claudius himself succumbed. He convened his civilian and military heads and in their presence recommended that Aurelian be appointed as his successor. Then he died, probably in late August 270.

When the news reached Rome, the Senate and population were shattered by the premature loss of a fine general and merciful emperor. They reminded themselves of the Sibylline prophecy and how Claudius had declared that it was for the emperor to sacrifice himself. Now he was dead in his hour of glory. The Senate needed no urging to appoint Claudius to a position among the gods. A golden shield was placed in the Senate house, mimicking that awarded to Augustus; several ancient writers attest the award to Claudius. The people subscribed to erect a golden statue ten feet tall in front of the Temple of Jupiter on the Capitoline, a commemoration without precedent. On the Rostra (the orators' platform in the Forum) was placed a column with a silver statue.

Such was the esteem in which the memory of Claudius was held by his subjects. The sweeping successes of Claudius against the Goths had earned their victor the appellation 'Gothicus'. After his death, a handful of Goths still menacing the Balkans made an attack on the town of Anchialus on the west coast of the Black Sea, but so great had been the extent of Claudius' victory that the local military were able to deal with the new alarm. In the next decades, newly appointed emperors starting with Constantine would be proud to trace their lineage, real or imagined, back to Claudius, and some incorporated the cognomen 'Claudius' into their official names. It has become fashionable to assert that the victories of Claudius have been exaggerated by Latin historians writing under the rule of later emperors who claimed descent from him. This raises the question of why anyone should want to claim lineage from Claudius unless his achievements had already been spectacular, and the statues described, no longer extant but doubtless well known to chroniclers of the 4th century, and inscriptions tell their own story.

The eastern problem

Gallienus and Claudius had been happy to leave the Palmyrene empire in place so long as it acknowledged the real emperor and safeguarded the eastern frontier. However, Zenobia's kingdom was growing into a real threat after the death of Gallienus. It is quite likely that the Palmyrenes felt obliged to the emperor who had appointed Odaenathus as ruler of the east, but not to those who had murdered that emperor. The distractions that the barbarians gave Claudius also afforded the Queen of Palmyra her chance.

Zenobia's son Vaballathus, in whose name she nominally ruled, had been given various high-sounding eastern titles, such as 'Corrector Totius Orientis', 'Imperator', 'King of Kings' and 'Lord of Palmyra', but these probably represented an attempt to impress their subjects with the continuity of reign between the late Odaenathus and his son. The problem was that, although Zenobia and Vaballathus were still endorsed as Rome's eastern rulers in the middle east, and expecting their authority to be recognised in provinces from Asia Minor to Egypt, many Roman forces declined to accept the Palmyrenes as their overlords. Zenobia decided to enforce her writ.

Zenobia first marched westwards and seized Syria, including the important city of Antioch (ca. 269). Forces under her general Zabdas then moved to occupy the Roman province of Arabia. The local frontier commander, Trassus, and his legion were defeated heavily near the town of Bostra. Trassus was killed and Bostra sacked (270; see map on page 37). At the same time, the mint at Antioch stopped issuing coins in the name of Claudius. The southern town of Petra was next to fall, and the Palmyrenes now controlled all of Judaea where they leaned on Egypt. Although coins were minted at Alexandria, in Egypt, for Claudius, this key province was also soon to change sides. Timagenes, a Roman officer, had rebelled in Lower Egypt in favour of Zenobia, who sent Zabdas to give aid in a move timed in early October 270 to capitalise on the death of Claudius. A combined force of 70,000 Palmyrenes, Syrians and barbarians overthrew the defence of 50,000 Egyptian troops in a pitched battle. The Palmyrenes then withdrew, leaving behind a garrison of 5,000 men.

During 269/270 the Roman fleet based at Alexandria had been conducting operations in the Aegean and eastern Mediterranean to aid Claudius by ridding the eastern Mediterranean of the Gothic sea pirates. The admiral Tenagino Probus (named as Probatus in the 'Augustan Histories', but known more accurately from inscriptions in Egypt) was in charge. After dealing with the Goths and their Heruli allies, Probus used his naval troops and a force of Egyptian volunteers to eject the Palmyrene garrison from Alexandria in early November 270 and then collected reinforcements from Egypt and the neighbouring Roman provinces of Africa to withstand the inevitable counter-attack. The Romans won a convincing victory over the returning Palmyrenes and pursued their eastern enemies. However Timagenes was able to use his local knowledge to mount a surprise attack on the Roman force in the mountainous area near Babylon; not the well known city, but a Roman garrison fort at the southern tip of the delta of the Nile river. The Romans were routed and Probus was captured and committed suicide. Thus within one month Egypt had returned into Palmyrene hands, threatening the corn supply to Rome. This could not be allowed to continue.

NOTES

1   Principal original sources for this and succeeding chapters: (i) Eutropius, *Breviarium*, translated by H W Bird (Liverpool University Press, 1993); (ii) Festus, *Breviarium*, translated by T M Banchich and J A Meka (De Imperatoribus Romanis, 2001), www.roman-emperors.org/festus.htm; (iii) Orosius, Paulus, *Seven Books of History Against the Pagans*, translated by R J Defarrari (Catholic University of America Press, 1992); (iv) *Scriptores Historiae Augustae*, translated by D Magie, Vol. III (Loeb, Harvard University Press, reprinted 1982), selected extracts; (v) Syncellus, *The Chronography of George Synkellos*, translated by A Adler and P Tuffin (Oxford University Press, 2000); (vi) Victor, Aurelius, *De Caesaribus*, translated by H W Bird (Liverpool University Press, 1994); (vii) Zosimus, *Historia Nova*, translated by J J Buchanan and H T Davis (Trinity University Press, 1967). Available only in the original Latin or in Latin translation from Greek: (i) Zonaras, Joannes, *Corpus Scriptorum Historiae Byzantinae*, translated by M Pinderi, Vol. II (Impensis, 1844); (ii) Anon., *Epitome de Caesaribus*, Appendix to Aurelius Victor (Teubner, 1911); (iii) Eusebius/Hieronymus, *Die Chronik des Hieronymus* (ed. R Helm, Akademie Verlag, 1984); (iv) Jordanes, *Romana et Getica*, recensuit T Mommsen (Berolini: Weidman, 1961).
2   Zosimus, *New History* (translator unknown), Green & Chaplin, 1814. Found in 'Translations in the Library of Nicene and Post-Nicene Fathers': www.ccel.org/fathers2/p/pearse/morefathers/.
3   Dodgeon, M H, *The Roman Eastern Frontier and the Persian Wars, AD 226–363: A Documentary History* (ed. S N C Lieu, Routledge, 1993).
4   Petrus Patricius, *Fragmenta Historicorum Graecorum*, ed. Mueller, 1883. Latin.

5   Vegetius, *Epitome of Military Science*, translated by N P Milner (Liverpool University Press, 1993).
6   Among others, Jordanes, *On the Origins and Deeds of the Goths*, translated by C C Mierow (widely distributed on the Internet: www.romansonline.com/sources/.
7   Dexippus, *Fragmenta Historicorum Graecorum*, ed. Mueller, 1883. Latin.
8   *Panegyrici Latini, In praise of Later Roman Emperors*, translated by C E V Nixon and B S Rodgers (University of California Press, 1994).

CHAPTER V

Aurelian – The Early Years

Our only source of knowledge for the early life of Lucius Domitius Aurelianus Augustus (Aurelian) is the writer known as 'Flavius Vopiscus of Syracuse', one of the six named authors of the 'Augustan Histories'.[1]

The poor reliability of this source was mentioned in the Introduction. Nevertheless, the stories concerning Aurelian's early life remain of interest. The military career of the future emperor, as narrated, is certainly consistent with the career that might have been expected, while the entire biography must have been at any rate credible to the author's contemporary readers. In the absence of any other significant information, it is impossible to say how much of the early life as narrated by Vopiscus is accurate. The wise biographer does not blindly accept that which he reads but, being aware of his ignorance, does not blindly reject it either.

Aurelian, then, was born on 9 September,[2] probably in the year 214 or 215 at Sirmium (modern Mitrovitz in the old Yugoslavia) in the Roman province of Pannonia.[3] Some other sources claim his birthplace in the province of Lower Moesia, later to be called Dacia Ripensis. He came of humble origins. His father was a farm worker for a senator named Aurelius. His mother was a priestess of the temple of the Sun god in their village.

The historian Vopiscus, following a two-century old tradition established by his better-known predecessor Suetonius, likes to mention the omens that portended the elevation of the future emperor. These make fascinating reading today, providing an insight into the signs that the superstitious ancient peoples found significant.

Aurelian's mother often quarrelled with his father and one day, with reference to their poverty, snapped at him 'Behold the father of an emperor'. She made the baby clothes from a purple cloak, which had previously been dedicated by a recent emperor, probably the Sun-worshipping Septimius Severus, to the Sun god. One day an eagle snatched up the purple-clad baby and placed him unharmed on a local shrine, which fortunately was unlit. When Aurelian was a child, a snake wound itself around his wash basin, and could not be dislodged. His mother claimed the snake as a member of the household. This bizarre tale draws its point from the well attested fact that snakes symbolised the 'genius' of the family head, and were sometimes kept as pets.

When he was older, Aurelian joined the Roman army as a humble foot soldier. This must have been around about the year 235, for the customary time to join the army was age 20, and was close to the end of the reign of the emperor Severus Alexander and the beginning of the period of crisis. He was described as 'comely, good to look upon with manly grace, tall in stature and possessed of many strong muscles'. He distinguished himself early by his military prowess. As part of a garrison of 300 men, he intercepted a raid by the 'Sarmatians' when they burst into Illyricum and he allegedly killed forty-eight barbarians in one day, followed by another 950 over several more days. This (we are told) gave rise to a children's song:

> *Thousand, thousand, thousand, we have beheaded;*
> *A single man a thousand we have beheaded;*
> *A thousand cups he may drink who a thousand has killed;*
> *No one has scarcely so much wine as the amount of blood that he shed.*

It doesn't rhyme in Latin either.

While the claim is ridiculous, it is quite clear that Aurelian's bravery and skills were early recognised. He must have received several rapid promotions, first to centurion and including a spell as deputy to one or more military tribunes, for the next we hear of him is as a military tribune stationed at Moguntiacum (modern Mainz, Germany) with the 6th Legion Gallicana which is otherwise unknown. There he aided the destruction of the Franks in Gaul during their invasions of 254–258 and was credited with killing 700 barbarians and the capture of 300, a feat that should surely be attributed to his unit rather than to their commander. This resulted in a new song:

> *A thousand Sarmatians, a thousand Franks,*
> *Again and again we've killed.*
> *We request a thousand Persians.*

The old barriers to promotion for simple legionaries, which had formerly required the higher officers to be of senatorial or knightly rank, had disappeared completely. It was now possible for the humblest soldier to aspire to rise all the way to the highest ranks. Ignoring specialist positions, the line of promotion as an officer began with the post of centurion, then led to junior tribune, senior tribune who advised the legion commander, commander of the legion, described variously as the prefect or the legate of the legion, and finally 'Dux', a general in command of at least one legion and auxiliary forces, and who often commanded the troops along an entire frontier.

It was as a military tribune that his terrible ruthlessness, severity and strictness for discipline emerged, a discipline without contemporary equal. Aurelian was nicknamed 'Hand to sword' ('Aurelianus manu ad ferrum') so that he might easily be distinguished from a fellow tribune, coincidentally also named Aurelian. Vopiscus cites an alleged letter from Aurelian to his deputy concerning military discipline: 'If you wish to be tribune, indeed if you desire to live, restrain the hand of the soldiers!' The deputy is advised to keep the soldiers from stealing from each other and from the citizenry. If they want plunder, they must seize it from Rome's enemies. They must look after their pack animals and behave with propriety. In turn, the officers must look to their men's well-being, their weapons and their uniforms. They must be treated as soldiers, not as slaves.

Aurelian himself set an example. He revived, as a new punishment, the ancient cruelty of bending over two trees with ropes, tying one foot of a miscreant to each and cutting the ropes, tearing the victim into two. This chastisement was inflicted on an adulterous soldier and served, we are informed, to 'inspire great terror in all'. The historian adds that soldiers in a unit that he had once punished never repeated the offence.

Another omen concerning Aurelian's future elevation came when, having being wounded so that he could not readily ride a horse, he rode in a carriage towards the great city of Antioch. A purple cloak spread out for him fell upon his shoulders. A century-old edict prohibited the use of a carriage within a city's walls, so Aurelian was forced to transfer to a horse. He was inadvertently given the emperor's own steed. When he realised the error, he switched at once to another mount, but this second portent was equally noted.

General for the emperor Valerian

Aurelian's career continued to flourish. He must have been promoted to the post of prefect (commander) of a legion, for Vopiscus informs us that he now became deputy to one or more Roman generals, who had the command of legions and auxiliary troops. It was at about this time – perhaps when he had become a full general – that Aurelian was appointed as an envoy to the Persians, where he received as gifts a sacrificial saucer from the Persian king, presumably Shapur, and an elephant. The first gift was commonly reserved for Roman emperors, the second could not legally be held except by a Roman emperor for military use. Aurelian was the first individual to own an elephant, and he passed it on at once to the legitimate emperor, not named but probably Valerian. Again, the omens for Aurelian's advancement were noted by his biographer.

65

Vopiscus records an exchange between the emperor Valerian and one Antoninus Gallus, otherwise unknown, concerning who should be guardian of the emperor's son, Gallienus. Gallus had argued that Aurelian would make a better choice than his master's selection of Postumus, the future rebel. Valerian replied that Aurelian 'is excessive; he is overbearing; he is heavy-handed' and expressed his fears that Aurelian would treat his pleasure-seeking son too severely. We may guess that Vopiscus' choice of phrase ('pleasure-seeking') is another dig at the despised Gallienus.

Another letter quoted by the historian is from Valerian to the city prefect, named as 'Ceionius Albinus', possibly M Nummius Ceionius Annius Albinus, known to have held the office in 256. During these difficult years, Valerian wished to reward those officers who had remained loyal, not only with promotions but also with more tangible benefits. However, he feared putting too heavy a tax burden on the provinces if the cash element were taken too far. Aurelian, however, was deemed to be an exceptionally deserving case, being both brave and capable, and Valerian therefore promoted him to 'Inspector of military camps' while enjoining the city prefect to provide victuals and cash to Aurelian while the latter was at Rome.

Ulpius Crinitus

It is now that the senator Ulpius Crinitus comes to the fore. Although unknown outside the 'Augustan Histories', and his existence is strongly doubted by modern historians, he was apparently the commander-in-chief (Dux) of the Illyrian and Thracian border under the emperor Valerian. Aurelian was made his deputy. When Crinitus was sick, Valerian ordered Aurelian to tackle a Gothic incursion around Nicopolis with full command. Aurelian was entrusted with the 3rd Legion and some 2,500 auxiliary troops as well as the forces of four friendly German chieftains.

As substitute and as deputy for Crinitus, Aurelian commanded troops, repelled barbarian invasions, had the authority to distribute the booty from defeated Goths to his troops and enriched his provinces with captured spoils including horses, cattle and slaves. He was also able to provide the emperor personally with an immense quantity of loot seized from the barbarians, while Crinitus thanked Valerian for giving him such a talented deputy.

Yet Aurelian himself had always been a poor man, although doubtless he had gained personally from the wealth recovered from Rome's enemies. Perhaps all poverty is relative. At any rate, Crinitus decided to adopt him as his heir, maintaining a long-established tradition whereby distinguished aristocrats without sons continued their family line for posterity; Aurelian was already his protégé. Valerian planned to make Aurelian a consul, Vopiscus tells us, although Aurelian does not appear to have received his first consulship until 271, when he was already emperor. Owing to his general's relative poverty, Valerian instructed the treasury prefect to hand over specified sums of cash so that Aurelian could hold celebratory races in the Circus and provide a huge banquet for the senators and knights. The consulship was to be taken with Ulpius Crinitus in order to 'fill out' the consulships of Valerian and Gallienus, starting on 22 May 257.

The appointment must have been delayed, as the historian now cites an audience of Aurelian with Valerian in 258 from the book of the 'Master of Admissions', a record of discussions kept by the freedman who decided whom the emperor would see. Valerian and his highest officials were resident at the Public Baths at Byzantium when Aurelian was received. The emperor publicly thanked his general for freeing the State from Gothic incursions and gave him numerous rewards together, we are told, with his appointment as consul. Aurelian arose and thanked his emperor with 'soldierly words', saying that he had done it all for the approval of the State and of his conscience.

Ulpius Crinitus now stood up and announced the adoption of Aurelian as his son, with the blessing of the emperor. Crinitus himself was supposedly of the Ulpii family whose most famous son had been the emperor Marcius Ulpius Trajanus (Trajan), so that it would certainly have been a signal honour to Aurelian. It is often supposed – without any authority – that Crinitus' daughter was now married to Aurelian. Certainly, Aurelian appears subsequently as a married emperor. Many years later, Aurelian would place a painting, showing his adoptive father with Aurelian, in the new Temple of the Sun at Rome (see Chapter VIII). Crinitus now drops out of history.

General for the emperors Gallienus and Claudius

After the death of Valerian, Vopiscus omits to mention any part that Aurelian played under the rule of Gallienus, nor of his part in the conspiracy that felled the latter. We learn only that he held many commands as general, but the emperors are not mentioned. One might conjecture that Aurelian fell out of favour with Gallienus, explaining the biographer's silence and the general's role in the conspiracy, but this seems to be unlikely. The general Ingenuus who rebelled against Gallienus (see Chapter III) was, presumably, the successor to Ulpius Crinitus and his deputy Aurelian as c-in-c of the Illyrian and Thracian border. Aurelian may have aided Aureolus and Domitianus, Gallienus' generals, to suppress the eastern usurper Macrianus and his sons. One might also suppose that Aurelian would have been present as a senior cavalry officer when Gallienus dealt with the massive Gothic incursion of 267. He must have accompanied the emperor when Aureolus revolted, in order to be part of the conspiracy against Gallienus.

We are now returning to more certain historical ground,[4] and not relying solely on Vopiscus. Under the reign of the new emperor Claudius, Aurelian remained loyal. Claudius entrusted the wars against the Goths and Heruli, who had poured out of the Sea of Azov around 267 (see last chapter), to Aurelian. He was appointed full commander of the legions in the area and, against his old adversaries, Aurelian again acquitted himself well. When some of the heavy cavalry force ran into a serious disaster towards the end of the campaign, Claudius dismissed its commanders for being 'rash' and acting without orders. Aurelian was assigned as general of this large, elite force, presumably replacing Cecropius, the last known commander of the heavy cavalry. This was a huge distinction and a mark of trust by the emperor. Late in 269 Claudius left Aurelian in charge of mopping up operations against the Goths whom Claudius had defeated in Thrace and Moesia. Then Claudius died in August 270, supposedly recommending that Aurelian be the next emperor.

Quintillus (270)

Quintillus was the brother of Claudius. Stationed at Aquileia to protect the north-east of Italy from incursions, Quintillus promptly proclaimed himself as emperor after the death of Claudius. He was hailed as such by the Roman Senate and coins were issued in his name, but he made the error of remaining at Aquileia.

Aurelian had probably been the author of the conspiracy that saw the murder of Gallienus and the accession of Claudius. He had remained loyal to the new emperor. After the death of the latter, he claimed to be Claudius' chosen successor, in rivalry with Quintillus, but felt it first necessary to complete the campaign against the barbarians in the Balkans for which Claudius had left him in charge. Aurelian continued to augment his 'illustrious' (Vopiscus) reputation by crushing the retiring Goths, perhaps relieving the sieges of the cities of Anchialus and Nicopolis, before he moved to Sirmium in Pannonia. He and his cavalry had destroyed the Gothic forces completely and recovered huge quantities of booty. Aurelian was acclaimed as the true emperor, the legitimate heir of the dying Claudius, by his army in September and was rapidly supported by all the other Roman legions, including those of Quintillus. Aurelian was 56 years old.

The army of Quintillus refused to heed their commander's speeches claiming accession and it was put to him that he ought to stand down in favour of the better man, rather than initiate another bloody civil war. Quintillus went to the extreme length of committing suicide by allowing his veins to be opened in the traditional Roman manner. His reign was certainly not longer than two or three months, from archaeological evidence dating the death of Claudius and the accession of Aurelian.

The accession of Aurelian is known from the evidence of Egyptian papyri to have been actually somewhere between September and December 270. However, he declined to recognise the rule of Quintillus, and chose to backdate his reign to the death of Claudius, sometime around August 270. Rather curiously, Egyptian papyri recognise in turn, first the rule of Claudius, then by consuls (sic) from October to December 270, and then joint rule by Aurelian and the Palmyrene Vaballathus. Almost certainly this reflects changing attitudes by the Palmyrene administrators at that time controlling Egypt.

Aurelian's army

This is a good place to discuss the nature of the Roman army that Aurelian had inherited. Most readers are doubtless familiar with the general appearance of the army of the first half of the 1st century AD, say from Augustus to Nero, through numerous depictions with varying degrees of authenticity in films. Readers who live in Britain may also have seen the much more accurate re-enactments by the 'Ermine Street Guard', which also features in documentaries.

The army of Aurelian would certainly have been readily recognisable by a Roman soldier of the 1st century.[5] Although there had been some changes in protective armour and in tactics, it remained fundamentally the same fighting force although, as already mentioned, an elite formation of heavy armoured cavalry now formed its core. In Republican times, the Romans already had to provide for military operations 'contarii', cavalrymen with a large sword and lance ('contus'). By the end of the 2nd century AD there existed units of 'cataphractarii', lightly armoured riders whose attire can still be seen with some inscriptions. However, the Persians were using 'clibanarii', heavily armoured cavalrymen whose horses were also covered with armour. Gallienus greatly increased the number of clibanarii units for his new mobile army, but the new 'Dalmatian cavalry', lightly mailed cataphractarii, predominated.[6]

Roman horses were comparatively small and were saddled, conferring much greater stability to the rider than a bare-back mount. Even so the stirrup, which greatly aids violent manoeuvres on a horse, had yet to be invented so that neither the Roman cavalry, nor their opponents, possessed this steadying item of equipment which would not appear until the 8th century. Therefore the saddles had special horns to support the body. The famous legions remained as ten cohorts, now each of 555 men (the first cohort possessed 1,105 men), with 726 heavy armoured cavalry and with numerous attachments of light auxiliary forces, such as light cavalry. The total force probably exceeded 7,000 men.

The old distinction between the legions, manned by 'citizens', not necessarily from Italy, and auxiliary forces (who were not citizens, but could expect Roman citizenship after an honourable discharge) disappeared in 212, when the emperor Caracalla declared all free men within the empire to be citizens. However, there still remained a clear distinction between the first-class forces employed by the legions and the distinctly second-class units of various irregular militia. The legions were provided with much better equipment, almost invariably of iron, whereas the auxiliaries were often provided with cheap, mass produced items. The auxiliaries were used mostly to help guard the frontiers of the empire.

We know of no pay increases received by the ordinary Roman soldier at all, after Caracalla's steep increases in the second decade of the 3rd century. Yet the debasement of the currency had reduced the soldier's real pay by 99.5%! In compensation, the soldier no longer had to pay for his own rations, bedding, clothing and weapons, and in fact received increased rations at no charge. Savings were provided in the form of frequent imperial hand-outs of gold and silver bullion, often made up into commemorative medals. Even so, the temptations for army units to indulge in corruption and to terrorise their neighbourhood must have been strong.

By the time of Aurelian, the standard legion had been found to be too inflexible for many purposes, and it was already the custom to create larger army units out of 'vexillations', detachments of specialist troops sent from one legion to aid the requirements of another formation. An elite force, such as Aurelian's main army, might contain vexillations of extra cavalry, archers, who were usually detached from the eastern legions where archery had attained a high degree of proficiency, and even slingers, who threw heavy stones. The advantages of firing long-range missiles against a packed enemy force were slowly becoming apparent, and would achieve much greater prominence in the next century and thereafter. Again, a force built up to lay siege to a city would require extra vexillations of artillery units, predominantly of catapults that hurled huge boulders, or 'Scorpions', devices rather like over-sized crossbows that could project an arrow with deadly force and high precision over long distances.

Each legion was intended to be a self-contained unit, so far as practical. Many of the soldiers would be trained as craftsmen, from engineers to surveyors; from medical orderlies to road builders. When on the march, the army would carry all necessary equipment with it in a baggage train that would often include the coins for the soldiers' pay. This provided a strong incentive not to desert the standard. At the end of each day, typically after a march of twenty-four miles on good Roman roads, the soldiers would set up camp. In territory threatened by an enemy, the camp would be surrounded by a complete wooden barricade made up from the two posts that each soldier carried on the march. The fence would be surrounded by a hastily dug ditch, while other soldiers stood on guard over the constructors of the camp. The marching army required a huge supply chain, some details of which have come down to us from the 4th century, but all would be provided in good time, usually by tax levies in kind on the local community. The army had to secure its supply line in enemy lands, although it was also possible to forage in fields of cereal crops. Contrary to common belief, the Roman soldiers were not pre-dominantly vegetarian – unless forced to be – but ate the same foods, meat, cereals and shellfish as the remainder of the population.

Each legionary was encased in heavy armour, protected by a shield and provided with a short stabbing sword with which he had been trained for his role as a skilled exponent of sword play within a line of similar swordsmen. There were three lines, which regularly rotated to the front row that actually did the fighting. Roman legionaries were not expected to indulge in slashing or two-handed sword sweeps, tactics that they viewed with contempt. The infantry would also carry one or two spears of different types, used for stabbing or for hurling against compact enemy lines where accuracy mattered little. An enemy shield transfixed by a spear became virtually unusable, and its bearer would have to discard it.

No soldier had to accept the personal protective equipment with which he had been issued, if he wished to provide himself with a superior sub-stitute, and the officers, who were better paid, in particular often wore the finest armour available. The metalwork did not roll off from a modern steel mill. It all had to be laboriously hand-finished with hammers, and therefore considerable variations arose in the standard issue, quite apart from natural developments in design. We no longer know how many armouries the Romans possessed, but it is generally supposed that they were small and operated by free, or freed, men, not by slaves, under contract to the army. In the general economic decline of the 3rd century, we may suppose that many of these small units would have ceased production – or even have been unable to move their output to where it was needed – so that skilled manufacture of armour and swords must have diminished just when it was most needed. Later Diocletian (284–305) would find it necessary to organise state factories to manufacture the army's weapons and armour. There would then be twenty factories in the western half of the empire and fifteen in the east, counting both general and specialist manufacturers, operated by free workers subject to military discipline.

The best form of bodily protection was provided by linked mail, where thousands of tiny rings, made from extruded bronze wire and sometimes as small as 3mm (0.12 inch) each, were linked together. The rings could be bent to form the necessary circles, but the Romans employed the far stronger technique of riveting the links. Linked mail had been known

71

since the 6th century BC, and provided immensely strong and flexible protection that could be extended to cover the torso, the upper arms and the thighs. The mail was very hard-wearing, but difficult to repair once damaged. It was also very heavy, weighing typically 6.8kg (fifteen pounds). It is evident that hand-made production of such mail must be terribly slow – 180 man hours per unit, according to modern reconstruction – and correspondingly expensive. The mail could be re-used time and time again, but if a legion so attired were to fall in battle, it would take a very long time to re-equip the replacement troops.

Scale armour was much easier to produce, and therefore cheaper than mail, and was widespread throughout the civilised world. Small metallic fish-like scales were allowed to dangle freely from rows of horizontal metal rings in such a way as to overlap each line below. The scales could be easily damaged, but were readily replaced. The scales provided lesser protection than mail against a direct sword thrust, while their big disadvantage was that they were almost useless against a thrust upwards, such as might be made by a foot soldier armed with a spear against a mounted cavalryman. By the time of Aurelian, much greater protection was afforded by attaching the scales to vertical rings, as well as horizontal, but the result was far too stiff to permit ready movement of the body and the armour was employed best by cavalry troopers who had less need to bend. Scale armour would be used primarily by the auxiliary forces, but it was also used by both the Roman heavy cavalry and the Persian and Palmyrene horsemen to protect their mounts. The horses must have found the weight of both their own armour and of the armoured rider to be quickly exhausting.

The Romans invented the 'cuirass' type of laminated (overlapping) armour in the 1st century AD, where large strips of overlapping metal were held in place by rawhide thongs. These provided excellent protection of the torso, and separate laminated metal strips could protect the upper arms. Moreover, the armour was very flexible. It took only sixty hours to produce, one third of the time needed for mail, was lighter at 5.5kg (twelve pounds) and conferred almost as much protection. Even so, it must have taken some time to re-equip all the legions, and scale armour persisted in the eastern provinces for many years after the first introduction of the cuirass. The general type went through at least two revisions, until the best version had been reached before Aurelian's time. A further addition by then had been the use of laminated metal strips to protect the sword-arm. The upper thighs of the legionary were protected by 'pteruges', strips of tough leather, while metal guards, rather like cricket pads, shielded the lower legs.

With so much effort and cost expended on the armour, it is evident that every effort would be made to re-use it whenever possible. It is likely that some of Aurelian's men – especially those clad in mail – would be wearing armour that had seen service one, perhaps two, centuries previously. The knowledge of this must have created a tremendous reinforcement of Roman military tradition.

The army's helmets were generally of a standard type, of iron for the legionaries and of bronze for the auxiliary troops. Again the style will be familiar from films, with the two hanging cheek pieces. However, some of Aurelian's heavy cavalry may by now have had their heads almost completely enclosed, bar part of the face, with a new design. Sword slashes by cavalrymen had become much more of a commonplace to both cavalry and infantry, so that the old metal extension of the helmet at the back of the neck had been strengthened and widened on the helmets of Aurelian's soldiers.

The legionary shield had finally settled down to the familiar, curved rectangle, with a bronze boss in the middle to protect the bearer's hand. The shield could be used to punch an opponent, as well as for self-defence. By contrast, the cavalry seem to have used oval or even circular shields. Auxiliary forces may have used any pattern.

The old, deadly, double-sided Roman thrusting sword, a weapon that readily inflicted a mortal wound, was made of iron and had a handle finished with ivory, doubtless also often re-used. Shields and swords were manufactured to be strong, so that they did not break easily in combat. Archaeological finds suggest that some Roman swords at this time were being replaced by an inferior slashing type, of barbarian pattern. Few Roman swords of this period remain after centuries of rusting, and the evidence is confusing as to the users of the new weapon. The cavalry, mounted on their horses, naturally needed a longer sword, but probably preferred to use spears, either for thrusting or for throwing. Similarly, the old, short legionary dagger had been dropped by the 2nd century, but reappeared in the 3rd as a strange, barbaric, long (41cm; 16 inch) substitute. It appears that, as the importance of the infantry declined, their weaponry slowly became worse.

Roman units possessed their own standards known as 'eagles', long poles bearing elaborate images and decorations and borne by an appointed standard bearer. The standards were believed to carry the 'genius' of the unit, so that loss of the eagle implied much more than disgrace, but a spiritual loss too. Roman soldiers were expected to guard their standards zealously, and their government would go to great lengths to try to recover any that had been captured.

Vegetius[7] has passed down to us the standard Roman tactics at this time. The heavily armoured Roman infantry stood on favourable ground 'like a wall' in lines. Behind the wall were placed reserves of armoured infantry to patch up any break in the wall under attack, or for any other tactical purpose required by the legionary commander. The heavily armoured cavalry were also placed behind the infantry wall. They would be brought forward to attack straggling lines of advancing or retiring enemy soldiers or cavalry. Light auxiliary forces, such as slingers, archers and light cavalry, were placed in front of the wall. They advanced to challenge and harass the foe. If successful, they pursued the retreating enemy forces; otherwise, they retired behind the armoured wall as the enemy advanced. The heavy cavalry would be moved forward to attack the advance, before retiring again behind the wall. The armoured legionaries of the wall would now engage in battle with javelins and then with their swords. Assuming they were successful and the enemy fell back, the heavy cavalry would smash into the retiring troops from the sides, while the light forces would continue the rout as far as necessary. Under no circumstances was the wall expected to break ranks and pursue the enemy.

It is only in recent years that attempts have been made to reconstruct the actual mechanism by which individual Roman soldiers fought. The Roman sources provide very sketchy information about sword fighting, and the bayonet remains the only comparable modern weapon. Modern military manuals state explicitly the effect of the 'terror of cold steel' on the enemy, an effect far greater than the less-feared (but much more effective) impersonal missile, such as a spear or a bullet. Roman armies and their adversaries had to confront this terror all the time, and it was probably only the possession of effective armour that made it bearable.

The idea projected by Hollywood films, that individual soldiers charged at each other and engaged in individual combat with opponents, is mistaken, for no sane soldier would leave his back exposed to an unseen enemy. The soldiers fought in lines at all times. The sources tell us that some battles went on for many hours. Yet how can heavily armoured men fight under conditions of, literally, life-and-death for so long without becoming rapidly exhausted? The Romans used three lines of swordsmen who would rotate regularly to relieve one another, but the lines would have needed time to rotate while their less-organised adversaries must have collapsed from physical and nervous exhaustion within an hour. Sabin[8] has calculated that, if just 5% of the troops on each side stood in the front row, they struck out just once every five seconds, and that only 1% of the strikes caused the opponent to die, each army would still suffer 5% casualties within just ten minutes. Yet victorious armies rarely suffered more than 5% losses in total.

In fact, continuous battle is a physical and nervous impossibility for armies armed with swords, and it seems that the opposing lines of soldiers stood off from one another separated by a few metres, with weapons bristling, until part of one line nerved itself to move forward and engage its opposite numbers. Since few of the soldiers would willingly risk their lives in combat, especially to cold steel, it would require a great deal of incentive to induce any part of the line to advance. Usually a standard bearer would lead the way, a grade of officers picked for their bravery and known to have an exceptionally high casualty rate. Most of the advancing soldiers would rank self-protection with their shields far higher than aggressive use of their swords during the engagement, so freedom of movement was essential. If they were successful, the enemy would fall back a little; if unsuccessful, the advancing party would retire again. One line might be pushed hundreds of metres if the other side was clearly superior.

With both sides mostly separated by a few metres, it is evident that the use of missiles such as javelins could be effective, and we know that this was a common cause of casualties even during the main battle. Roman javelins were designed to snap after first use, so that they could not be re-used by the enemy. This type of skirmishing could indeed go on for hours, and even have to end at the onset of darkness without either side having gained an advantage. Casualties during this period would be light, not exceeding for both sides the 5% ultimately sustained by the winning army. However, if at any point one of the enemy lines collapsed or fell back in panic, the encouraged Roman troops could crash in, causing further panic and the less-organised enemy to start to run. It is now that the victors could hack down their fleeing opponents. In earlier times, casualty figures among the defeated army then rose to around 10% dead, but the relentless and efficient Romans sought to maximise their advantage through the use of cavalry to pursue the vanquished, inflicting losses of around 15% dead on their foes and completing the rout of the remainder. Even higher losses were often inflicted on the poorly armoured barbarians. By contrast, the strict discipline and available reserves of a Roman army meant that it was less likely to fall back, and even when it was defeated it would normally have inflicted terrible losses on its victorious opponents.

It was the custom in ancient times for victorious armies always to plunder their defeated foes; the eagerly sought prize and recompense for their hard-fought victory. However, the disciplined Romans did not begin the pillaging until the enemy had entirely fled or surrendered. When the officers now gave the signal, there was systematic looting of the enemy camp or city by selected troops while the majority stood guard against a surprise attack. Thus there was no free-for-all such as had resulted in the undoing of countless less-drilled armies. The booty was later sold and the proceeds distributed to all the soldiers, including those who had been sick or sent on special duties.

The Roman army put great store on rigidity in its orders of march or battle, holding that slackness created weaknesses that led to defeat. Military discipline had always been severe, but it had been allowed to lapse through the chaos of the middle of the 3rd century. It was Aurelian's achievement that it was so strongly re-instilled into the army. It is worth emphasising here the advantages that a properly organised, well disciplined permanent Roman army backed by the resources of an empire had over its barbarian counterpart: guaranteed supplies, medical assistance, superior armour and weaponry created by skilled craftsmen, and the military advantages conferred by its constant training, practised tactics and superior order in battle. By contrast, the barbarian rabble, no matter how brave, fought as individuals and were generally equipped only with a spear (the crudest form of aggressive weapon) and a shield made of skins bound over a wooden frame. They lacked the technology to manufacture swords and armour, and only rarely could support horses for use as cavalry. They relied on a single massed shock-charge to break down their opponents and were extremely vulnerable to expert Roman archers, recruited from the east. The barbarians were baffled as soon as their food ran out and the land about them had been laid waste – usually by themselves.

The Roman army drawn up in full armour and ceremonial finery behind its standards must have been a glittering sight indeed, and the historian Dexippus gives us an account (see next chapter), probably as an eyewitness, of its effect on an awed barbarian mob. This was the army that Aurelian now controlled, rejuvenated by his reassertion of discipline and still the most powerful military machine on the planet.

NOTES

1   'Vopiscus of Syracuse' in *Scriptores Historiae Augustae*, Vol. III, 'The Deified Aurelian', translated by D Magie (Loeb, Harvard University Press, 1932, reprinted 1982).
2   Chronicler of 354 in *Monumenta, Germaniae Historica, Chronica Minora*, Vol. 1 (ed. Mommsen, 1892). Latin.
3   (i) Zumptio, C T, *Annales Romani*, 3rd edn (Berolini, 1862). Latin; (ii) *Dictionary of Greek and Roman Biography and Mythology*, Vol. I (ed. W Smith, J. Walton, 1870); (iii) *Prosopographia Imperii Romani* ('PIR', 2nd edn, 1933). Latin.
4   Principal original sources (see Chapter IV, Note 1).
5   (i) Simkins, M and Embleton, R, *The Roman Army* (Osprey 'Men at Arms' series, Vols 46, 1984 revised edn and 93, 1979); (ii) Jones, A H M, *The Later Roman Empire*, Vols 1 & 2 (Blackwell & Mott, 1964; reprinted Johns Hopkins paperbacks, 1986).
6   Eadie, J W, 'Development of Roman Mailed Cavalry' in *Journal of Roman Studies*, 57: 161–73 (1967).
7   Vegetius, *Epitome of Military Science*, translated by N P Milner (Liverpool University Press, 1993).
8   Sabin, P, 'The Face of Roman Battle' in *Journal of Roman Studies*, 90: 1–17 (2000).

CHAPTER VI
Aurelian the Emperor (270–275)

Aurelian was now the sole recognised emperor,[1] the twenty-ninth to rule, within that part of the empire that still acknowledged Rome's authority. The mints of Cyzicus and Siscia (see maps pages 29 and 37) had already issued coins in his name; after the death of Quintillus the other Roman mints of Mediolanum (Milan) and Rome followed suit. However, he had no time to savour his success, as barbarians were threatening everywhere. He did not even have the time to travel to the capital city to get himself formally recognised by the Senate. Instead, a deputation of senators came to greet Aurelian at the northern Italian city of Ravenna in November 270.[2] The new emperor hoped to maintain the friendly relationships that his predecessor (Claudius) had fostered with the Senate after the ill-feeling generated previously by Gallienus, and planned to share his first consulship as emperor at the beginning of the new year with the leading man of their order, T Pomponius Bassus. 'How should I rule wisely?', asked the emperor modestly. 'Make use of gold and iron,' replied one of the senators. 'Iron for those who are enemies, gold for those who co-operate.'

The order of events that follows is hopelessly confused in the literature. We shall follow the traditional sequence, but an alternative will be outlined later. Aurelian set out against the Juthungi tribe, from north of the Danube, who had opportunistically invaded northern Italy after the death of Claudius; the latter had died while moving to meet the threat. Since the defection of Postumus, the system of fortifications protecting the gap, the Agri Decumantes, between the Rhine frontier and the Danube had effectively been abandoned, despite attempts at restoration by Postumus, and the Alpine passes were undefended. Allegedly as many as 80,000 combined tribesmen on foot and horse had attacked the frontier cities in the province of Raetia and then devastated the area from the Danube in Raetia as far south as the Italian river Po. The tribesmen began to withdraw, burdened with their loot. Aurelian collected together an elite force of fleet-footed infantry that raced silently ahead to ambush the invaders on their retreat across the Danube. The Juthungi walked straight into the trap. As their hordes began the crossing of the river the Roman army, positioned in the forests in a crescent spread over both sides of the

77

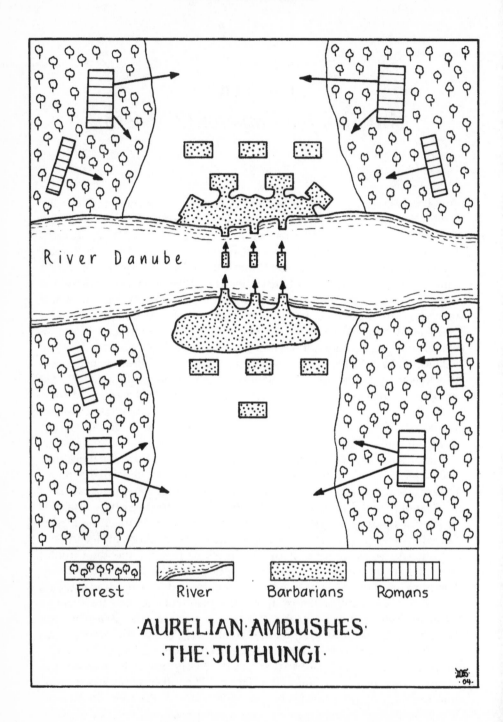

Forest   River   Barbarians   Romans

·AURELIAN·AMBUSHES·
·THE·JUTHUNGI·

water, closed the two arms of the crescent behind the barbarians to create a steel ring surrounding the enemy who were caught with half their number on each side of the river (see diagram opposite).

After many of the Juthungi had been killed while attempting the passage of the Danube, the survivors sent envoys to the Romans. We have a full account from a fragment of the 'Histories' of Dexippus.[3]

The swaggering emissaries were not at all fearful of their fate, merely concerned that the tribute paid to them by earlier emperors might be forfeit. However, Aurelian had determined to set an example. He deliberately set himself raised high on a dais, cloaked in purple, while the entire army was arranged around him in the form of a crescent. The officers stood by their horses. Behind Aurelian were displayed all the insignia of the legions – golden eagles, the portraits of emperors past, and the names of great generals displayed in gold letters; the whole paraded on spears made of silver.

Then the Juthungi envoys were commanded to appear. They were struck dumb at the sight and remained for a long time silent. Finally Aurelian gave them leave to speak, which they did through an interpreter. The spokesmen attempted a vainglorious justification of their actions, boasting of the strength upon which they could call (40,000 horsemen and 80,000 footmen in all, although not all were then present), and that they were prepared for war, trusting in their strength, their fierceness and their ancestors. However, in view of the uncertainty of the outcome, they were willing to offer peace in exchange for restoration of their tribute.

The emperor was not prepared to put up with this nonsense, and replied forthrightly on these lines (shortened and paraphrased):

> If you really want peace, why are you demanding money, and then threatening war if you don't get it? But the Romans are skilled at war, and you will fear it. You have grabbed booty by fire and sword and are only frustrated by our power and your rashness. We have already destroyed 300,000 Goths [a reference to Claudius' crushing victory at Mt Haemus in 269/270, in which Aurelian himself had played a major role], and monuments show our glory. Let us not forget either that we have brought swift reprisal to the Alamanni [a reference to their attack during the reign of Gallienus].
>
> Your passage across the Danube into our lands broke the treaty you had with us, although we had done you no injury. Thus we can rely on the offended gods to help us. We cannot predict the outcome of the battle, but we trust in our strength and our ancestors. You, however, are encircled by our men, and time and famine both work against you. Soon you will surrender to us anyway. The whole of your peace petition is nothing, unless a facade to conceal your fear. Given our position of strength, why do we even consider it?

The envoys departed 'greatly dismayed', Dexippus assures us, having hoped with bold words to retain their booty and reclaim their tribute. Aurelian himself departed – he had to attend to the pressing business of getting himself appointed emperor at Rome. The war he left to his generals.

Imagine his frustration, then, when news arrived that some of the Juthungi had broken out to the rear of the trap, back towards Italy where they ravaged the area around Mediolanum. Aurelian at once returned to the scene with a flying force of light troops, while the legions followed at their best speed. The barbarians were broken up in a series of minor skirmishes.

Aurelian was finally able to reach Rome as the undisputed emperor at the end of 270, when his position was confirmed by the reluctant Senate, which, it may be recalled, had previously supported Quintillus. This is the evidence of Zosimus, and is supported by common sense, for new emperors who did not move quickly to get their status affirmed tended to face usurpers. However, it is also possible that Aurelian did not finally arrive in Rome until the following year (see below).

Immediately urgent messages reached the new emperor that the Vandals and perhaps Sarmatians were planning to enter the Balkans again by passage across the Danube near Aquincum (modern Budapest). Aurelian at once hastened northwards via Aquileia and into Pannonia, sending instructions ahead for a scorched-earth policy. All food supplies in the provinces of Upper and Lower Pannonia were to be moved at once into the cities there so that the barbarians – who would never think to bring their own supplies – could not make use of them. All citizens were to be ready to retire smartly into the same walled towns. Then the emperor himself arrived with his army and there resulted a pitched battle with the marauders. When darkness fell, and the two sides separated, the Romans were unsure who had won, but the Vandals re-crossed the Danube during the night and sued for peace. This time, interestingly, Aurelian consulted his own weary troops as to the measures that should be taken. Again, we have the story from a fragment of Dexippus' history. The emperor invited his troops to examine the enemy camp, and to pick out whether there was anything they wanted to grab for themselves, but the soldiers decided to opt for a peaceful resolution. The barbarian survivors were permitted to return home empty-handed on condition that they refrained from further pillaging, furnished high-ranking hostages against their good behaviour – a common practice in Roman times – and also provided 2,000 cavalrymen for the Roman army. A party of 500 Vandals failed to honour the truce and was massacred by the Romans. This temporarily secured the Danube frontier, and also made possible the establishment of a market where the barbarians could conduct trade with the province. Particularly in red wine, one might guess. For this achievement Aurelian appears to have been awarded the title of 'Sarmaticus Maximus', although this early distinction is surprisingly rare on later inscriptions about him.

German invasion of Italy (winter 270–271)

At once there arrived advance intelligence of a fresh impending attack on Italy by the Alamanni. Gibbon believes that these were the survivors who had broken out of the ring constructed earlier by the army encircling the Juthungi, but Aurelian would have needed two large armies if one was to be left containing the Juthungi and another to fight the Vandals. Aurelian posted a considerable garrison on the Danube and his army rushed back from Pannonia, although the emperor himself was delayed for a few days. In fact there was a formidable incursion across the Alps into northern Italy by fresh waves of Alamanni, Marcomanni and Juthungi tribesmen, who had by-passed the garrison at Ariminum on the north-east Italian coast before bursting into the fertile Italian plains. Since the Alpine passes are blocked until March, we must assume that the invasion occurred in the spring of 271 unless, as is possible, the snows melted earlier in the warmer seasons of the Roman imperial age.

Aurelian raced back in person from the Danube with a flying cohort of light auxiliaries, while the legions he had sent back earlier arrived in the nick of time after a long march. The emperor's tactics are unclear despite the several ancient accounts, unusually in general agreement, of what happened next. The Romans may have blocked the retreat of the invaders at a spot near Placentia in north-west Italy, which the Germans had sacked, or they may have been pressing hard on the barbarian heels as they advanced, nibbling them from the rear. Aurelian send a message to the barbarians, saying 'if you want to fight, I am prepared, but you would do better to surrender, and I give guarantees as your lord'. Their arrogant reply was: 'We have no lord, and in the morning indeed be prepared, for you will see how free men can fight.' Rather than face an open battle the barbarians retreated into the forests. At evening they ambushed and severely defeated the Roman army, probably while it was still hastening to the threatened area.

The news caused panic at Rome, where the citizens remembered only too well the invasion of the Alamanni deep into Italy little more than a decade earlier. Felicissimus, the mint-master there who had been accused of debasing the coinage to pocket some of the silver supplied for the purpose, created a dangerous riot, perhaps aided and abetted by senators who feared the return of Aurelian. Some say that Felicissimus had filed off the emperor's coin marks. It has been conjectured that Aurelian might have threatened to close the mint to end thefts of coins and silver. What we do know, from the evidence of the coins themselves, is that Aurelian's first issue of coins, the 'Divus Claudius' series to commemorate his late mentor, the newly deified emperor Claudius, was the worst issue ever for quality. Another cause of dissatisfaction at Rome would have occurred if the Palmyrenes, controlling Egypt, had stopped the normal despatch in spring of the grain ships to Rome. This would have caused a fear of starvation, but assumes that Queen Zenobia was ready to make the final break with Rome. Her coins issued at this time still acknowledged Aurelian as emperor.

The emergency required that the Senate consult the Sibylline Books again. Yet some of the senators hesitated, for fear that divine aid might lessen the emperor's reputation for which the senators might in turn have to pay. According to the 'Augustan Histories',[4] the emperor himself 'marvelled at you, O Senators, to have hesitated so long about opening the Sibylline Books, as though you were debating in the church of the Christians, and not in the Temple of all the gods'. He went on to offer any sum of money or human or animal sacrifices that might be desired by the rituals. The story is doubtless apocryphal, but gives an insight into the views of at least the pagan writer on key differences between Christianity and the Roman religious tradition.

So the Sibylline Books were at last consulted with the appropriate ceremonies, and two regular festivals, the Ambarvalia and the Amburbium, were brought forward, involving the ritual procession of sacrificial animals that would subsequently be slaughtered. Areas around which the animals had first been paraded could not, according to the prophecies, be passed by the barbarians. The 'Augustan Histories' date the consultation to 11 January 271, but this must be far too early.

Meanwhile, the successful, yet undisciplined, Germans had broken into small parties to plunder the north of Italy. The 'Augustan Histories' attribute this to the success of the rituals; we do not know of their effect on the superstitious minds of the barbarians. Aurelian reorganised his forces and dogged the rear of the careless tribesmen as they advanced down the great Aemilian and Flaminian roads leading to the capital from the north-east coast of Italy. Thus the Romans were able to deal with the barbarians in small parcels, each delivering a shattering blow with overwhelming numbers on the Roman side. Pressed hard, the Alamanni were unable to pillage the defenceless towns of Pisaurum and Fanum Fortunae on the Aemilian Way. As they turned westwards onto the Flaminian Way towards Rome, Aurelian caught the main body up and fought a pitched battle by the Metaurus river. The barbarians were pressed into the river and many were drowned. Inscriptions at Pisaurum and at Fanum Fortunae, which had both miraculously survived the barbarian passage, commemorate the Roman victory. As the remnants of the Alamanni withdrew northwards, Aurelian struck again near Ticinum; again, an inscription marks his success. Few of the raiders would return home across the Alps. For these successes, Aurelian was awarded the title of

'Germanicus Maximus', while 'Victoria Germanica' appears on his coins. The victory had strengthened his position against pretenders, and the German tribes would not trouble Italy again while Aurelian remained emperor. Yet, after centuries of undisturbed peace, this was the third time in twelve years that the defenceless capital city of Rome had nearly been seized by barbarians. The new emperor determined not to leave Italy again until after he had fortified Rome.

The alternative view

Many modern historians, including the great Gibbon, have remarked on the similarities of the invasions of the Juthungi at the end of 270 and of the Alamanni at the beginning of 271.[5] Could Aurelian really have had time to mop up both invasions and to deal with the Vandals in between? The alternative view is that the confused ancient descriptions of the invasion by the Juthungi and the Alamanni really describe the same event, probably occurring after Aurelian's rough handling of the Vandals. However, if this is the case then the surviving fragments of Dexippus, the most reliable historian of that period, need rearrangement of their order and Dexippus has confused the Danube river with the Metaurus. The problem remains unresolved.

Aurelian visits Rome[6]

Aurelian could not wait to mop up the remnants of the Germans in view of the uprising in his rear. He marched straight on to Rome where the mint-worker rebellion on the Caelian Hill was suppressed in heavy fighting. Allegedly some 7,000 of Aurelian's soldiers alone were killed, and the output from the mint was interrupted. Aurelian now turned his wrath on those thought to be behind the rebellion, and a number of senators lost their lives (Zosimus claims three deaths), while others had their properties confiscated. One of the senators to be executed was he who had previously advised Aurelian to use 'gold and iron' – as the 'Continuator of Dio' tells us, he tasted the iron of his own recommendation. The same source describes how the ex-consul of 263, M Nummius Albinus, old, bed-ridden and terminally ill, was asked how he hoped things would turn out. 'If the fatherland is well,' he said, 'to be sure I will die unwillingly. However if things turn out otherwise, I die gladly. For I would rather perish than learn of the fatherland overthrown.' These two snippets are all that survive from the original lengthy account, by the Continuator of Dio, concerning the reaction of the patriotic aristocracy to the arrival of Aurelian. The loss of the bulk of this source must be accounted a serious blow to modern history. The reliable 4th-century historian Ammianus Marcellinus alone informs us in colourful language that, after Aurelian had found the treasury in Rome empty after the 'deplorable' events of the emperor Gallienus, he 'fell upon the rich like a tidal wave'.

The problems at the mint at Rome were dealt with by temporary measures. Gaius Valerius Sabinus replaced Felicissimus as the mint master in 271 and evidently held Aurelian's confidence. He would be retained for at least three years in his post according to the evidence of inscriptions.[7] The mint at Rome was closed and its operations moved to the mint at Mediolanum. The new output of 'silver' coins returned to the marginally superior output seen under Gallienus.

Some opportunists thought that Aurelian could not survive as emperor after the disaster with the Alamanni and the disturbances at Rome; they decided to stake their own claims to the throne. Septimius rebelled in Dalmatia, Domitianus (Gallienus' old general who had previously defeated the Macriani) in southern Gaul. Urbanus also mutinied; we are not told where. All these rebellions were quickly extinguished. Zosimus places the insurrections between Aurelian's arrival at Rome and his attack on Palmyra.

There is very little information about these usurpers, and Zosimus, a reliable 5th-century historian, was until recently the only definite source. The rebellion of Septimius is also mentioned by the *Epitome de Caesaribus* (early 5th century). The 'Augustan Histories', normally so ready to come up with details of pseudo-emperors, surprisingly have no data on these insurrections at all. However, in the year 1900 a poor quality coin was found in the Loire valley, issued in the name of Domitianus. The details appeared to have been stamped over another emperor's image, and the coin was taken to be a modern forgery. Soon after, it mysteriously disappeared.

Very recently, this coin was re-discovered in a small museum at Nantes and was undergoing critical re-examination when, on 24 February 2004, the British Museum revealed a coin that it declared to be 'sensational'. It had been found as part of a hoard in a field near Oxford, England, and had originally been a late 3rd-century antoninianus with a silver wash. The silver had deteriorated, leaving the stamped bronze image of a Roman emperor's face, hitherto unrecognised but of the 'radiate' style typical of the second half of the 3rd century. The inscription is 'Imp(erator) C(aesar) Domitianus P(ius) F(elix) Aug(ustus)', providing the very first direct evidence that Domitianus had actually gone so far as to declare himself emperor (see coin portrait, illustration number 18 in the plate section). The French coin has since been shown to have been cast from the same die as the Oxford coin.

This discovery vindicates Zosimus' text, and renders much more plausible the existence of the otherwise unknown Septimius and Urbanus. Domitianus must have been serving in the Alps as a frontier general, perhaps at Cularo, as most of Gaul was still held by the Gallic–Roman empire. The hypothesis that he was a rebel against that empire, rather than against Aurelian, unnecessarily complicates the evidence of Zosimus.

It was at this time that Aurelian earned his reputation for ruthlessness. He had been emperor for some nine months by now, and had not enjoyed a moment's freedom from fighting foreign or domestic enemies. Some said that the senators had been killed on charges that were trivial or unsubstantiated, others that Aurelian might be a good healer, but his cures were bad or, at any rate, too bloody. As Vopiscus puts it: 'The most excellent emperor began to be feared, not to be loved.'

His character

Aurelian was not a new crusader, seeking to overturn existing conventions and establish some kind of 'better way'. On the contrary, he was a deeply conservative man of originally farming stock, whose principal desire was simply to restore the Roman empire to the golden age that had existed in his youth, he would recollect, during the reign of Severus Alexander. He showed the greatest reverence for tradition and for the Senate – provided it behaved itself – and his main concerns were to stamp out corruption and to restore discipline to the army. We might perhaps call him a fervent Roman patriot.

It is evident that the new emperor now took great pains to maintain friendly relations with the Senate, and to reward loyalty. Several senior senators are known to have taken consulships during Aurelian's reign, including T Pomponius Bassus, the 'leading man' of Claudius' reign who now was granted the honour of sharing Aurelian's first consulship, and Julius Placidianus, who had held the garrison at Cularo for Claudius, and who may have been instrumental in the suppression of the recent Gallic rebellion of Domitianus. Inscriptions show that those who served in one position under Aurelian frequently reappear with other important posts later in his reign. Aurelian was loyal to his supporters, and in turn inspired great loyalty in them. There would be no more rebellions against his rule.

Aurelian's attitude towards military discipline and official corruption was much fiercer. If the carrot did not work, there was always the stick or, perhaps, if the 'gold' did not avail, there was always 'iron'. His strength of purpose and fiery temper were remarked upon by all the ancient writers. Here are some of their views:

- 'Effective in war, unrestrained temper, excessively cruel.' (Eutropius)
- 'Ferocious, blood-thirsty, necessary rather than kind at all. Always harsh.' (Eutropius)

85

- 'Severe and incorruptible.' (Victor)
- 'Stern, savage, bloodthirsty.' (Vopiscus; similar in *Epitome De Caesaribus*)
- 'Was not accustomed to threaten in vain, nor, if he did threaten, to pardon.' (Vopiscus)

Aurelian's own slaves and manservants who committed crimes were killed in the emperor's presence, to maintain order and, many said, out of sheer cruelty. One maid who had been found guilty of adultery was put to death; we may recall that a soldier who had so acted had been torn asunder from two trees. There can be no doubt that Aurelian exercised the fiercest control over morality and military discipline. The armies had been increasingly a law unto themselves and the new emperor's drastic tightening of control was declared on coins, where Aurelian is proclaimed as 'Restitutor Exerciti' (Restorer of the Army).

Early on, Aurelian was required to quell a mutiny among some fractious troops. He addressed them in person and took a hard line. Lifting his purple cloak with his right hand, he declared that god (Jupiter) alone could bestow the purple. It was for god alone to determine the length of rule of his chosen, and not even fifty mutinies like theirs could divert this divine will.[8]

We know that Aurelian had a wife, Ulpia Severina, whose profile with plaited hair appears on some of the emperor's coins. She is shown as a typical Roman matron and is traditionally the daughter of Aurelian's adoptive father, Ulpius Crinitus. She may well have originated from the Danube area, like her husband, where Trajan's forename Ulpius was very common. Aurelian also had a daughter, but no sons. He held a yearly celebration of the Sigillaria for his wife and daughter 'as though he were a private citizen'. The Sigillaria occupied the last few days of the lengthy December celebration of the Saturnalia, and was traditionally the occasion when small gifts were exchanged. Although we know little of Severina, it seems that she was at least well respected and possibly played an important role behind the scenes, as she is titled 'Augusta' (empress) on coins issued late in 274 and 275. There are several eastern inscriptions invoking her name, while she was honoured on coins produced at Alexandria even after Aurelian's death. An inscription found in Spain describes her as 'Mother of the Camps, of the Senate and of the Country'. There was also at least one sister. Family ties must have been put to a severe test when the relentless emperor ordered one of his own relatives killed. It may have been his sister's son or his sister's daughter; the literature is confused and no reason is stated anywhere. However there had already been at least three rebellions against his rule.

Yet, as we shall see, he was capable of showing great clemency towards vanquished enemies. It is not clear from the ancient historians whether this represented a triumph of compassion or of policy, but in either case it meant that potential enemies were always willing to throw themselves on his mercy rather than trust to taking up arms against his well publicised military skills. Moreover, there is no doubt that he was much loved by his own army despite his fearsome reputation for discipline. There was never a serious army rebellion against his rule. His friends, too, must have been kindly disposed towards their illustrious companion. He gave sufficient wealth to them to alleviate their poverty, but not so much as to cause envy outside their circle. Perhaps Aurelian remembered the similar kindnesses he had himself received from the former emperor Valerian and from Ulpius Crinitus.

We know little of Aurelian's personal tastes. It is likely that his personal hero was his adoptive forebear, the emperor Trajan. The 'Augustan Histories' tell us that he enjoyed best a simple glass of red wine. He liked actors on the stage and was fascinated by a professional eater who devoured fabulous quantities of food in front of him. When he was ill, he never called a doctor but treated himself, usually by fasting. The Romans had great confidence in the beneficial effects of 'purging the system' by abstinence from food.

Maintaining a long tradition, Aurelian awarded himself his first consulship on 1 January 271. He may have taken steps to strengthen the heavy cavalry force that Gallienus had initiated. As their former commander he must have had expert knowledge and a lively interest, although he appears always to have used light cavalry in the few actions of which we still have a record. There is no direct evidence that Aurelian created any heavy clibanarii cavalry units, although he probably created the 'Equites Promoti Clibanarii Comitatenses', which still existed at the end of the 4th century.[9] It was the custom for emperors to name new or reorganised army units after themselves. Inscriptions record a 'Cohors Plimasensis Aureliana' and a 'Legio III Augusta Aureliana', as well as an imperial guard, the 'Protectores Aureliani Augusti'.

He must also have made many key military and civilian appointments, but the literature records very few: Bonosus was esteemed as a military commander and would in later years come to command the critical Raetian frontier. However, Aurelian's recorded description of this man was 'Born to drink, not to live', and he provided Bonosus with a wife, a Gothic noble, so that he could go and spy on the Goths' conversations while drinking with them. The woman had been supplied as a hostage by the Vandals who had surrendered to Aurelian near the Danube at the beginning of his reign.

Mucapor was a high-ranking officer and a member of the headquarters staff. Pompeianus would be commander against the Palmyrene empire. Probus became commander of the 10th Legion, perhaps in Pannonia, and later led the naval invasion force that recaptured Egypt before being appointed to command of the Rhine armies. Saturninus was appointed to command of the eastern frontier, provided that he never set foot in Egypt. This province, the main supplier of corn to Rome, and with a reputation for disturbances among its peoples, was always deemed by all the emperors to be of special significance. The emperor in person long reserved for himself the right to be governor of Egypt.

A few other senior officials, such as provincial governors and urban prefects, are known from contemporary inscriptions.

Strategies

At long last Aurelian had time to take stock of his position.

1. The frontiers were for the time being quiet, and free from serious threat of barbarian incursions.
2. Queen Zenobia ruled the eastern part of the Roman empire, and was becoming more and more ambitious.
3. The breakaway Gallic–Roman empire now comprised only Gaul and Britain but still held many of the best Roman troops in garrisons along the Rhine frontier.

The fact that Aurelian controlled neither the east nor the west parts of the empire meant that, on the one hand, he lacked their resources, such as tax revenue and troops, while, on the other hand, the breakaway empires posed a threat to his own rule which meant that he could never deploy his entire army against any one barbarian menace. Gallienus had tried to restore the whole realm, but had failed. The time was now ripe for a further attempt to be made. Reunification would make the whole empire better able to withstand barbarian attacks.

What to do first? Aurelian at present commanded only one third of the empire's resources. He certainly could not undertake a war on two fronts. It is likely that events in the breakaway empires made up Aurelian's mind for him, as we shall see, but it would have been a logical decision anyway to take on Zenobia's kingdom first as it controlled more wealth than the Roman and Gallic empires put together, and so more gold and silver with which to restore the shattered western economies and to pay the army. Moreover, all the grain for the Roman population had traditionally been supplied from Egypt, now under Zenobia's sway.

After the death of two short-lived emperors, combined with various power struggles in the army, the Rhine armies had appointed C Pius Esuvius Tetricus, allegedly a civilian, to hold the purple for the Gallic–Roman state in the spring or summer of 271. Tetricus was governor of the province of Aquitania and resident at Burdigala (Bordeaux) on the west coast of Gaul at the time and he may have moved his court there. Tetricus' reign was strewn with internal dissensions, perhaps even mutinies according to Orosius, and it appears that his heart was not in his new position. It is likely that he was in correspondence with Aurelian; certainly the latter felt it safe to leave the Gallic empire to its own devices for a while, perhaps calculating that the rebels in any case possessed too few troops to threaten Rome.

As already recounted, the Palmyrene empire had been flexing its muscles during the short reign of Claudius. Queen Zenobia now controlled the important Roman eastern provinces of Syria and Egypt. The mint at Antioch had issued coins in the name of Aurelian (senior) and Vaballathus (junior) from December 270, but Aurelian's tactical blunder against the Alamanni in spring 271 had far-reaching consequences. As well as the handful of pretenders, listed above and speedily overthrown, Zenobia and her young son Vaballathus now started to project their own claims. The Palmyrene monarchs in spring 271 backdated the accession of Vaballathus to the death of his father Odaenathus in 268; thus Vaballathus appeared to be senior to Aurelian in terms of years of reign. The complications of dating Egyptian papyri at this time are described in Chapter VIII. Coins from August 271 and an Egyptian papyrus dated 17 April 272 (Egyptian equivalent) are dated: 'The second year of the emperor (Aurelian) and 5th year of (Vaballathus)'; the papyrus adds for Vaballathus: 'most glorious king, consul, emperor, general of the Romans'.[10] Slowly, the name of Aurelian fades away from official inscriptions in the east.

Zenobia herself claimed to be a descendant of Cleopatra. She was, we are told, of 'incredible' beauty, with penetrating black eyes, a face dark and swarthy, and pure-white teeth. Possessed of a proud spirit, she was stern when necessary, merciful when possible. She was a keen huntress who spoke little Latin, but read Greek as well as using her Syrian native tongue. Her three sons, Vaballathus, Herennianus and Timolaus, had been raised to understand Latin, and knew little Greek. Privately, the family lived in oriental style, but the queen adopted the manner of a Roman emperor when she appeared in public. She promoted religious tolerance, so that Christianity and the Roman gods flourished in the east as well as the Palmyrene cults of worship of the Sun and of Bel. Zenobia was also a keen fan of Greek culture, and she was assisted by a learned adviser, Cassius Longinus, who had been born in ca. 213. Longinus was a Greek rhetorician and Neoplatonic philosopher who had taught at Athens for about thirty years. After the sack of Athens, he moved around the year 267 to Rome, but was soon enticed by Queen Zenobia to transfer again to Palmyra, where he became her chief counsellor and tutor to her sons. He wrote many books about philosophy, though few now survive.

Zenobia, in the name of Vaballathus, now attempted to seize all Asia Minor (271). By the end of the spring most of the provinces were in their

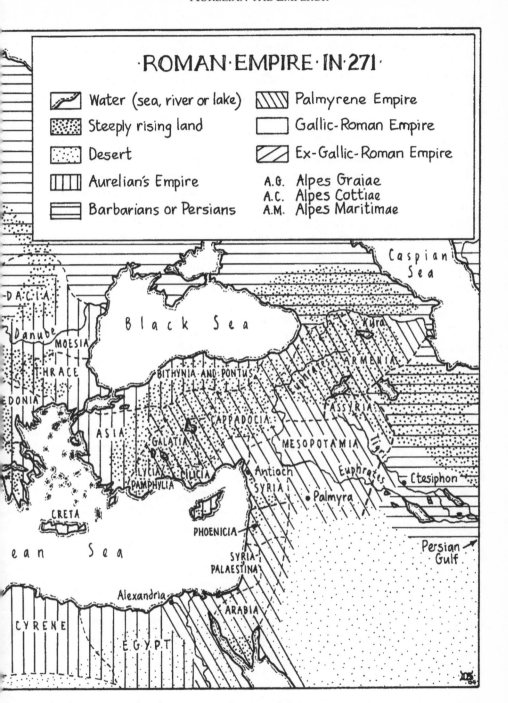

·ROMAN·EMPIRE·IN·271·

Water (sea, river or lake)
Steeply rising land
Desert
Aurelian's Empire
Barbarians or Persians

Palmyrene Empire
Gallic-Roman Empire
Ex-Gallic-Roman Empire
A.G.   Alpes Graiae
A.C.   Alpes Cottiae
A.M. Alpes Maritimae

91

hands, but Bithynia and the city of Chalcedon remained uncaptured, while the mint at Cyzicus continued to produce coins for Aurelian. Probably they wished to create an 'Independent Eastern Empire' to rival the 'Independent Gallic Empire' of Tetricus. Zenobia, then, was for all the reasons stated above to be the first target.

Aurelian's wall of Rome[11]

Because Aurelian planned to be away from Rome for some time, and the temper of the barbarians was uncertain, he felt it necessary to make proper provision for the defence of the capital city against another incursion by would-be plunderers. There had been barbarian attacks on Italy in 259, when the Alamanni nearly reached Rome, in 268 and in 271. The old wall named after Servius Tullius from the days of the Roman Republic (see Chapter I) failed to encompass the densely populated city, whose population had fallen from its peak, but was still at least of half a million people. It was therefore necessary to build another wall, and for this Aurelian enlisted the aid of the Senate.

Work on the new city wall began in 271, but the pressing military needs of the time meant that the wall was constructed predominantly by civilian labour. The wall had to be created in some haste and, for speed of construction, incorporated many existing monuments such as Hadrian's huge mausoleum and the Egyptian-style pyramid built earlier by the senator Gaius Cestius as a tomb. Aurelian's wall was built on foundations that were four metres (thirteen feet) deep, with a core of soft volcanic tufa aggregates, cross-running lines of tiles for binding, cemented with concrete and faced with re-used bricks, and was finally finished, we are told, during the reign of the emperor Probus (276–282). The failure of the state-owned brick-building industry to provide the necessary raw materials for the wall has been taken as an indication of one of the economic failures of the time. The work was of uneven quality, reflecting the varying standards of workmanship. In some places, the wall does not even join up with re-used older constructions, and it is supposed that there must once have been wooden bridging.

The new wall mostly followed the old customs boundary, where taxes were levied on goods going in and out of the city, and may have created its own new customs line. The Janiculum area west of the Tiber river held many water-mills for the production of flour. The mills had probably been introduced under the reforms of Alexander Severus to supply bread to Rome's population, and were powered by one or both of the major viaducts that crossed the area. The importance of these mills can readily be gauged from the fact that Aurelian's wall crossed the Tiber to enclose them, and the peculiar line of part of the wall that exactly follows two branches of the aqueducts. Another large extension had to be made to

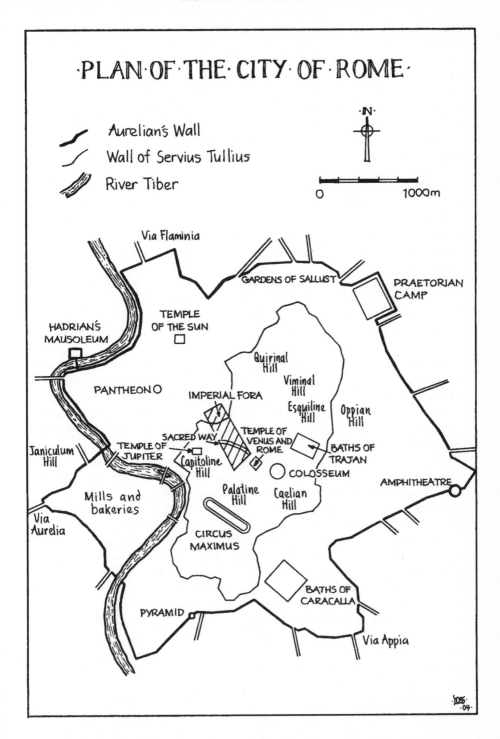

PLAN·OF·THE·CITY·OF·ROME·

Aurelian's Wall
Wall of Servius Tullius
River Tiber

·N·

0   1000m

Via Flaminia

GARDENS OF SALLUST

PRAETORIAN
CAMP

HADRIAN'S
MAUSOLEUM

TEMPLE
OF THE SUN

PANTHEON O

Quirinal
Hill

Viminal
Hill

IMPERIAL FORA

Esquiline
Hill

Oppian
Hill

SACRED WAY

TEMPLE OF
VENUS AND
ROME

BATHS OF
TRAJAN

Janiculum
Hill

TEMPLE OF
JUPITER

Capitoline
Hill

COLOSSEUM

AMPHITHEATRE

Mills and
bakeries

Palatine
Hill

Caelian
Hill

Via
Aurelia

CIRCUS
MAXIMUS

BATHS OF
CARACALLA

PYRAMID

Via Appia

·JOE·
·04·

encompass the barracks of the Praetorian Guard. The wall also ran along the river bank. When complete, the wall was 3.6 metres thick, 6 metres high and 19 kilometres (12 miles) in circumference. The 'Augustan Histories' claim that the wall was '50 milia' long. This has been translated as '50 miles' in the past, and would represent a ridiculous exaggeration, but an alternative translation is '50,000' feet, equivalent to 15.3 kilometres (9.5 miles). There were 381 artillery towers, spaced at thirty metres, for Roman military catapults that could not, however, hit enemies sheltering close to the wall. The top of the walls could be reached only by access through the towers. There were no towers along the river wall, which would be described by Procopius in the 6th century as a major weakness.

This huge construction was completed without disturbance from barbarian tribes, against whom it was intended to provide only a temporary defence. Such a giant circumference could hardly withstand a determined siege by professional troops equipped with the latest siege machinery, but could stop an ill-disciplined barbarian rabble from suddenly breaking in. Equally, the presence of the new wall could not prevent a determined besieging force from starving out the occupants, but barbarians rarely tarried in their search for plunder, and in any case the wall was required only to delay the external enemy until the emperor could hurry back with his main army.

The wall would be inadequate against Roman legions. Little more than thirty years after its completion, the usurper Maxentius would double the height of the walls against the army of his rival Constantine. The imposing walls that we see today are predominantly those of Maxentius, although parts of Aurelian's original construction are still visible. Moreover, the manpower demands of the 381 artillery towers for catapults and their crews were such that later defenders preferred to employ archers. There were originally no fewer than twenty-nine entrances through the walls, a serious structural defect. Four great gates guarded the four main roads in and out of Rome; twelve lesser gates served the secondary roads. The remainder defended lesser roads or even access to private houses, and would be blocked up by Maxentius. Strangely enough, Maxentius still lacked confidence in the wall of Rome and sent his army out to face Constantine in 312, when it would be heavily defeated.

Although the wall had been extended far beyond the confines of that of Servius Tullius (see diagram on page 93), Aurelian did not yet extend the 'pomerium', the ceremonial boundary of the city inside which auspices were taken. Traditionally, this could be extended only by a Roman who had annexed foreign territory. The last had been the emperor Trajan about 170 years previously, and Aurelian had yet to manage such an accomplishment.

Wall-building was not yet a regular feature for all Roman towns, although it would shortly become so. Walls surrounding other cities followed the general pattern of those built for Rome, but were smaller. At this time Aurelian was more interested in improving communications, and several, perhaps all, of the major Roman roads linking his part of the empire were put into good repair.

The Goths tamed

Having put all civil affairs into good order, and having arranged for Rome's defences, Aurelian himself set out with huge forces, doubtless comprising the army's elite units including the heavy cavalry, in the autumn of 271 towards the east. The army's advance into Asia Minor was interrupted when it arrived in the Balkans, in order to clear out more Gothic invaders from Thrace and adjoining provinces. The intruders had made a bad mistake in choosing to invade at that time. With his large army, Aurelian was minded to cross the Danube and chase the barbarians; all were destroyed in a series of major engagements during the course of which the Gothic leader Cannabaudes was killed. For these victories, the Senate awarded Aurelian the title 'Gothicus Maximus'. The emperor issued coins with the legend 'Victoria Gothica'.

This was a major victory over the Goths, reinforcing those previously delivered by Gallienus in 268 and Claudius in 270, and it is interesting to speculate whether it was the fact of Aurelian carrying the war into their own lands that determined the lengthy peace that followed. Far too often, the barbarians had been able to make raids of their own time and choosing, and then melt back into their homelands if things went wrong. The Gothic intrusions had finally been checked for decades according to the reliable late 4th-century historian Ammianus Marcellinus. The termination of these incessant invasions must count as one of Aurelian's greatest achievements, although the Gothic historian Jordanes prefers to omit any mention of these crushing defeats from his highly biased 6th-century account of his compatriots' history.

Reorganisation of the Danube provinces (271 or 273)

The Roman province of Dacia had been conquered almost 170 years earlier by the emperor Trajan as a mountainous buffer state between the barbarians and the Roman provinces south of the Danube river. This had not been a great success, the province had been weakened under the rule of Gallienus, and the long line of its border tied up an excessive number of Roman troops garrisoned there. Furthermore, the provinces south of the Danube had been 'devastated' and 'ruined' (Vopiscus) by barbarian incursions. Dacia was not even a useful buffer state, as recent barbarian invasions had been largely seaborne. Aurelian therefore made the strategic decision to abandon Dacia. All troops, and all those civilians who

95

wished to move, were relocated to two newly created provinces south of the Danube. Trajan's old military supply bridge over the river must also have been destroyed. The Danube is half a mile wide at this point, and the huge (52-metre; 57-yard) timber spans resting on concrete piers would not be equalled for a millennium.

This must have been a difficult decision for the emperor, involving not only the obvious loss of Roman prestige but the abandonment of a territory created by his adoptive predecessor, Trajan. The new provinces Dacia Ripensis and Dacia Mediterranea were carved out of the existing provinces of Upper and Lower Moesia and from Thrace, although it is no longer clear whether Dacia Mediterranea was created at exactly that time or within the next decade; it definitely existed by 283. In any event, the operation re-populated the southern bank of the Danube. The capital of the new 'Dacia' was placed at Serdica (modern Sofia), and a mint was opened there. Some of the original Dacians elected to remain in the abandoned province, where they created a friendly trade and buffer zone in which the barbarians might become civilised. Even the modern name, Romania, of this former province reflects its history.

The year in which this resettlement occurred has been hotly disputed, with dates from 270 to 274 being advanced.[12] Logic suggests that the abandonment of the original province would have occurred either in 271, when Aurelian was moving against Palmyra and therefore needed every spare legion on which he could lay his hands, or possibly in 272 or 273 after the Carpi tribe had caused disturbances in the same area (see Chapter VIII). However, many coin hoards have been found in Romania, which date to 272/273, and may represent measures by the remaining locals against the uncertainty created by the Carpi.

Whatever the date of the evacuation of Dacia, the two legions once stationed there (V Macedonia and XIII Gemina) were now available south of the Danube, in the new province of Dacia, to augment the existing eight legions already guarding the Danube frontier. Aurelian also circulated coins bearing the legend 'Dacia Felix (fortunate)' and adopted the title 'Dacicus Maximus'. It was long believed that these were propaganda exercises, to disguise the loss of face involved in the evacuation, but it has recently been determined that the coins date from the first year of Aurelian's reign and therefore could have had nothing to do with the evacuation. The handful of inscriptions bearing the legend 'Dacicus Maximus' all date from late in Aurelian's reign and cannot reflect his defeat of the Carpi (see next chapter) who occupied the original province of Dacia, as one inscription is known which claims both 'Carpicus Maximus' and 'Dacicus Maximus' for the emperor. Instead the title may acknowledge a second victory over the Goths who moved into the original Dacia at about this time given that the title 'Gothicus Maximus' was, so to speak, already taken.

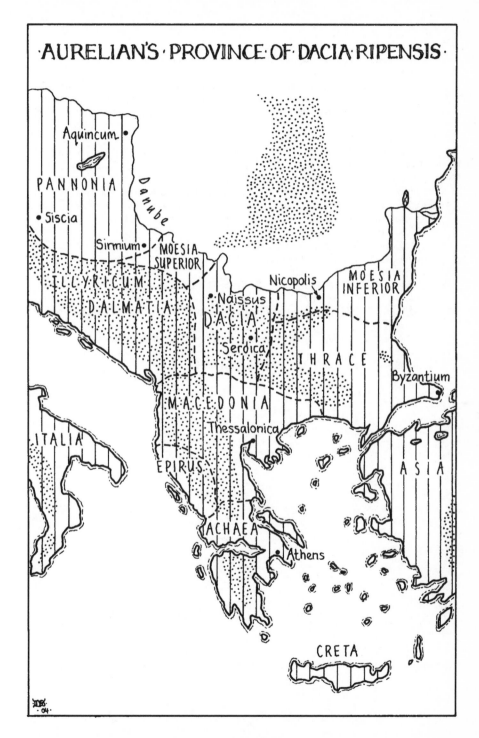

AURELIAN'S · PROVINCE · OF · DACIA · RIPENSIS ·

NOTES

1 Principal original sources (see Chapter IV, Note 1).
2 Continuator of Dio, *Fragmenta Historicorum Graecorum* (ed. Mueller, 1883). Latin.
3 (i) Dexippus, *Fragmenta Historicorum Graecorum* (ed. Mueller, 1883). Latin: (ii) Petrus Patricius, *Fragmenta Historicorum Graecorum* (ed. Mueller, 1883). Latin.
4 'Vopiscus of Syracuse' in *Scriptores Historiae Augustae*, Vol. III, 'The Deified Aurelian', translated by D Magie (Loeb, Harvard University Press, 1932, reprinted 1982).
5 (i) Gibbon, E, *The Decline and Fall of the Roman Empire*, Vol. I, Chapter XI (Everyman's Library, 1910, 1980 reprint); (ii) Saunders, R T, 'Aurelian's Two Juthungian Wars', *Historia*, 41: 311–27 (1992).
6 (i) Continuator of Dio, op. cit.; (ii) Marcellinus, Ammianus, *The Later Roman Empire*, translated by W Hamilton (Penguin, 1986); (iii) Polemius Silvius, *Monumenta, Germaniae Historica. Chronica Minora*, Vol. 1 (ed. Mommsen, 1892). Latin.
7 CIL 05:6421. Watson, A, *Aurelian and the Third Century* (Routledge, 1999). Also gives CIL 10:1214, but the author cannot trace this inscription.
8 Continuator of Dio, op. cit.
9 Eadie, J W, 'Development of Roman Mailed Cavalry', *Journal of Roman Studies*, 57, 161–73 (1967).
10 Rea, J P (ed.), *The Oxyrhynchus Papyri* (London), No. 2904 (XL, 1972), dated to 17 April 272.
11 Richmond, I A, *The City Walls of Imperial Rome* (Clarendon Press, 1930).
12 Cizek favours the evacuation of Dacia in 273. See Cizek, E, *L'Empereur Aurélian et son Temps* (Les Belles Lettres, 1994).

CHAPTER VII
Aurelian in the East

Zenobia and the Palmyrene empire[1]

Aurelian probably spent the winter of 271/272 in quarters in the Balkans. He would not attempt to move an army across enemy territory until the spring when supplies and supply lines would be easier. Zenobia currently occupied Asia Minor, Egypt and Syria, and her armies had advanced as far west as the city of Ancyra in the province of Galatea. Aurelian could scarcely seek to recover the eastern part of the empire from the trained and battle-hardened Romano–Palmyrene forces without a massive show of strength, and it is certain that he must have weakened the Danube garrisons to do so. Hence the need to evacuate the old and troublesome Roman province of Dacia. By the time spring arrived, he had formulated his course of action. There would be a two-pronged attack on the Palmyrene empire, with Aurelian's main force pushing through Asia Minor into Syria, and a fleet under general M Aurelius Probus to reconquer Egypt, restore the corn supply to Rome and divert the Palmyrene forces. This Probus was not the old admiral Tenagino Probus, who had lost his life defending Egypt against the Palmyrenes.

Just as the emperor Claudius had been fortunate to have the future soldier-emperor Aurelian as his right-hand man, so Aurelian was equally endowed with the future soldier-emperor Probus, who was, like Claudius and Aurelian, another of the line of talented Danubian generals. It is probable that Probus and his fleet sailed from the naval base of Byzantium at the head of the Aegean Sea in April 272, as we know from papyri that the Romans landed in Egypt in May.[2] Zenobia must have got wind of the fleet movement, probably from spies, for coins issued from the mint at Alexandria no longer recognise Aurelian as emperor; only Vaballathus as 'Augustus'. Other Alexandrian coins show Zenobia titled as 'Augusta' with the goddess of the moon on the reverse side. Aurelian's portrait was also dropped from coins issued at Antioch in summer 272, where Vaballathus becomes 'Augustus'. The die had been cast; the 'King of Kings' had now openly declared himself as the lawful Roman emperor, in direct opposition to Aurelian.

It was already the Palmyrene custom to align their administrative titles with Roman usage. The Palmyrene empire commanded many former Roman troops, and it is likely that they would have been of doubtful loyalty had they been asked to choose between Rome and Palmyra; hence the royal family's current selection of the Roman titles 'Augustus' and 'Augusta', by which they could represent themselves as the legitimate Roman emperors.

Naturally both sides consulted the omens and remarkably some of them have come down to us, through the historian Zosimus. Aurelian must have been encouraged by the Temple of Apollo at Seleucia in Cilicia: 'One hawk many doves commands, whose end on his destructive pounces must depend.' Hmm.

The Palmyrenes were less fortunate at the same temple, when they asked whether they would control the entire east: 'Accursed race! avoid my sanctuary you whose treacherous deeds the angry gods disdain.' The shrine to Aphrodite Aphacitus was also unpromising for Zenobia. There was a pool of water there into which the supplicant could throw gifts of gold, silver or precious cloth. If the gifts sank, they were acceptable to the god. But if they floated . . . Palmyra's last offerings floated. Perhaps they should have proffered gold.

The Palmyrenes had left only a small garrison to hold the important province of Egypt. Probus and his fleet arrived in the late spring and by mid-June 272 the key city of Alexandria had fallen into Roman hands. The remainder of the country had been rolled up by the end of the same month and, according to inscriptions, a certain S Ammianus was installed as the new Roman governor.

Aurelian's Roman armies crossed the Bosporus from the mint town of Byzantium into the province of Bithynia. Zenobia and her general, Septimius Zabdas, retreated before Aurelian and his fearsome reputation. In any case, it appears that the towns of the former Roman provinces had less enthusiasm for the eastern rulers, and Aurelian and his army were given a rapturous welcome by the provincials wherever they appeared. The province of Bithynia had remained loyal, while the neighbouring Galatea collapsed almost at once. The key town of Ancyra was immediately retaken.

The city of Tyana in the province of Cappadocia controlled the key pass, the Cilician Gates, over the Taurus mountains into the plains of Cilicia. Its only previous claim to fame had been that it was the birthplace of 'Apollonius of Tyana', a philosopher, or perhaps fanatic, who had been nearly contemporary with Christ. Tyana put up a brief resistance which infuriated the short-tempered Aurelian. He swore that he would not leave a dog alive in the city when he had finished with it. The traitor Heraclammon offered to show the Roman troops the way over the walls where a huge pile of earth rose up to the top like a siege mound. The tale

100

goes that Aurelian himself ascended the mound – apparently the towns-people were too naive to watch it – and waved his purple cloak as a sign to those both inside and outside the city that it had fallen. The story beggars belief but, by whatever means, the defence was circumvented and the emperor's troops seized the city. They must have looked forward to the traditional reward for taking a defended town, namely the opportunity to plunder it, but remarkably Aurelian ordered them only to kill all the dogs in fulfilment of his promise. The story is contained in the unreliable 'Augustan Histories' and also in the surviving fragments of the much more dependable 'Continuator of Dio', and thus did the emperor deflect his soldiers' rage into laughter.[3] Then Aurelian explained to the assembled soldiers: 'We are fighting to free the cities and if we prefer to pillage them, they will have no more faith in us. Let us rather seek plunder from the barbarians and we shall spare those whom we regard as our own.'

The career of traitor was not an appealing one in ancient times. Quite apart from the lack of opportunities to display your talent, most contemporary peoples, including the Romans, Greeks, barbarians and Persians, regarded those who betrayed their own side with such contempt that the usual reward – whatever might have been promised – was to put the traitor to death as soon as he, or she, had served their purpose. An alternative was to hand the miscreant back to his own side for proper treatment. Given these inducements, it is surprising indeed that any felt inclined to betray their own people. The moral was written for all to see by any who cared to read Livy's famous history of early Rome.[4]

Yet there never seemed to be a shortage of applicants for the post of 'next traitor', who could be relied upon to guide an invading force through a disused well, or up a stairway that was not guarded. The ancient peoples, as defenders of a besieged city, never seemed to block up or guard all its entrances, a puzzling omission that would result in the loss of many apparently impregnable cities over the centuries. Again, there is abundant evidence from early history that the besiegers rarely tied their noose at all tightly; it always seemed to be possible for small parties to get in and out, presumably under cover of darkness.

Aurelian killed the traitor who had let his soldiers into Tyana, with the explanation: 'He who has not spared his Fatherland could not have kept faith with me.' The action clearly met with the approval of his biographer in the 'Augustan Histories'. The benefit of rewarding treachery, so that it might encourage the next renegade to aid the emperor, had yet to be recognised. However, the emperor commanded that the traitor's property should be restored to his children, so that no one could accuse Aurelian of killing merely to steal. This merciful example towards Tyana heartened all the other cities of the region to open their gates to Aurelian, and probably encouraged the surrender of Egypt to Probus (mentioned above) without resistance. Aurelian advanced to Syria.

Zenobia, then, had surrendered virtually all her western possessions without a fight. However, she was determined to hold Syria and therefore Immae, in the plain east of the huge city of Antioch, was the site of the first set-piece battle (May/June 272). The Palmyrene forces comprised light archers and heavy armoured cavalry, copied from the Persians, who were the highly experienced elite of their army. Aurelian could not match the last – he had only light cavalrymen and the heavily armoured foot troops of the legions – so he defeated them by a remarkable stratagem. First, he placed the legions across the Orontes river. We now follow Downey's reconstruction of events in 1950 (see diagram opposite).[5] Zenobia's army had been drawn up on the Orontes plain, west of the lake of Antioch and to the north of the city. This barred Aurelian's direct route to Antioch, and provided ideal terrain for the use of the Palmyrene heavy cavalry. Aurelian therefore by-passed the plain by following the Roman road on the other side of the lake, and then planned to attack Zenobia's forces from the east, cutting off their retreat south to Antioch. Zenobia's general Zabdas understood the threat and sent cavalry along the Orontes river/ main Roman road east from Antioch to intercept the Roman legions in the plain east of the Lake of Antioch. Aurelian must have sheltered his infantry by placing them north of the tributary that runs east out of the lake.

Returning to Zosimus, the Roman light cavalry were told to continue to challenge and evade the enemy horsemen while the latter were still fresh. The Palmyrene cavalry were burdened by the weight of their armour – on horse and man – in the blistering heat of the summer day. The Roman light forces manoeuvred at speed around their opponents, retiring before sudden Palmyrene advances. After an hour or two of this, both sides had retired as far east as the small village of Immae and the Palmyrene cavalry were so utterly exhausted that they could scarcely move. At this point the Roman horsemen charged in and knocked off those of their adversaries who had not already fallen from their staggering mounts. The heavily shielded Roman infantry then marched forward and massacred the helpless archers at close quarters; the archers may still have been in the Orontes plain, and now cut off from Antioch, or they may have been caught disorganised while chasing east of Antioch after their cavalry. Zabdas, Zenobia and the surviving Palmyrene forces – light archers could presumably run faster than armoured legionaries – retired to reorganise.

Zabdas at first fell back to the walled city of Antioch but, knowing he could not expect a generous reception there, he took the precaution of dressing up one of his men as 'Aurelian', so that the townsfolk would believe that Zabdas had captured the real emperor. The Palmyrenes retired by night by the main road south to another city, Emesa. Thus it was that the surprised Aurelian, who had anticipated another battle or a siege, found himself entering Antioch to a hero's welcome. A few Palmyrenes

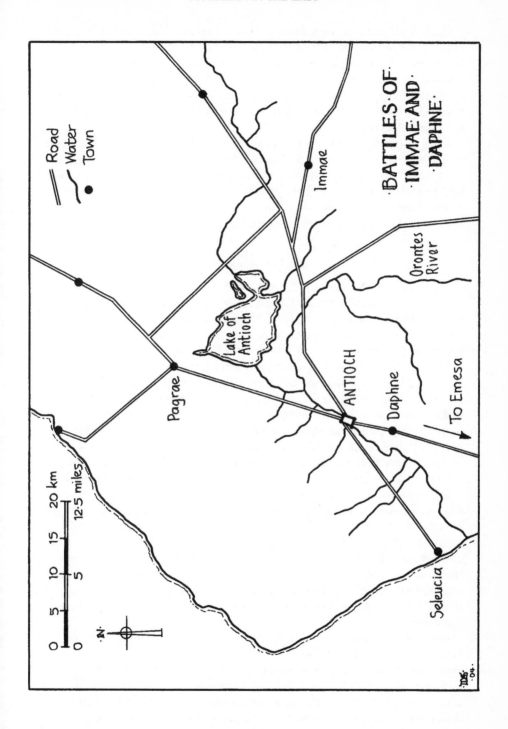

remained behind as a rearguard on the road south, where they occupied a hill above a small town, Daphne, from which they hoped to harass his exit from Antioch. The legionaries locked their shields together in the famous 'tortoise' formation and ascended the hill safely through a hail of missiles. Once at the top, their luckless adversaries found that they had no escape. They were easily routed and many fell to their deaths from rocky crags as they sought to flee.

Again Aurelian showed his statesmanship. When the emperor learned that many of the citizens of Antioch had fled for aiding Zenobia, he proclaimed an amnesty on the grounds that necessity rather than choice had guided their actions. This generous offer prompted many exiles to return home. Somewhat surprisingly, the Christian Church at Antioch also invited the pagan Aurelian to arbitrate on one of its internal disputes.

Paul of Samosata[6]

Paul, a native of the eastern Roman town of Samosata, had been elected bishop by the local Christian community at Antioch in 260, replacing Demetrian who had died in office. His religious views appeared to some of the local worshippers to be heretical. In the words of the early Christian historian Eusebius, Paul was a follower of 'Artemas and his gang', who held that Christ was merely a man on earth. A Synod was held at Antioch in 264, for which the learned and senior Bishop of Alexandria, Dionysius, was too sick to attend, and Paul 'covered up his heresy', as Eusebius puts it. He was permitted to continue in office. However, by now the Sun-worshipping Queen Zenobia seems to have become his patron, and power went to Paul's head, resulting in a further Christian investigation.

A new Synod was held at Antioch in 268 or 269 and this time the learned Malchion managed to nail down Paul's excuses and explanations. Paul was disqualified as bishop, excommunicated, and a letter was sent to all the provinces explaining the decision. The Synod declared that they might have been able to accept his ambition and arrogance, and the fact that he was a terrible example to the pagans; they could have swallowed his consorting with pretty young girls in his private house or that hymns in the church at Antioch could be sung only to Paul and never to God; they might overlook the fact that he used religion merely as a means of making money. Paul could be forgiven for all these disgraces, but his heresy was intolerable.

Paul was replaced as bishop at Antioch by Domnus, the son of Demetrian. Yet Paul refused to vacate the church building, and was supported in his defiance by Zenobia. It was only after Aurelian and his army had entered Antioch that the local Christian community was able to appeal to its emperor. They begged the emperor to remove the heretic, to which Aurelian sagely replied: 'The building [i.e. church] is to be given to those to whom the bishops of Italy and of the city of Rome should adjudge it'.[7] As the otherwise hostile Eusebius would later remark, this was a perfectly just solution. Only now did Paul abandon the building.

Resumption of war with Palmyra

The battle of Immae, east of Antioch, had been the decisive moment of the entire campaign, and had demonstrated conclusively the discipline of the legions and the superior tactics of their supreme commander. Nevertheless, the war was not yet finished. The Palmyrene forces were now based at Emesa (modern Homs). Emesa was a walled Roman colony founded by the emperor Caracalla and possessing a dominant Temple of the Sun, in which its most famous former citizen, the Sun-worshipping emperor Elagabalus (218–222), had once been a priest. The city's inhabitants would certainly be favourable to the Roman cause.

Reinforcements for the Roman army poured in from the other liberated cities. Thus strengthened, and with Zenobia's forces correspondingly weakened, Aurelian marched south to Emesa, picking up without a fight many minor towns en route. In the plain outside Emesa Zenobia and Zabdas were able to put up a force of 70,000 Palmyrenes and their allies. Against them, Aurelian drew up the forces of an empire: Dalmatian cavalry, crack legions from the Illyricum area, his Imperial Brigade, Moorish cavalry, newly recruited soldiers from the recovered provinces of Asia and Syria and, strangest of all, wild club-men recruited from Palestine. Even so, his forces were numerically inferior.

After battle had been joined, the Roman cavalry gave ground a little so that their advancing infantry could not be encircled by the large numbers of armoured horsemen of the Palmyrenes hovering on the perimeter. The latter chased the retiring cavalry and thus disrupted their own troop lines; probably the foot soldiers followed too quickly. At this critical juncture, the Romans claimed to have seen a 'divine form' giving them encouragement. The Roman infantry promptly smashed in and routed Zenobia's forces. In the confusion, the club-men turned their weapons onto the armour of the enemy cavalrymen, so terrifying them that they fled in disorder back into the city. The result was an overwhelming victory for the Romans.

Zenobia, Zabdas and, no doubt, Zabbai (the second-in-command, known only from an inscription at Palmyra) considered a continuation of the fight from Emesa itself, but took the advice of other councillors: that Emesa would not welcome them, Egypt had already fallen to another Roman army that might take them from the rear, while a flight to Palmyra would give them time to reconsider their options properly. This was the advice they followed, so that Aurelian was able to enter Emesa in person to a rapturous welcome from its inhabitants. He made his way into the

105

Temple of Elagabalus to pay his vows and, legend has it, saw the same entity who had so heartened his troops in the battle and to whom he would build a local temple. So precipitous had been the flight of the Palmyrenes back to their own citadel that the Romans were able to seize huge quantities of their possessions and resources that had been abandoned.

Now Aurelian could attack Zenobia's base, her colossal city of Palmyra (summer 272). Friendly Bedouin tribesmen assisted with the movement of his entire army across the eighty to ninety miles of desert between Syria and Palmyra – other Arabs hindered them – and they supplied the Roman army with provisions. The city itself was hugely stocked with supplies, armaments and catapults that could hurl burning pitch. At first Aurelian tried negotiations. He sent a letter to Zenobia saying: 'You should have done voluntarily what is now commanded with my letters. I order you to surrender.' He went on to say that, if she did, the lives and rights of the citizens would be respected. The only penalty would be that Zenobia would have to hand over all her personal wealth, a marvellous array of jewels, gold, silver, silks, horses and camels; her life and the lives of her children would be spared.[8] The emperor evidently felt that the troops would demand some recompense in the form of booty for all that they had endured.

Zenobia replied, in an insolent letter written in Greek: 'It is not I more greatly affected with losses. For those who died in battle were mostly Romans.' She added that she had no intention of surrendering to a letter and that the descendant of Cleopatra would rather die as a queen than live as a commoner. Besides, reinforcements were expected from Persia; surely bluff after the rough treatment handed out earlier by Palmyra to Shapur. The reply outraged the short-fused Aurelian who now set in hand preparations for a full siege, supervised by himself. Plans were made to intercept any new arrivals from Persia. At one point, he appears to have received a minor arrow wound when he strayed too close to the city.

The siege was a protracted affair in the blistering desert heat, for so well stocked a city with such steep walls could not readily be taken by storm. The delay appears to have caused criticism at Rome, for Aurelian felt obliged to announce:

> The Romans say I have only to bear a war against a woman, yet her forces are as great as a man's. And what manner of woman! How wise in debates, how agreeable in disposition, how grave towards military matters, how bountiful, when the need may arise, how severe, when strictness requires. The peoples of the East and Egypt so feared her that not Arabs, not Saracens, not Armenians, would wage war with her.

106

The Romans made no effort to mount a serious assault as Palmyra had the reputation of being impregnable. For a while the citizens of Palmyra were able to defy the besieging Roman army from their huge, walled city, during which they hoped that the attackers would run out of supplies and have to retire. When it became clear that this would not happen, disputes arose within the city as to the best course of action, some advocating surrender trusting to Aurelian's reputation for mercy; others wanting to seek aid from the Persian empire. However, Shapur had died at about this time, and the Persians were distracted by disputes about the succession. Aurelian was able to suborn some of the Saracen and Armenian reinforcements to change sides and even employed some Persians as archers.

While these disputes were in progress, one of the city defenders made a habit of cat-calling at Aurelian from high up on the city walls whenever the emperor came forward to review progress. One of his gifted marksmen told his superior 'Sir, I could get him!' The archer fitted an arrow to his bow, shielded by other soldiers in front, drew a bead on the critic and let fly. The cat-caller fell dead from the battlements.

Eventually supplies within Palmyra became low and Zenobia herself mounted one of the swiftest dromedaries and fled eastwards in search of assistance. Again, the exits had not been well stopped by the besieging force. The Roman light cavalry chased after Zenobia in hot pursuit and actually caught up with her just as she ran into a boat waiting on the river Euphrates. The soldiers dragged her off the boat and brought her back to an agreeably surprised Aurelian. Later, Zosimus tells us, he had second thoughts, reckoning that posterity would give him little credit for having conquered a mere woman.

After this setback Palmyra surrendered to assurances from the emperor, and Zosimus gives an account of the fearful citizens emerging from the city gates with gifts and sacrifices for their conquerors. Yet Aurelian again showed clemency. He accepted the sacrifices and returned the gifts, although he did require payment of a large tribute. The people of Palmyra were allowed to return home to their city, and a Roman garrison was put in charge there. Palmyra was now to be ruled by Marcellinus, the Roman governor of the Euphrates border. A certain Sandario was appointed local commander at Palmyra of the garrison of 600 bowmen. It is also possible that the Roman army made a show of force against Persia before departure from Palmyra (see below). Zenobia, her young son Vaballathus through whom she reigned and her board of counsellors were taken as captives, and Aurelian and his army returned to Antioch, or perhaps Emesa, where a treason trial was held of the captives.

Zenobia claimed that she was just a poor, weak woman who had been led astray by her advisors and her life was spared, despite loud demands for her death from the army. The principal advisers, however, were all executed. Prominent among them was the Greek counsellor and

107

philosopher Longinus, whose loss was later regretted by Aurelian's biographers. There remains extant a letter from Libanius, a pagan orator of the 4th century, asking for a promised copy from one Eusebius of one of Odaenathus' speeches, drafted by Longinus.

The emperor may also have had two of Zenobia's three sons killed at this time, an event tentatively proposed by the 'Augustan Histories' but unlikely as her third son, Vaballathus, survived to be appointed the client king of Armenia; some of his medals still survive. The other two had probably died before the war with Aurelian. General Zabdas disappears from history at this time, and was presumably also among those executed.

Aurelian still seemed to be concerned with his reputation concerning the fact that he had 'only' overcome a woman. The 'Augustan Histories' and other writers remark on the admiration of the emperor for Zenobia, and he is quoted as saying that he spared her life in view of her previous services with Odaenathus for Rome against Persia. He was also determined to parade the fallen queen: in the east so that all might know of her downfall and, especially, at Rome. In the meantime, Aurelian took the designations of 'Parthicus Maximus' and 'Palmyrenicus Maximus', apparently interchangeable titles that described the downfall of Palmyra, while a coin shows the legend 'Victoria Parthica' – the Palmyrene empire was still mis-named as that of Parthia.

Persia, more barbarians, Palmyra re-visited and an Egyptian revolt

The eastern Palmyrene empire had been recovered for Rome with surprisingly little bloodshed – at any rate among the Roman forces – and it seems likely that Aurelian tarried awhile in the east, where he made a successful, punitive sortie into Persia presumably in response to aid they had provided to Zenobia. Only two of our ancient sources mention the campaign against Persia: Aurelius Victor and the 'Augustan Histories'. He seized some of the 'dragon flags' used as standards by the Persians; the metal head had an open fang through which air passed into a long silken streamer, creating a hissing sound. An alternative possibility is that Aurelian used his imposing and victorious army to conduct negotiations from a position of strength with Hormizd, the new king of Persia and a son of Shapur. Independent confirmation of Aurelian's successes in Persia comes from the victory title that Aurelian adopted, 'Persicus Maximus', found on a coin (the same title found in inscriptions appears always to be used as a substitute for 'Parthicus Maximus').

Aurelian's huge achievement had been to reunite the eastern part of the empire, and its grain, wealth and tax potential, with the central authority of Rome herself. The Roman army had also become greatly enlarged by the addition of the eastern legions; moreover two additional legions were created for Syria and for Arabia, while the threats to Rome from the east had been greatly reduced. For all this, the grateful Senate bestowed upon Aurelian the important title of 'Restitutor Orientis' (Restorer of the East), an appellation that appears on many coins. That was a mighty enough achievement for any emperor, but Aurelian must have felt that now he had a tidy force with which he could really start to put right all the disasters that had befallen the empire.

The energetic emperor and his tireless army marched back from Syria to the lower Danube area, where another invasion of barbarians, this time the Carpi, had been timed to take advantage of the reduced garrisons there. The Carpi were a tribe centred in northern Dacia that had stirred up trouble previously under the emperors Gordian III and Philip between ca. 240 and 250, and had also made attacks during the reign of Gallienus, who had probably abandoned the northern half of Dacia to them. During the crossing of the Bosporus, separating Europe from Asia, one or more of Aurelian's ships sank including one that carried several important captives from Palmyra. Zenobia herself, however, survived.

Although it was by now autumn, the Romans conducted a vigorous campaign against the Carpi, who were destroyed. It may well have been at this time that Aurelian decided to abandon the southern half of Dacia, although surely the evacuation would not have occurred during winter, instead of doing so when he was heading east to overthrow Zenobia (see Chapter VI). The emperor also settled many captured barbarians south of the Danube, not quite unprecedented but probably the first on such a scale, and indicative of the contemporary shortage of manpower available to the Romans in this critical area. The Senate, in Aurelian's absence, enthusiastically added the title 'Carpicus' to his already prestigious list. When he heard of this, Aurelian joked: 'It remains only for you to call me "Carpisculus" [a form of boot]'. He may have felt that his other titles had been devalued by a reward for a border skirmish, although the affair was certainly sufficiently serious to merit recognition by several of the ancient historians.

Word came through to Aurelian from the Roman governor of the Euphrates border, Marcellinus, that the Palmyrene aristocracy had taken advantage of the emperor's absence to create a riot, culminating in the massacre of his garrison at Palmyra. The rebels had tried to persuade Marcellinus to join the revolt, but he fobbed them off with ambiguous answers while waiting for the return of his master. A certain 'Septimius Antiochus' was appointed by the Palmyrenes as their new emperor; he assumed the purple toga in late 272/early 273. An inscription at Palmyra claims that Antiochus was a son of Zenobia, in which case the latter must have remarried after the death of Odaenathus and Antiochus would have to be less than 5 years old. At once Aurelian, who was then near the Rhodope mountains west of Byzantium in Thrace, turned about with his armies and retraced his steps to Palmyra. Stern and grim, he arrived at the city of Antioch without warning (spring 273), in the middle of a horse race, terrifying the local population, and then moved on. Palmyra was unprepared for such a speedy return and fell into his hands almost at once. It is even likely that there was little popular support for the uprising, as an inscription in Palmyra, dated to March 273, shows that the chief priest of the god Bel gave support to the emperor's designs.[9] However, this time there was to be no mercy. The legions annihilated those inhabitants who resisted, plundered all the valuables and razed the fortifications of the giant city to the ground. Later, Aurelian would give orders that its Temple of Bel should be rebuilt; modern archaeology suggests that it had been little damaged, but probably all the fittings had been looted. A handful of survivors were permitted to return, but Palmyra never fully recovered. Those of the Arab inhabitants who survived resumed their nomadic life. Even the trade route that Palmyra once dominated was moved farther north, to the town of Batnae.

The emperor Diocletian (284–305) would partially rebuild Palmyra, adding military buildings, baths and an imperial palace. The city would recover further under the rule of the Byzantine empire, and then under the Umayyeds. It was finally abandoned by the Islamic Abbasid dynasty, which preferred to rule from Baghdad, and was sacked by Tamerlane, a murderous Mongol conqueror of the 14th century. When the ruins of the city were rediscovered by Wood and Dawkins in 1751, they were said to contain the most magnificent remains of classical antiquity, although only some thirty to forty families still resided there. Even today, the ruins remain a sombre spectacle surrounded by arid desert and overlooked by an Arab castle built in medieval times, presumably from the rubble of the city, and perched on an equally desolate hill. The town of Tadmur, not to be equated with Solomon's 'Tadmur-in-the-Wilderness', resides nearby. The Temple of Bel provides the best-preserved ruins, and was for generations a home to Bedouin tribes, until evicted by the French colonial authorities in the 1920s.

The usurper Antiochus had been spared because, according to Aurelian, he was too mean a person to merit punishment. Antiochus was probably only a toddler anyway. A worthier opponent may have presented himself in the shape of a wealthy Greek paper merchant, Firmus, who had had the temerity to foment a revolt in Egypt (273), probably in conjunction with the uprising in Palmyra. Egypt was famous in antiquity for the quarrelsome nature of its inhabitants. Firmus had a reputation as a big drinker, one who had liked in happier times to compete with Aurelian's generals. He forged close relationships with the Blemmyes tribe in lower Egypt and managed to put up an ill-disciplined rabble who sacked the major city of Alexandria prior to their leader's assumption of the purple. Ammianus Marcellinus[10] records that Alexandria had been so divided that eventually civil strife broke out

110

resulting in the destruction of the royal palace and one quarter of the city (273). The fabulous 500-year-old Alexandrian library, located in the palace grounds and filled with predominantly Greek-language books, was also destroyed. This loss, together with that of the neighbouring museum, must be accounted a major blow to civilisation. Then Firmus began to mint coins and raise a proper army. Again, Rome's corn supply was threatened.

The rebellion was not a good idea with the real emperor so close. Aurelian immediately hastened round from Syria and crushed the ragged forces put into the field against him. Firmus, described by the emperor as a 'brigand', was seized and tortured to death. A papyrus of this period marks the presentation of a crown to Aurelian to commemorate a victory, presumably that just described. The date of the papyrus seems to be 272/3. The production of coins from the mint at Alexandria, which had just hit a new low, suddenly greatly increased at this time (Aurelian's '3rd year' of rule).

The nomadic Blemmyes tribe had been a constant nuisance to the southern frontier of Egypt, and it is quite possible that Aurelian now formed a friendly relationship with the king of Axomis (modern Axum), a town in Ethiopia, who claimed to control them. Axum is not easy to find in a modern atlas, but lies at about 13°N 38°E on a tributary of the Nile between Khartoum and the Red Sea, more than 2,000 kilometres (1,250 miles) to the south of Alexandria.

While he was deep in the south of Egypt, Aurelian might have heard of the celebrated hermit, St Anthony.[11] Anthony was an Egyptian who had been born in about 252 at a village by the middle Nile. His parents died at about the same time as the arrival of Zenobia's general Zabdas, who seized the country for his mistress. A keen student of the bible, Anthony elected to give up his parents' farm around about the year 270, and moved to a remote mountainous area in the desert where he became a hermit for some thirty-five years, subsisting only on bread and water. Here he attracted both pilgrims and the sick who hoped to be cured. In 305, long after the recovery of Egypt by the Romans and the death of Aurelian, Anthony moved down from the mountains to establish cells for fellow hermits. St Anthony is often described as the founder of the monasteries, but his 'monks' were required to live in strict isolation. He made one visit to Alexandria to support the local Christians in the face of persecution, before retiring again to the desert mountains twenty miles west of the Red Sea. A second visit to Alexandria for the same purpose as the first followed some forty years later. It must have been a healthy life. He died in 357 at the age of about 105.

Now Aurelian departed with the bulk of his armies to return to Europe. He had recovered all the east from Palmyra and had chastised the Persians, but the boundaries between the Roman and Persian empires

111

remain unclear to us today. We know that Odaenathus had driven Shapur completely out of Mesopotamia, but Aurelian would later nurture plans to expel the Persians from the same province. It is possible that the Persians had taken the opportunity while Palmyra was besieged to grab back some of Mesopotamia, and that Aurelian's expedition to Persia shortly afterwards was in response to this.

NOTES

1   (i) Principal original sources (see Chapter IV, Note 1); (ii) General source: Dodgeon, M H, *The Roman Eastern Frontier and the Persian Wars AD 226–363: A Documentary History* (ed. S N C Lieu, Routledge, 1993).

2   Rea, J P (ed.), *The Oxyrhynchus Papyri* (London), No. 2921 (XL, 1972), dated to 17 April 272 acknowledges Aurelian and Vaballathus as joint rulers in Egypt; No. 2902 (dated to 24 June 272) gives Aurelian as sole ruler.

3   (i) *Scriptores Historiae Augustae*, Vol. III, 'The Deified Aurelian', translated by D Magie (Loeb, Harvard University Press, 1932, 1982 reprint); (ii) Continuator of Dio, *Fragmenta Historicorum Graecorum*, (ed. Mueller, 1883). Latin.

4   Livy, *The Early History of Rome*, translated by A de Sélincourt (Penguin Classics, 1960).

5   Downey, G, 'Aurelian's victory over Zenobia at Immae AD 272', *Transactions of American Philological Association*, 81:57–68 (1950).

6   Eusebius, *The History of the Church*, translated by G A Williamson, (Penguin, 1965, reprinted 1989), Chapter 7.

7   The quotation is from Eusebius, op. cit. (no translator given: Translations in the Library of Nicene and Post-Nicene Fathers: www.ccel.org/fathers2/, and appears also in Zonaras, Joannes, *Corpus Scriptorum Historiae Byzantinae*, translated by M Pinderi (Impensis Ed. Weberi, 1844) Vol. II. Latin.

8   Letters to and from Zenobia: (i) Petrus Patricius, *Fragmenta Historicorum Graecorum* (ed. Mueller, 1883). Latin; (ii) Continuator of Dio, op. cit. (iii) *Scriptores Historiae Augustae*, Vol. III, 'The Thirty Pretenders' and 'The Deified Aurelian' (see 'principal original sources').

9   Gawlikowski, M, 'Aurélian et le temple de Bel', *Syria*, 48: 412–21 (1971).

10 Marcellinus, Ammianus, *The Later Roman Empire*, translated by W Hamilton (Penguin, 1986).

11 (i) Brauer, G C, *The Age of the Soldier Emperors* (Noyes Press, 1975); (ii) 'Anthony of Egypt, Saint' in Encyclopaedia Britannica© CD 2000 Deluxe Edition 1999–2000.

CHAPTER VIII

Restorer of the World

Restoration of the western empire (273/4)[1]

With peace finally settled upon the eastern part of the empire – and this time for good, at least so far as Aurelian was concerned – the emperor was able to move his large armies back through the Balkans and into north Italy. The time had now clearly come to re-unite the remnant of the breakaway Gallic–Roman empire with the main empire.

The Gallic–Roman empire was rotting from within. Only Gaul and Britain remained of the original three countries that had defected to Postumus. Spain had returned to Aurelian's nominal rule, although cut off by Gaul. Postumus was dead and two successors had been speedily murdered. The value of the coinage had also shown a recent marked decline; the 'silver' coins contained even less silver than those of Gallienus and the gold coins, although pure, had lost one third of their weight since the death of Postumus. The loss of the silver mines of Spain must have been a severe blow, only partly compensated for by the supply of silver, as a removable minor impurity, from the lead mines of Britain. The citizens of Gaul would have looked with envy at the sudden new prosperity of the remainder of the Roman empire, with peace restored and markets re-opened, and the influx of wealth from Palmyra.

Nevertheless, the legions on the Rhine remained a formidable force – thus far deployed only toward the German barbarians, against whom they enjoyed some success – and they were actively recruiting Frankish and German auxiliaries to bolster their strength. The present emperor in Gaul, Tetricus (271–274), had been plagued by internal dissent and threatened by his own army officers and, as already remarked, he seems to have had little enthusiasm for his role in the first place. Although he had appointed his son as caesar, he had initiated a secret correspondence with Aurelian with a view to surrendering power to the official emperor, but needed to choose his moment with care. One of the supplicant's letters to Aurelian contained this line from Vergil: 'Snatch me, invincible one, from these evils.' It was at about this time that Faustinus rebelled at the Gallic mint of Augusta Treverorum in Gaul, although the ancient writers disagree about whether the revolt was against Tetricus or, a little later, against Aurelian.[2] The revolt was soon suppressed.

Aurelian and his armies pressed into the Gallic empire from north Italy early in 274, and probably followed Claudius' previous route west of the Alps to Cularo, up the valley of the Rhone river to Lugdunum (Lyons), which was captured, almost certainly without resistance. Then the army moved north along the valley of the Saône river. His ultimate objective must have been an advance along the Marne river towards the key rebel mint city of Augusta Treverorum, see map page 35. Tetricus led out his Rhine armies for the purpose, as his biographers remarked, of maintaining appearances. Battle was joined near Catalaunum (Chalons-sur-Marne) on the Marne, about half-way between the modern cities of Paris and Nancy and thus deep within Gaul. But Tetricus and his close staff suddenly defected to join Aurelian, evidently as part of a pre-arranged plan as otherwise they could hardly have reached him without being set upon. Bereft of their leaders, and without any formal battle plan, Tetricus' army was speedily routed and apparently chopped to pieces.[3] The massacre can have formed no part of Aurelian's plan, as he still needed a strong defence of the Rhine, but he had finally reunited the western empire with Rome.

Why did Tetricus change sides in the middle of the battle, and not before? There has been speculation that he actually made a real stand, and was captured during the battle, but this scarcely fits with Aurelian's subsequent amiable treatment of Tetricus. The Gallic ex-emperor's coins were allowed to continue to circulate, his name was not erased from monuments, his administrative appointments were not changed (judging by inscriptions) and later Tetricus would be given an important governorship by Aurelian. Hardly the treatment of a rebel captured in battle. The reason that Tetricus did not change sides earlier was that he wanted to undermine the resistance of the Rhine legions. An earlier defection would have simply resulted in the generals of the Gallic empire appointing one of their number to make a proper battle.

Aurelian did what he could to restore the defences of the Rhine and put walls around some towns in Gaul. He felt it prudent to make one important administrative change: contrary to the normal habit of placing mints next to their armies, the mint at Augusta Treverorum was closed and the former mint at Lugdunum, far to the west, was reopened. Temptation had been placed out of reach of the Rhine armies, and it appears that Aurelian's loyal general Probus, the future emperor, was put in charge of this powerful force.

The ancient literature is again very vague about dates, but the evidence of coins shows that the Gallic mint at Lugdunum had started striking coins in the name of Aurelian in February 274. Inscriptions in Gaul now recognise Aurelian as 'Restitutor Galliarum' and, perhaps genuinely and not out of propaganda, as 'Restitutor Libertatis'.[4] A surprisingly high percentage of those surviving inscriptions dedicated to Aurelian are known from Gaul and Germany, and all are dated to 274/275. It would appear that the locals were only too happy to celebrate the restoration of the real emperor. What about Britannia (Britain)? There is not a shred of evidence to suggest that Aurelian and his armies crossed to that island, but inscriptions that now began to appear in Gaul glorifying their new emperor contain, among other titles, that of 'Britannicus Maximus', traditionally celebrating a conquest. It seems very likely that the downfall of Tetricus had persuaded Britain to rejoin the official Roman world. Britain had shown little enthusiasm for the break in the first place, but so long as the Gallic–Roman empire remained in place, it was cut off from central rule.

The Roman empire restored (274)

Aurelian and his hardy, well disciplined legions had by now accomplished a feat that had no parallel in Roman history. Together they had seen off numerous bands of barbarians and reunited the entire Roman world. For this extraordinary achievement, the Senate and Roman people bestowed on Aurelian the highest honour that had ever been genuinely granted: 'Restitutor Orbis' – Restorer of the World. Postumus, Valerian and Gallienus had all awarded themselves the same title without any justification. The emperor was also granted a 'Triumph', a parade in which the emperor and his victorious legions were allowed to march proudly into Rome to the cheers of the entire population. As was customary in such Triumphs, there were led in processions before the conquerors representatives of all those whom they had conquered, together with samples of the booty that had been seized.

The timing of the Triumph is now a matter of conjecture, although it was certainly in 274. None of the customary coins issued to mark the occasion are known to have survived. It would probably have occurred shortly after the reunification of the empire, in spring, but others have suggested dates as late as August or September, when Aurelian would have celebrated his 'quinquenalia' (five years of rule). In any case, it was the grandest Triumph that Rome had ever seen, or would ever see again. And, unlike the Triumph of Gallienus that had actually been largely earned by the eastern king Odaenathus, Aurelian had fully deserved his. The 'Augustan Histories' provide a full account of the spectacle.

The procession began at daybreak in Rome, and was led by four royal chariots, all liberally covered with their original ornamentation of gold, silver and jewels, and half seized from Palmyra. The first had been owned by Odaenathus. The second had been donated to Aurelian by the king of the Persians. The third had been crafted for Queen Zenobia so that she might use it when she entered Rome. As the writer remarks: and so she did, but not in the way she had planned. A fourth royal chariot, taken from the late Cannabaudes, king of the Goths, was led by stags and carried the emperor himself. It was driven all the way up to the temple on the Capitoline Hill, where the stags would be sacrificed to Jupiter Best and Greatest. Zonaras claims that Aurelian's chariot was led by elephants, following the precedent set by the victorious Republican general Pompey.

There followed assorted wild beasts: in order, twenty elephants, 200 tamed beasts from Libya and Palestine, four tigers, assorted giraffes, elks and other animals, and finally, as a taster of what was to come, no fewer than 800 pairs of gladiators. The tamed beasts would later be donated to the Roman citizenry, so that there accrued no costs to the treasury for maintaining them.

Next in line were numerous bound captives taken from all the defeated nations and barbarians, each carrying placards to state their origin. From the east, there were Palmyrenes and Egyptians; from the barbarians, groups labelled variously as 'Goths', 'Alans' (i.e. Vandals) and 'Suebians' (i.e. Alamanni and Juthungi) from north of the western Danube, Roxolani and Sarmatians, presumably including the Carpi, from north of the eastern Danube, and 'Germans' and 'Franks' from east of the Rhine. One placard claimed that some captives were 'Amazons', a legendary race of female warriors, but the victims were actually female Goths captured while fighting in male attire. Now came representatives of all the races and tribes that were friendly to Rome, again carrying their placards to identify themselves to the cheering Roman population. The list of representatives from the east was a long one, for the ease with which Rome had overthrown Palmyra had caused a sensation. There were Axomites and Blemmyes from deep to the south of Egypt; Arabs, Saracens and Persians, and even Hiberians from the Russian Caucasus, Bactrians from their valleys east of the Aral Sea and Indians from their sub-continent.

And now came Tetricus and his son, not bound but wearing Gallic trousers. They were followed by the sad figure of Zenobia, former Queen of the East. Zenobia was loaded with jewels so heavy that she could barely stagger. Feet and hands were bound with golden fetters, a gold chain around her neck was supported by a Persian clown. There may have been some murmurs at the fact that a Roman senator was being led as a captive in a Roman Triumph, but Tetricus was spared the humiliation of Zenobia and probably his place in the procession was purely representative of Aurelian's achievements; after all, Tetricus had himself placed the breakaway empire into the real emperor's hands.

The remainder of the procession must have been glorious indeed. Gold crowns were displayed, presented by various Roman cities. Then came representatives of the Roman people themselves, their guilds and

116

associations. Then a squadron of armoured cavalry, followed by the splendour of the regal booty that Aurelian and his army had seized, predominantly from Palmyra. One of the items taken from the east was a spectacular type of vivid purple garment that would later be displayed at Rome in the Temple of Jupiter. Subsequent attempts by the Romans to emulate its hue never succeeded.

The conquering army came next, whose marching feet were normally prohibited from the streets of Rome. It was customary for the troops to make wisecracks about their victorious general during a Triumph, but Aurelian must have been so far ahead that he could certainly not have heard the jokes above the tumult. Finally came the senators, subdued we are told, and perhaps fearing for the future now that their emperor had come home.

Having made his sacrifices in the Temple of Jupiter, Aurelian dedicated a gold statue in the Roman Forum, by the Temple of Concord, to the 'Genius of the Roman People'. The French author Homo[5] wrote in 1904 that there existed also a Statue of Mercury erected by Aurelian in 275 beside the Sacred Way in the same Forum, but it seems to have disappeared since. The procession reached the Capitoline Hill at nine in the evening, when it would certainly have been dark, and arrived at the imperial palace late indeed. On the following day there were the usual celebrations: plays in the theatres, races in the Circus, wild beast hunts and gladiatorial fights, including a naval battle. Many of the gladiators would have been taken from the former captives.

There survives a monument commemorating the Triumph, erected in the Sacred Way running through Rome's various imperial forums by his urban prefect Orfitus in 274. The stone, one of only three known for Aurelian from the Sacred Way, is primarily interesting for the few titles that Orfitus acknowledges for Aurelian, and is reproduced on pages 119–20, together with its translation. Note the absence of any claim to victory over Tetricus, or over Gaul.

Aurelian showed astonishing clemency towards the defeated Zenobia, widely attested in the ancient literature. He gave her a pension, made her marry a Roman senator and she became a typical Roman matron on a gifted estate at Tibur (modern Tivoli), twenty miles from Rome, bringing up her children as Roman citizens. Less surprising was the honour shown to Tetricus and his son. Tetricus was made 'corrector' (governor) of the Italian province of Lucania in south-west Italy while his son became a senator. They threw a banquet to celebrate the creation of a splendid mosaic in their huge villa on the Caelian Hill in Rome, showing Tetricus and his son handing over the keys of Gaul to Aurelian while receiving back the senatorial toga. Prominent among the guests was the emperor himself, who asked whether it was better to be a ruler in Gaul or a senator at Rome. The answer, required both by tact and honesty, was the latter.

Aurelian in Rome (274)

Aurelian had returned to Rome for his Triumph. He had previously appeared in 271, to settle the rebellion there and to make preparations for his march against Zenobia, and presumably he had dropped in, so to speak, while switching his armies from Palmyra to north Italy prior to the invasion of Gaul. However, now he was able to give his full attention to trying to set right the economic woes of the empire. Years of constant civil wars had taken their toll on every part of the Roman economy. Taxation was steep, the money was virtually worthless and inflation was rampant. To give a measure of the extent of the debasement of the denarius, where in the 2nd century AD this coin would buy a day's unskilled labour, now the same labour cost about fifty denarii. The net effect of these problems was to blight trade, stifle investment and render general misery to the population as a whole. The only saving grace appeared to be that the relentless plague of the previous twenty years had finally dissipated.

Next on Aurelian's agenda, then, was economic recovery. And seizure of the riches of Palmyra, coupled with restoration of the lost tax revenue from the more prosperous east, made this goal more readily achievable than for many years.

Coinage[6]

Under his predecessor, Claudius, the silver currency of the empire had become little more than a small circle of base metal with a 2% wash of silver that easily rubbed off. The main difficulty was a shortage of silver bullion, and unfortunately Palmyra's wealth did not remedy this particular problem. It is believed that the silver mines in Dalmatia and Spain were becoming exhausted or, at any rate, short of workers. However, there was plenty of gold to reform the aureus coin, while Aurelian was at least able to stabilise the silver currency at a level acceptable to all.

Gaius Valerius Sabinus had served as Aurelian's trusted mint master, replacing the rebellious Felicissimus, since 271. He was based at the largest mint in Mediolanum after the emperor's closure of the mint at Rome following the disturbances there. The mint at Mediolanum was moved to Ticinum in early 274, and Sabinus moved with it. The mint at Rome had also reopened (perhaps in 273), but never regained its former pre-eminence. It is certain that Sabinus must have taken a major hand in the reforms that were to follow, the most significant attempt to improve the currency that had ever been undertaken in imperial times. Previously the name of the game had been almost relentless debasement. Strangely, the Greek historian Zosimus is the only ancient writer to comment on the overhaul of the coinage, although chemical analyses – and the physical appearance of the new coins – tell their own story. The emperor himself would undoubtedly have taken an interest in the design of the coins, and it is perhaps significant that he almost always appears in armour. Some of the new coins were issued in the name of his wife, Ulpia Severina.

Authentic Aurelian Inscription

CIL VI 1112

Triumphal inscription set up in 274 in the Sacred Way, in the Roman Forum.

IMP•CAES•L•DOMITIO
AVRELIANO•PIO•FELICI
INVICTO•AVG•PONTIF•MAXIMO
GOTHICO•MAX•GERMANICO•MAX•
pARTHICO•MAX•CARPICO•MAX•
trIB•POT•V•CONS•ii•DESIG•III•IMP•III•
p•p•prO•CONS•RESTITVTORI•ORBIS•
fortissimO•ET•VICTORIOSISSIMO
PRINCIPI
virius•orfitus v•c•PRAEF•VRBS•
denotus•numini•maiESTATIQ•EIVS•

Items in lower case are missing from the damaged monument, and have been filled in by analogy with similar inscriptions elsewhere. Orfitus is known to have been city prefect in 273/274. He had previously been a consul when Claudius was emperor (270).

Translation: To emperor caesar, L. Domitius Aurelian, pious, lucky, invincible emperor, chief priest, vanquisher of the Goths, Germans, Parthians (=Palmyra), Carpi. Executive tribune for the 5th time, Consul for the 2nd time, consul designate for the 3rd time, hailed conqueror for the 3rd time. Father of the Country, Governor, Restorer of the World, our most strong and victorious prince. Virius Orfitus, the most honourable, City Prefect, set it up to the glory of his majesty.

CIL XII 5548

IMP/CAES
LUC/DOM
AURELIANO
P•FEL•INV
AUG
PONT MAX
GERM•MAX
GUTICO•MAX
CAR•MAX
PRO•V•INP
III COS
PP
XXXVIIII [sic]

The inscription above was found in Narbonensis Gaul, and therefore must have been written after the re-unification of Gaul with Rome in 274. That which follows was found at Uzappa, in the province of Africa.

EDN HD012439

IMP•CAES
L•DOMITIO
AVRELIANO
PIO•FELICI
AVG•PONTI/
FICI•MAXIMO
GERMANICO
MAXIMO•GOTHI/
CO•MAXIMO•TRI/
BVNICIAE•POTES/
TATIS•PATRI•PATRIAE
COS•II•MVNICIPES•VZAPPEN/
SES•DEVOTI•NUMINI•MAIESTATI/
Q•EIVS•D•D•P•P

Aurelian and Sabinus made their major attempt to reform the currency, in which no one retained any confidence, after Aurelian's restoration of the empire in 274, or possibly even the previous year when the treasures of Palmyra had been newly brought to Rome. The new antoninianus was stamped from a superior die and appears to have contained originally 5% silver, including the wash on the surface, although the leaching effect of the soil over the centuries means that those coins recovered today contain only about 4% of silver. The issuing mints mostly stamped the legend 'XX.I' (20:1) on the new coins, a guarantee that they were worth at least one twentieth (5%) of the same size coin made from solid silver. The weights of coins were also stabilised so that there was much less individual variation from one to another. Indeed, the most casual inspection of examples stored in the British Museum shows that the new coins were markedly superior in weight, uniformity and physical appearance to their predecessors.

The new solid gold aureus was set to fifty per pound weight of gold, and also bears a guarantee: 'IL' (1:50). The number of 'silver' coins that would buy an aureus is unknown. The new production of superior quality 'silver' coins meant that there was once again a demand for lesser coins for minor purchases. Copies of the debased denarius were again issued, bearing the inscription 'VSV' which is taken to stand for 'usualis', or usual value. The details of how the token bronze small change was fixed in relation to the other coins are unclear; it is thought that Aurelian decreed that five denarii were equivalent to twenty sestertii, thereby fixing the relative values of the new 'silver' coin and the bronze change. He would not be the first emperor to set relative coin values by decree.

Aurelian also called in the useless currency that had been circulating, replacing it with his better-quality money. These measures helped to improve confidence in the coinage, and Aurelian's coins remained the standard issue until the reforms of Diocletian at the end of the 3rd century. It is baffling to discover that, uniquely, the new Gallic mint at Lugdunum issued 'silver' coins of inferior quality to Aurelian's new coinage, and that these coins also lacked the silver guarantee. Moreover, coin hoards suggest that the older, debased coinage of Tetricus was actually preferred in Gaul to the superior new coins. This preference has been the cause of much speculation, with new rebellions in Gaul being postulated (perhaps that of Faustinus, already mentioned) but without any definite conclusion yet being available. It is also unclear to what extent Aurelian's new coins were circulated in Britain. A large coin hoard in England, which had been buried at the beginning of the 5th century, shows a wide range of Roman coins, including some dating as far back as Republican times, but only two show Aurelian's head. Again, recoveries of coins from Roman military sites in Britain show few from the period of Aurelian's reforms, while there are many 'radiate copies', inferior imitations made by local mints.

·ROMAN·MINTS·IN·275·

- Water (sea, river or lake)
- Steeply rising land
- Desert
- Roman Provinces
- Barbarians or Persians

- ● Current Mints
- ■ Former Mints

A.G. Alpes Graiae
A.C. Alpes Cottiae
A.M. Alpes Maritimae
D.R. Dacia Ripensis
M.S. Moesia Superior
Se Serdica
Me Mediolanum
Ti Ticinum

Caspian Sea

Black Sea

Kyra

Danube
MOESIA INFERIOR
D.R.
Se
THRACE
EDONIA
Byzantium
BITHYNIA AND PONTUS
ARMENIA
Euphrates
ASSYRIA
Cyzicus
ASIA
CAPPADOCIA
GALATIA
MESOPOTAMIA
Tigris
LYCIA
PAMPHYLIA
CILICIA
Antioch
Euphrates
Ctesiphon
SYRIA
CRETA
Tripolis
PHOENICIA
ean   Sea
Persian Gulf
SYRIA-PALAESTINA
Alexandria
ARABIA
CYRENE
EGYPT

Aurelian's treasury issued many new coins, from mints at Mediolanum (later at Ticinum, and the most important mint), Siscia (second largest), Rome, Cyzicus and Serdica, the last being a new mint set up for evacuees from the old province of Dacia and its garrisons. After the fall of Zenobia, Aurelian had regained the use of the mints at Antioch and Alexandria. The latter was always an oddball, issuing coins with Greek, rather than Latin, lettering. There was also a mint at Tripolis, in the eastern province of Phoenicia, after 273, but its output was small and it was soon closed. Another small mint was that at Byzantium which had been closed before the new currency came into being. Aurelian wanted to maintain tight control over the mints, after the disasters of the riot at Rome and the unrelated seizure of Augusta Treverorum by the Rhine armies. Four civic mints producing bronze small change would survive for a while in Asia Minor but, after the emperor's death, even these would be closed down by his successors.

Generally speaking, the army's requirements were requisitioned from the local population where the troops were stationed. An Egyptian papyrus records a rare government payment for army clothing demanded during the reign of Aurelian, but the sum paid, even in the new coins, would have been hopelessly inadequate.

The measure of Aurelian's military achievements can be seen from the inscriptions on the coins from this period:

- Restitutor Orbis (Restorer of the World)
- Pacator Orbis (Pacifier of the World)
- Restitutor Gentis (Restorer of the People)
- Restitutor Orientis (Restorer of the East)
- Pacator Orientis (Pacifier of the East)
- Pax Aeterna (Eternal Peace; how often wished by previous emperors on their coins, and how rarely achieved)
- Pax Augusti (Peace of the Emperor).

Legal reforms

Aurelian cracked down hard on corruption, extortion and on plots against himself. He was especially harsh with government officials convicted of fraud, theft or extortion, punishing them much more severely than was required by the military code. Although details are scanty, it is evident that considerable physical suffering was inflicted, rather than simply recall to Rome or a nominal fine. We may assume that provincial administration took a turn for the better. Aurelian also introduced the title of 'corrector', a new name for a regional governor first seen with his recent ally Tetricus. The title would become popular with later emperors. A startling change was the appointment of the senator C Firmus as 'corrector' for Egypt from early 274, evidenced in an inscription. Egypt, the granary of Rome, had always been a highly sensitive province, and emperors since Augustus himself had always chosen to rule it personally. The senator's name was the same as that of the Egyptian pretender in 273, with all the possibilities of confusion that might occur in ancient histories or modern assignments of inscriptions.

The senators at Rome had been little more than figureheads for years, rubber-stamping the decrees of emperors present in Rome or absent on campaigns. Aurelian showed considerable tact and diplomacy in seeking their aid and advice, but their representation in the civil service and in the army continued to be restricted in favour of equestrians who had demonstrated their abilities. It seems that the emperor had reversed his own earlier enthusiasm for retaining the improved mutual co-operation seen between his predecessor Claudius and the Senate. Vopiscus ('Augustan Histories') claims in one place that the Senate held him in fear; in another that he was regarded as the senators' taskmaster. Another of Aurelian's laws was that imperial rescripts (judgements passed by the emperor) had the full force of law indefinitely, and were not specific for the current year in which they were legislated.

He enacted many new laws. One popular measure was to cancel all arrears to the Roman treasury by burning the public records, following precedents set first by the ancient Greeks and in imperial times by Hadrian (118) and Marcus Aurelius (178). He also suppressed the nuisance caused by embezzlers and informers. Most Roman emperors had relied on the evidence of spies for reasons as diverse as stopping treason and checking tax evasion. However, the whole system was extremely unreliable as it gave ample opportunity for informers to give false information for reasons of spite or greed; they received a 25% cut of any fines arising from successful prosecution. The Romans did not, of course, have a proper police force, an invention whose time was not to come until the famous Bow Street Runners of the late 18th century.

Many other ordinances were directed at improving public morality, and some survived to be incorporated into the 6th-century Codex by Justinian, an east-Roman emperor who published Roman laws.[7] Marriage laws and the rights of minors and of the family head were reinforced. Aurelian planned to restore to married women their 'Senaculum' (an open-air meeting place) provided that those who were also priestesses should rank highest. Free-born women were not allowed to serve as concubines, and the purchase of eunuchs was restricted to senators, apparently on the prosaic ground that the price had become so high that no one else could properly afford them.

It seems that the emperor was a stern ruler at Rome, who tried to bend military law to fit civilian cases. The restrictions of Roman Law were put aside whenever Aurelian felt that either his person or the State was

Aurelian's Law

The eastern Roman emperor Justinian (527–565) authorised the production of several volumes of a 'Digest' of existing Roman Law, organising and summarising both Republican Law and those decrees of his imperial predecessors that were still valid. The Digest has survived intact, while a 'Codex' lists individual one-off judgements assigned to those emperors who created them. Among the legal pronouncements of this huge work only seven are attributed directly to Aurelian, while two decrees by later emperors refer to earlier judgements by Aurelian. All are found in the Codex.

As described earlier in this book, Aurelian was not one of Rome's great reformers. He was far more interested in the restoration of the normal Roman way of life for civilians, while his foreign military campaigns left him little time to formulate laws at Rome. The evidence of Justinian's Digest and common sense both suggest that he created far fewer Roman laws than did other emperors of equal or even lesser period in office. However Vopiscus, Aurelian's unreliable biographer, attributes to Aurelian the passage of 'many' enactments (listed earlier), including the important principle that imperial pronouncements should have effect until countermanded. This rescript still exists in Justinian's Codex and is dated to the beginning of Aurelian's rule.

The surviving Aurelian directives in the Codex were not written by the emperor personally; they were drafted in legal language by his legal staff and signed by Aurelian. Thus the words are not his, and his signature has not survived into the Codex.

Directly attributable to Aurelian is a law concerning marriage gifts. Can a marriage gift made on the day of the wedding, but when it is unclear whether the gift was donated by bridegroom or husband, be later taken back by the husband? This was an important issue in an age of marriage dowries, perhaps later followed by divorce. Aurelian's answer: the husband can withdraw the gift if he made it in his house (now the joint home), but not if it was made in the bride's house.

Another petition concerns the contested release of a slave, set free by the will of his deceased master but disputed by the heir. Aurelian's response: by taking possession of the estate, the heir has agreed to the terms of the master's will. Other laws pertain to aid by the emperor to restore to those debarred by youth their inherited property even if they had proved to be incompetent in its administration (the restitution could not be complete, so as not to deceive those dealing with the inheritors); a commercial dispute about a sale (the emperor's permission could stand as substitute for the local governor's decree); an apparent decision about the disputed possession of a farm (the text is now corrupt) and an opaque judgement concerning the role of the father with respect to his emancipated son and the son's nomination as a decurion: 'when you say you have appealed, you show that the lawsuit pertains to you. For you were only able to oppose the nomination of the son and not to give agreement to the office conferred on him'.

The emperor Constantine quotes and softens an important Aurelian edict when the latter had attempted to re-tax abandoned Roman lands. Aurelian had declared: If the original owners could not be discovered, the local community was to be held liable for the tax.

The joint emperors Diocletian and Maximian quote a decree of Aurelian: that children of the 'First Centurion of the (Army) Reserve' could not be held liable for their fathers' debts if they had taken neither his position nor his possessions, even if no other heirs existed.

threatened. Despite all the honorary titles awarded to him, such as 'Restitutor Orbis' as we have seen, he declined to use any title 'save that of the sword'. Contemporary accounts suggest that Aurelian felt that he could rule all the Roman world, not as sovereign but as conqueror. Aurelian was the first princeps to call himself 'Dominus' (Lord), a practice later adopted by other emperors such as Diocletian; the first to behave openly like a king. However, the royal diadem was not overtly used on coins until the ascent of the emperor Constantine. Aurelian's wife, Severina, appears on coins as 'Domina'.

Aurelian took consulships in the years 271, 274 and 275.[8] They are numbered in sequence I, II and III in the Fasti, so it seems unlikely that he could have held a 'suffectus' or 'ornamenta' consulship. (See Appendix B for a description of the consulships.) His co-consul in 274 was Capitolinus, about whom nothing else is known although his name appears on an inscription with Aurelian. His loyal general Marcellinus, who had refused to join the second Palmyrene rebellion in 273, was Aurelian's co-consul in 275. As the emperor dated the Tribunicia Potestas from late 270, he should have possessed a total of six 'Potestas' awards (270–275 inclusive), but inscriptions tell us that he actually held seven. Reconciliation of dates shows that Aurelian took the honour on an extra occasion, during 274 and probably on the event of his Triumph. We know that other emperors occasionally did the same. More baffling are the dates that appear in papyri from Egypt, where Zenobia ruled through her son Vaballathus. The Egyptian scribes – who dated according to the year of their ruler with each new year beginning on 28 August – started by making the first year of Aurelian's reign equal to the fourth year of Vaballathus', having backdated the rule of Vaballathus in spring 271 to the death of Odaenathus in 267/8, but then other dates go awry.

The confusion was convincingly cleared up by Professor Rea in 1972.[9] Aurelian's first year was correctly counted from the year in which he was recognised by the Senate, late in 270. Thus year September to August 270/271 = 1 Aurelian = 4 Vaballathus. However Aurelian subsequently wanted to pretend that the reign of his rival, Quintillus, was unlawful, so that he, Aurelian, counted his first year from early August 270. Thus year 270/271 was now 2 Aurelian = 4 Vaballathus. This would have been confusing for the eastern scribes, particularly because Aurelian's writ did not yet run in Egypt. They kept to the original system.

Bread and circuses

Successive emperors had always found it necessary to keep the huge population of the city of Rome sweet, largely because of the disturbances they created when upset. Rome was still the capital of the Roman world, even if emperors rarely had time to reside there, and the capital city was resplendent with its treasures. No sane emperor could have wanted a general uprising at Rome. A policy of 'bread and circuses', i.e. the distribution of free bread or corn and the provision of an endless supply of entertainment in the Roman amphitheatres, had been pursued since the time of Augustus. Although we have no precise figures for Aurelian's time, in year 354 we know that there were no fewer than 177 days per year allocated as public holidays or festivals in Rome, when games would be celebrated.[10] It may well have been the interruption of the grain supply to Rome by Palmyra that had provoked the riots in the capital city in 271.

With the new wealth to hand, and the improved reliability of supplies from Egypt, once again under central administration, Aurelian was able to increase the free distribution of bread to the large qualifying population in Rome. When he had set out for the east, he had promised the people of Rome that, if he returned successful, he would give each man 'crowns weighing two pounds'. Somewhat naturally, they assumed he meant crowns of gold, but no emperor could afford that. Instead, he gave each man a crown made up of a special bread, promising a hereditary right to a day's allowance of bread forever more; more than 100,000 metal tickets were issued. The amount of bread that was sold by the bakers at one fixed price was increased by one ounce to two pounds per day, and this was of benefit to the entire population at Rome.

The importance of the mills and bakeries can be judged by the fact that two aqueducts entering Rome were assigned solely to provision of hydraulic power to the mills, and that the area containing the mills and bakeries, on the sloping ground of the Janiculum Hill west of the Tiber river, had to be especially enclosed by an extension of Aurelian's wall (see diagram on page 93.) Coins were struck to mark the emperor's liberality. They show the inscription 'Annona Aug.' (hand-out of the emperor). The cost of these donations was defrayed by extra taxes in kind on those goods imported from Egypt and on which the state had a monopoly of manufacture, such as glass, paper, linen and hemp. The tax was called the 'Anabolicum', often mentioned in papyrus inscriptions. The boatmen on the Nile and Tiber rivers were increased in number and organised into efficient guilds.

Aurelian also added pork to the Roman hand-outs with olive oil and salt included at regular intervals, and it has been speculated that the disasters preceding his reign had induced starvation among the city dwellers, making the distributions essential. The guild of pork butchers had enjoyed the same legal privileges as the bakers since the time of Septimius Severus (193–211). Thus there was already a channel for Aurelian's distribution of free pork. In addition the powers of the city Prefect of Supplies were increased, and it is thought that the bakers' and butchers' guilds were made into official bodies with compulsory membership. Although we do not know the original quantities dispensed, the free ration of pork at Rome in the 4th century amounted to five pounds per month, but was only available for some five months of the year. The pigs were derived predominantly from southern Italy and lost weight in transit, resulting in various compensatory regulations for the suppliers and dealers.

Aurelian even planned to add wine to the list of free handouts, financed by a tax in kind on wine imports, but this scheme may not have been implemented before the death of the emperor. He had proved to be one of the most considerate of all emperors, past or future, towards the people of Rome. Some of those consulted were critical about the extent of the emperor's generosity. 'If we give wine to the Roman people,' said one, 'there remains thus to give only chickens and geese.'

As a matter of fact, Aurelian almost certainly did go too far with his handouts, which increased the culture of dependency among Rome's city dwellers. This dependency arose from the Roman system of patronage, in which a patron, in this case the emperor, rewarded his clients, the people of Rome, for their loyalty. Aurelian's generosity generated a yearly burden for his successors, who might not be able to enjoy the fruits of a major conquest of a wealthy state. In later years other emperors would slowly cut back on Aurelian's munificence, but the free pork ration at Rome continued well into the 5th century. His idea of free wine was never copied by later emperors, although discounts of up to 25% were occasionally provided to qualifying inhabitants of Rome.

In addition to these perpetual benefits, Aurelian handed out clothing imported from various provinces, those made of pure linen from Africa and Egypt being most favoured. He also made some cash donations. According to the reliable 'Chronicler of 354' 500 denarii were issued per person on just one occasion.[11] The 'Augustan Histories' record three donations. In either case, the issue was accompanied by coins with the inscription 'Liberalitas Aug.' (generosity of the emperor).

Public buildings

Unlike his predecessors in more peaceful times Aurelian commissioned few public buildings, with the notable exception of a temple (see below). The most surprising omission is a triumphal arch, erected in the middle of Rome by most emperors to commemorate great victories. Those of Septimius Severus and Constantine can still be seen in much of their former glory in Rome today. Even the beleaguered emperor Gallienus had managed to award himself a triumphal arch for his victories in 264. Aurelian also resisted the temptation to erect a large statue of himself. Today, there is no known extant statue of the emperor Aurelian, so that we know his appearance only from his coins. Even inscriptions commemorating the emperor's victories are very scarce.

The Chronicler of 354 relates how Aurelian caused a new camp to be created for four guard units in the Campus Agrippae, where he would also build his temple. The Portico of the important Baths of Caracalla burned down and was rebuilt. Inscriptions tell us of new public baths built at Grumentium (Grumento, south-west Italy) and repaired at Caesena (Cesena, north-east Italy). The 'Augustan Histories' hint at a few major projects begun, but not completed. A public bath for winter was needed in one of the districts of Rome; it was planned but apparently not started. Work commenced on 'Aurelian's Forum' at the port of Ostia, but this was diverted into public offices. He also failed to adopt the practice of many of his predecessors by building a palace; indeed, he did not even like the old palace in which he resided. Instead he built a small villa and stables for himself and for his horses in the Garden of Sallust. The garden comprised imperial grounds on the slope of the Quirinal Hill that butted up against the Aurelian Wall which was, presumably, still under construction. Here he would exercise, even when unwell. He also favoured the Gardens of Domitia on the bank of the Tiber and containing Hadrian's mausoleum.

However, he started work on the reclamation of waste land in Italy by the local authorities in order to encourage agriculture. Use of the land was exempt from all charges for three years, but this tax avoidance scheme was abandoned in the following century owing to its cost to the treasury (a problem also known in our own time). Aurelian also promoted viticulture, possibly in connection with his scheme to distribute free wine, and arranged for the banks and the bed of the Tiber river to be made good in order to restore proper navigation. Aurelian had planned thoroughly his project for free wine. He intended to purchase untended woodland in Etruria along the Aurelian Way, which was not named after the emperor but was an ancient road, built about 220 BC, running along the north-west coast of Italy from Rome to Pisae (Pisa). Then many of his barbarian captives, held as slaves, would be settled to plant vines and subsequently to produce the wine. He even made provision for storage, labour and transportation of the finished product. It all ended when he died.

The rural population of the Roman empire must have greatly declined in recent years, due in part to deaths caused by plague, in part to high taxation of land and in part to barbarian raids resulting in the abandonment of much of the countryside for the greater security of the walled towns. However, the Roman government was not prepared to give up the lost tax revenue. It tried every means to assign the desolate land (and its tax burden) to those who would take it on, usually with temporary tax relief typically of three years. But when this failed, the Roman emperors were prepared to force the land onto others. Aurelian directed that the tax lost from deserted lands should be made up by the local council of each city, a policy that would also force them to send out their surplus

131

occupants as labourers to work on the land in an effort to bring agri-cultural land back into fruitful use and to reduce the burden of useless mouths in the cities. This edict had to be modified about two generations later by the emperor Constantine, to provide relief to those communities too poor either to find the tax or to buy the land; nevertheless, the modified decree survived into Justinian's 6th-century Digest of Roman Law.

Aurelian's religion

It had become customary to worship the 'genius' of living emperors, and to venerate deceased emperors as one of the pantheon (collection) of Roman gods. However, Aurelian's home provinces in the area of the Danube river had long been accustomed to worship the Sun. It is unclear what Aurelian's early religious beliefs were, but the coins issued in the first part of his reign (270–273) show the usual collection of Roman gods, with Jupiter, father of the gods, pre-eminent.[12] The champion Hercules is also widely represented, as for many of Aurelian's predecessors. The ruling emperor was supposed to have a special relationship with the gods, who would bring him luck, and the closeness of Aurelian, and other emperors, to different gods is often demonstrated in the coinage. His wife Severina is frequently depicted as Juno, the wife of Jupiter. Ruling emperors were always the chief pontiffs (Pontifex Maximus) of the pagan religion at Rome.

There was by now rather a large collection of deities, while Christianity had introduced the concept of just one God. The idea of a single ruling divinity seems to have taken hold with the pagan population too, with several eastern cults, such as Mithras, rising in popularity. In an effort to reunite the peoples of the empire under a common religion Aurelian re-introduced the cult of the Sun-god 'Sol', who stood above all other gods but did not replace them. The Sun was intended to be the dominant, universal religion of which all other religions were simply junior representations. Although a Roman cult, it sought to appeal to the western devotees of Apollo and to the eastern rites of Mithras and Sun-worship. Previously the emperors Severus, Elagabalus, Gallienus and Claudius II had all been Sun-worshippers, while the Greek god Apollo was identified with light and healing. The present emperor may have been influenced in his decision by the coincidence that Sun-worship at Rome in ancient times had been in the charge of the clan of the Aurelii.

Aurelian must have seen similar worship of Sun-gods while on service in the east, especially in Egypt, Emesa and Palmyra, and he was perhaps personally persuaded that this was the true religion. In the Sun-Temple of Elagabalus at Emesa he claimed to have seen the divine entity that had given him victory in the battle outside the city. Certainly he became a

132

devotee of Sol in 272/273 and, when he learned that Palmyra's temple of Bel had been looted by his victorious troops, he ordered its immediate restoration. The huge Temple of the Sun at Heliopolis in Phoenicia, 49 by 88 metres (54 by 96 yards) with fifty-eight Corinthian columns, was built in 273, when Aurelian and his troops would have been in the area. The ruins of this, and several other great temples, still remain at modern Ba'albeck in Lebanon.[13]

We must acknowledge here that it remains unclear which of several variants of the Sun-god Sol was intended to represent; perhaps all, including Bel who was not a Sun-god, were taken to be different manifestations of the same entity. There was an old Roman 'Sol', whose temple stood in the middle of the Circus Maximus, the giant race track at Rome. Apparently the solemn processions here were often confused by the Roman people with those of the Armilustrium, another parade on different dates by priests of Mars.[14] Aurelian reconciled the confusion by holding games, the 'Ludi Solis', at the Circus Maximus for his new god 'Sol Invictus' on the same days as the Armilustrium (19–22 October). Thirty-six races were run on the last day of the games!

Aurelian's early coins declare him to be a god (deus) while still living. He was proclaimed 'born to be god and lord'. However, later Aurelian did not claim that he was personally divine, but had rather been chosen by Sol to be its emperor on Earth. Later coins show the Sun handing the globe to the emperor, or authority to other gods. The Sun's image appeared on the reverse of many of Aurelian's coins. One coin shows Aurelian and Severina with the Sun shining between them. On another a combination Sun–Jupiter figure holds out a sceptre to the emperor. The legions had to adopt the new deity in their insignia and to start Sun-worship; probably not a hardship for his crack troops from the Sun-worshipping Danubian frontier. Aurelian reminded them that it was the Sun who appointed emperors, not the armies. Late coins de-emphasise the emperor's role, with inscriptions such as 'Sol Dominus Imperii Romani' (The Sun is Lord of the Roman Empire). Notwithstanding the emphasis on the Sun-god, other pagan cults continued to flourish despite their supposed junior status.

Aurelian also opened a splendid Temple of the Invincible Sun (Sol Invictus) in the Campus Agrippae, at the centre of Rome, with huge subsidies, a vast quantity of gold amounting to some 15,000 pounds weight, and gems, largely taken from Palmyra. The temple was dedicated after his Triumph at Rome in 274, perhaps on 25 December (see below), but must have been in construction for many years; perhaps since the emperor's first lengthy sojourn in Rome in 271. A few coins show Aurelian as 'Aurelianus Aug Cons', taken to mean that the emperor was the consecrator of the new temple; it would be unusual to remark that an emperor was also a consul. Games in honour of the Sun were to be held

every four years, commencing in 274. The temple was the most magnificent building to have been constructed in Rome since the Baths of
Caracalla, which had not been finished until the reign of Severus
Alexander (222–235). It had its own college of priests, the 'Pontifices dei
Solis' drawn from leading senators, and of equal rank to the earlier
pontiffs, now known as the 'Pontifices Maiores'. Members could serve in
both colleges. Aurelian was also the high priest of the Sun. The title
Pontifex Maximus made him high priest of both the Sun and of the
traditional Roman deities. Severina became 'Piissima' and the Temple's
birthday – presumably its day of consecration – was assigned to the feast
of the winter solstice on 25 December, made a public holiday and
celebrated with races in the Circus Maximus. A century later, the
triumphant Christian religion would appropriate this date for the birth
celebration of its own Son.

The Temple of the Sun has long since disappeared, buried between the
modern Corso and the Church of S Silvestro in Rome, but Palladio made
a sketch in the 16th century from the extant remains. It shows a circular
temple with magnificent porphyry columns, perhaps from Palmyra,
enclosed by a large, rectangular surround. Within the temple were placed
effigies of 'Helios-Sol', the Greek–Roman Sun-god, and 'Belos-Baal', the
eastern manifestation. The Temple also had a practical aspect. Vats of
treasury wine were stored in its porticoes for sale to the public.

It is evident that hitherto Aurelian and the Christian Church had
enjoyed good relations. The popes were known to the emperor and their
offices were unhindered. The emperor's desire to standardise Roman
religion under a unifying Sun as dominant god may have caused him to
become less tolerant, particularly as the Church would not have
recognised Aurelian's role as 'god's chosen one'. A possible further
problem was that Christian or Jewish writers had put together a series of
mock-prophecies that purported to predict the 'future' in verse, while
actually relying on a great deal of hindsight. That is, the prophecies
pretended to predict the future, but were actually written after the events
they described so that the verses provide historical data in typical vague
fortune-telling style. Some of these have survived, and are known as the
'Oracula Sibyllina'; their purpose was doubtless to ridicule or discredit the
real oracles. The pseudo-predictions end with the ascendancy of
Odaenathus, and therefore were probably written close to Aurelian's
reign.[15] He would not have seen it as a joke.

Eusebius tells us that Aurelian had planned to initiate a new
persecution of the Christians, but died before he could implement it. St
Augustine acknowledged, but disputed, the argument that, just as there
had been ten plagues of Egypt before the Israelites were permitted to
leave, so the Christians had suffered ten imperial persecutions, starting
with Nero. That of Aurelian was alleged to be the ninth in the series.

Orosius also attests that it would be the ninth persecution of Christians since that of Nero, and the divine warning to Aurelian was a thunderbolt that struck close by the emperor's feet, terrifying all around. Aurelian's contemporary, Lactantius, adds that the edicts had already been despatched, but had yet to reach the farthest provinces, when the emperor was struck down by divine retribution. The edicts lost their force when the reigning emperor died and the Christian tradition of several martyrs during the reign of Aurelian is almost certainly wrong.[16]

Felix I, an energetic and influential pope, had died on 30 December 274. He had been anointed in 269, and must therefore have been well known to Aurelian, even if only by reputation. It is tempting to question whether it was the death of Felix and the appointment in January of his successor, Eutychianus, who held office until 283, that caused the break between emperor and Church. Unfortunately, nothing at all is known of Eutychianus as pope, but he might have been more dogmatic with pagans than Felix.[17]

Fashion

An imperial court tends to set its own fashions that will be followed by the aristocracy. The lengthy sojourn of the emperor and the empress in Rome must have set its own precedents. The *Epitome De Caesaribus* states that Aurelian introduced the king-like habit of adorning his garments with gilt and jewels, a practice hitherto almost unknown. Among a series of petty snippets vouchsafed to us by the 'Augustan Histories', we learn that Aurelian would not wear silk clothing, nor give it as a present to others. Silk was imported from the east, mostly by ship or caravan from India, and was considered effeminate. His wife once asked her husband if she might keep a single robe of purple silk. Aurelian's illuminating reply was 'God forbid that a fabric should be worth its weight in gold'; the price of silk was at that time equal to its weight in gold. Married women were for the first time permitted to wear purple clothing; previously it had been restricted to a much favoured bright pink or else multi-coloured. Men were not allowed to wear effeminate boots, defined as those coloured in purple, wax, white or ivory.

The emperor's slaves remained clothed in the same style as when he had been a commoner. The household guard traditionally wore purple tunics, but Aurelian permitted the use of embroidered bands. Senators were allowed to employ personal message runners dressed like the emperor's runners. Aurelian introduced the idea of providing the common people with handkerchiefs, not so that they could blow their noses, but so that they could wave them when showing approval.

Aurelian's attitude to precious metals was also interesting. He observed that nature had provided more gold than silver, yet gold was often used pointlessly for ostentation whereas silver was reserved for its proper use; i.e. coinage and goblets. We are told that he considered banning the use of gold in the form of decorative leaf, coat buttons and other frivolous uses, but never carried through the threat. The use of gold for jewellery was presumably sanctioned, as soldiers were allowed to replace their silver clasps with clasps made of gold. His personal silver vessels never exceeded thirty pounds in weight. Inconsistently, though, he permitted the use of silver ornamentation on private coaches, where previously only bronze or ivory had been allowed.

Interruptions (late 274 or early 275)

Another barbarian invasion of the province of Raetia, and a rebellion at Lugdunum, the former seat of Tetricus in Gaul, required Aurelian's presence in the north after his residence in Rome. The latter might explain the unusual output of silver coins that lacked the silver guarantee, which was mentioned previously. Both difficulties were suppressed quickly and harshly; this emperor was always short-tempered. Literary evidence suggests that Aurelian may have taken the opportunity while in Raetia to restore the old, fortified boundary that covered the gap between the Rhine and the Danube. A subsequent invasion by barbarians, during the reign of the next emperor, was said to have broken through the 'Trans-Rhine' fortified line ('Limes'), which was supposed to have been abandoned during the reign of Gallienus. The 'Augustan Histories' claim that Aurelian delivered the Vindelici tribe in Gaul from barbarians, but this may have been confused with the invasion of Raetia. Gregory of Tours (6th century) cited the belief of 'the ancients' that Aurelian had placed a wall around the city of Dijon in Gaul.

The Sassanid empire (275)

It would appear that the Roman military believed that the vicious and rapacious Sassanid monarchy under the descendants of Shapur, who had died in 272, in Persia remained a threat to Rome's restored eastern provinces, and Aurelian amassed another substantial army to deal with the Persians. The force left for Asia Minor in the summer of 275. The armies passed through the Balkans where they may have dealt with an influx of barbarians. By autumn Aurelian and his legions had arrived at Caenophrurium, about half-way along the old paved road that ran between Perinthus (later named Heraclea) and Byzantium in Thrace, when he was suddenly struck down, almost out of the blue.

The death of Aurelian (September or October 275)

Aurelian's private secretary, Eros, had been accustomed to send out the emperor's legal pronouncements, and had been caught in some act of fraud or forgery, perhaps extortion from the provincials. Aurelian threatened punishment, and his secretary knew only too well the emperor's reputation for temper and the probability that vengeance would be exacted. Eros appears actually to have anticipated the threat; he had previously taken the precaution of forging a list, in the emperor's handwriting, of names of senior legionary officers selected for punishment by Aurelian. Eros showed the list to some of the emperor's headquarters staff. With what horror – or, perhaps, with what guilty conscience – they saw the list can readily be imagined. In panic the officers conspired together and then they ran into the emperor's tent where a Thracian general named Mucapor stabbed Aurelian to death.

The evidence of papyri is that Aurelian was killed sometime between 29 August and 10 October 275. He was 61 years old. The announcement of his death stunned the entire Roman world. Aurelian was buried in a splendid tomb not far from where he fell and statues on columns lined the route. So did a statue of Eros' fate. He was put on a stake and exposed to wild animals.

There is something strange about the murder of Aurelian as it has been handed down to us. The story of the mischievous secretary Eros and the sudden assassination by the general Mucapor is well attested by several Latin and Greek writers, so the basic facts are beyond dispute. Yet to try to reconstruct the scene in imagination is to cause bafflement.

Aurelian was on his way to a major military campaign against the Persians, and was in close contact with his top military officers. Suddenly, Eros rushes out with a forged list of names of officers selected for punishment. The list contains the names of all the top generals. Clearly that scenario is ridiculous. The generals would just laugh. The emperor is not about to execute all his military advisers just before a campaign. Is it a bad practical joke?

Let us try again. Eros rushes out with his forged list of names of half, or a third, or a quarter, of the top military officers. The named soldiers immediately jump up and kill Aurelian. Why did not the other generals present stop the murder, or even promise to reason with the emperor on their behalf? That scenario does not work either.

Try this: Aurelian has a normal appointment with a handful of unsuspecting officers who are innocent, or predominantly innocent, of any crime. Eros rushes out with his list of their names for punishment. Despite their innocence, not one protests at the panicky idea of immediately killing the emperor. That is not impossible, but is surely unlikely.

The 12th-century historian Zonaras provides a different explanation from the Latin writers. He claims that Eros forged a series of letters condemning individuals, rather than a list of condemned names, and that Eros then showed these privately to the officers concerned, inciting them to murder his master. Apparently not one stopped to consider his actions or to consult with others shown the same letters, despite the fact that they all rushed together into Aurelian's tent. Vopiscus maintains that Eros had a list of names for condemnation, comprising officers who were genuinely threatened, officers who were falsely threatened, and Eros' own name added to give credibility.

Was there an organised conspiracy? Eros knows of the plot, but keeps silent. When his own life is threatened for some unrelated misdemeanour, he rushes to the conspirators with his forged list of names. The plotters then kill Aurelian. In that case, why was no substitute emperor put forward, as had happened after the murder of Gallienus? The idea of a deliberate conspiracy does not seem to fit very well with subsequent events.

A much more promising supposition is that Aurelian had discovered corruption among several officers, as well as Eros, and he had summonsed them on some pretext. Now he confronted Eros with the charge. Eros rushes out to the guilty soldiers with his list, and they rush into the emperor's tent before Aurelian can punish them. This is plausible, but we now need to explain why two later emperors, Tacitus and Probus, found it necessary to continue to pursue apparently large numbers of conspirators implicated in the assassination of Aurelian. Perhaps the later victims were members of some kind of organised racket, rather than a conspiracy against the emperor personally, and its leaders had killed Aurelian when the true purpose of their planned meeting with the emperor had been revealed. This is substantially the argument that the ancient writer Aurelius Victor implies.

The only certainty in this tangle is that the murder was improvised hastily, and the principal agents were arrested almost at once having had no time to plan a careful escape or a successor emperor. The other officers with the accompanying army were evidently also taken by surprise.

Epitaph

Aurelian had been emperor for about five and a half years; accounts range from five years four months to six years. He left only a daughter, so there could be no dynasty. He died mourned by the Senate, despite their fear of his temper. To summarise his rule, we must first describe the actions of his immediate successor. The next emperor, Tacitus (himself a senator), proposed that Aurelian be deified. 'O Senators, I could justly prosecute even the gods, who have allowed such an emperor to perish, unless they

138

strongly preferred him to be with themselves. Therefore I propose divine honours . . .' The request was at once granted by the Senate. Tacitus then proposed that a golden statue of Aurelian be placed on the Capitol, and silver statues in the Senate House, in the Temple of the Sun and in Trajan's Forum. Apparently the silver monuments were indeed erected and dedicated, but the golden statue was never set up. Further, proposed Tacitus, every man should own a painting of Aurelian. Because he was speaking in the Senate House, we must assume that he meant every senator, for it would have been a Herculean undertaking even to provide just the citizens of Rome with individual paintings.

Two favourite slaves had been treated as freedmen by Aurelian. They were actually freed by special vote of the Senate after his death. A certain Aurelius Festivus claimed to be Aurelian's freedman after the death of the emperor, and wrote a book about the Egyptian pretender Firmus.

On the basis of just one inscription dedicated to Aurelian, from which his name appears to have been erased, it has been suggested that he may have been subject to a limited 'damnatio memoriae' (condemnation of memory; erasure of name from monuments).[18] However, there is no other evidence from the inscriptions themselves nor from the ancient literature, and, as we have seen, Aurelian was swiftly deified in accordance with the Senate's wishes. The inscription concerned was probably the target of a contemporary lout.

The 'Augustan Histories' and other writers describe Aurelian as 'an emperor who was necessary rather than good'; elsewhere, that he was one of the few good emperors, but he lacked the prerequisite quality of mercy that marked out the best of their class. A later emperor, Diocletian, who had served under Aurelian, stated that the talents of Aurelian were better suited to the command of an army than to the government of an empire. Aurelius Victor claims that the emperor had enjoyed 'exceptional popularity and prestige in the army' and that the announcement of his murder 'resulted with destruction to the instigators, with fear to the dishonest, with doubts to their imitators, with regret to each excellent man, to no one arrogance or ostentation'. Eutropius opines that Aurelian was 'deservedly' made a god. He had 'improved military discipline and lax morals'. The *Epitome of Caesars* compares Aurelian with Alexander the Great and Julius Caesar. Francis Bacon (1561–1626), reviewing and classifying great imperial rulers of past ages, added Aurelian to that group who had restored boundaries or freed lands from enslavement.[19] The only other Roman emperors in his short sub-list were Augustus and Vespasian. Gibbon declares that he died 'regretted by the army, detested by the Senate but universally acknowledged as a warlike and fortunate prince, the useful though severe reformer of a degenerate state'.[20]

His coins portray some of Aurelian's titles: 'RESTITUTOR EXERCITI' (Restorer of the army), 'RESTITUTOR ORIENTIS', 'RESTITUTOR ORBIS',

'PACATOR ORBIS' (Pacifier of the World) and 'DEO ET DOMINE NATO' (Born to be God and Lord). Aurelian's Danubian troops, the backbone of his army and of all his accomplishments, are celebrated with 'Virtus Illurici', 'Genius Illur(ici)' and 'Genius Pannoniae'. Vaguer military congratulations are 'Concordia Militum', 'Fides Militum' and 'Fortuna Redux' (Return of good fortune).

His military distinctions, the so-called 'Cognomina Victoriarum', from inscriptions include (in alphabetical order):[21]

ARABICUS MAX.	Second defeat of Palmyra 273?
BRITANNICUS MAX.	Rare, possibly voluntary return of Britain from Gallic–Roman empire
CARPICUS MAX.	Defeat of Carpi tribe, 273
DACICUS MAX.	Probably second defeat of barbarians (Goths? Carpi?) in Dacia after 273
GERMANICUS MAX.	Defeat of Alamanni in 271
GOTHICUS MAX.	Defeat of Goths in 271
PALMYRENICUS MAX.	Defeat of Palmyra in 272
PARTHICUS MAX.	Probably defeat of Palmyra in 272
PERSICUS MAX.	On coin: Defeat of, or successful negotiations with, Persia, 272. On inscriptions, always appears to be a substitute for 'Parthicus Max.'
SARMATICUS MAX.	Possibly defeat of Vandals in 270. Only the unreliable 'Augustan Histories' confer this title. The sole evidence from an inscription is that provided from a well worn stone at Suddak (modern Sadagh in eastern Turkey), discovered in 1868 and from which little can now be read. After addressing Aurelian as emperor, the partial inscription 'ARMA' appears in the position expected for the victory title 'sARMAticus max'. No surrounding letters can be read, and this assignment has been disputed in recent years.

The 'Augustan Histories' also award the titles of ADIABENICUS MAX. and ARMENIACUS MAX., but these titles have yet to be confirmed from inscriptions. However Vaballathus, whose name appears with Aurelian on some coins, was entitled ADIABENICUS MAX., which might explain the error. The four most common victory titles, and the only ones found in Egypt, are Germanicus Max, Gothicus Max, Parthicus Max (or variant) and Carpicus Max.

Other civil or flattering distinctions from his inscriptions include:

DOMINO NOSTRO (Our Lord)
GLORIOSISSIMUS, PERPETUUS VICTORIOSISSIMUS
INDULGENTISSIMUS (the most glorious, perpetually the most
victorious and the most indulgent to others)
INVICTO PIO (Invincible and pious)
PACATOR ORBIS (Pacifier of the World)
PATRI PATRIAE (Father of the Fatherland)
PIUS FELIX (Pious and fortunate)
PONTIFICUS MAX. (Chief Priest)
RECUPERATA REPUBLICA (The Commonwealth restored)
REPARATOR, CONSERVATOR PATRIAE (Repairer, Preserver of the
Fatherland)
RESTITUTOR SAECULI (Restorer of our times)
RESTITUTOR GALLIARUM, LIBERTATIS (Restorer of Gaul, or of
liberty in Gaul)
TRIBUNICIA POTESTATE (Executive tribune)
VIRTUS AUGUSTI (Virtue of Augustus).

Inscription after death:

DEO AURELIANO (to the god Aurelian).

Particularly interesting are thirty Roman milestones found in the west of the Roman province of Africa, to the south and west of Carthage.[22] These can be dated to 274–275; that is, after Aurelian's reunification of the empire, and Aurelian is addressed systematically as 'Perpetuus Imperator' (continuous or universal conqueror). These stones represent the first description of an emperor in such manner, although the title became popular with succeeding emperors. The stones also celebrate Aurelian as Restorer of the World, invincible, most victorious, most glorious and most indulgent to others. However his military victories, such as 'Germanicus Max.', are barely mentioned. It was a time to celebrate peace.

The lack of good written evidence that has survived to the modern era makes it difficult to judge Aurelian's temper or temperament, but the near-contemporary accounts are hardly likely to be seriously in error. Eusebius preserved in Greek the later Christian emperor Constantine's 'Oration to the Gathering of the Saints' (ca. 326) in which the earlier imperial persecutors of the Church were castigated. Aurelian is described, by Constantine, as 'the savage perpetrator of every wrong-doing. How marked was your fall when, in the middle of your unrestrained career, you were cut down on the highway in Thrace and filled the ruts of the road with your impious blood!'.[23]

There remains also a description by the pagan emperor Julian (361–363) of the 'Banquet of the Caesars', a fantasy in which he imagined the deified Roman emperors arriving as dinner guests at the hall of the ancient gods.[24] Aurelian rushed in, fearful that he would be detained at the entrance for close examination of his 'many unjustifiable murders'. However the Sun-god Helios, who might be supposed to owe Aurelian a favour, told the other gods to excuse Aurelian on the grounds that his punishment (assassination) had fitted his crimes; therefore, according to the old Delphic oracle, 'justice has been done'. This, then, was the view prevailing of Aurelian in the 360s.

The certainty is that single-handed, if an emperor commanding many legions can be called single-handed, he restored military discipline, crushed all his opponents, whether barbarian, Roman usurper, or alien state such as Persia and Palmyra, and reunited the two major separated parts of the empire with Rome. In the last he had, to be sure, been aided by the evident enthusiasm of the provincials for reunification with the central authority; the eastern and Gallic provinces had all welcomed Aurelian and his armies with open arms as soon as the troops of the pretenders had retired. The provincials did not want the empire to fragment; they wanted the certainty and security of the Pax Romana to continue. The 'Restorer of the World' found a world that wanted to be restored. Moreover, the Goths had been so severely handled that they remained quiet for decades.

In addition, Aurelian had tried hard to reform the currency and the economic climate of the Roman empire, and had increased the free rations for the dispossessed population of the city of Rome. Even the official religion had been made more welcoming to the provincials. We cannot guess what further administrative reforms Aurelian might have introduced had he survived, perhaps anticipating those of his successor Diocletian.

The restored and renewed empire would continue under his successors for a further two centuries. The judgement of posterity can only be that in Aurelian one of the great Roman superheroes, to be ranked with the Scipios, Julius Caesar or Augustus, strode upon the earth.

St. Valentine[25]

One of those perhaps martyred during Aurelian's rule was the bishop of Interamna Nahars (modern Terni), a large town sixty-three miles north of Rome on the Flaminian Way. Famous for his piety and charity, and known as a worker of miracles, the bishop, Valentinus, was invited to Rome to heal a sick child. He effected the cure and converted several of the local residents to Christianity, including one Abondius, son of a city prefect

142

named as 'Placidus'. Placidus ordered the arrest of Valentinus and, when he refused to sacrifice to the Roman gods, Valentinus was beheaded, then buried on the outskirts of Interamna Nahars. The date of the execution was 14 February.

We know that Furius Placidus was prefect of Rome in 273, in the middle of Aurelian's rule and therefore before the emperor had initiated any persecution of Christians; however, the events narrated may relate to a somewhat later date when Placidus might be described as ex-city prefect. It was the custom to refer to an ex-magistrate in later years by his highest previous title, and thus the death of Valentinus more probably occurred during the last great persecution (303–311) of the Christians under the emperors Diocletian and Galerius. The story was recorded by Hieronymous (Jerome) towards the end of the 4th century, apparently from information in existing Roman calendars. Thus began the legend of Valentine, patron saint of lovers. The traditions that justify his patronage are few in number and concern children as much as the amorous.

NOTES

1   (i) Principal original sources (see Chapter IV, Note 1); General sources: (ii) Dodgeon, M H, *The Roman Eastern Frontier and the Persian Wars AD 226–363: A Documentary History* (ed. S N C Lieu, Routledge, 1993); (iii) Drinkwater, J F, 'The Gallic Empire', *Historia-Einzelschriften*, 52:13 – 276 (1987).
2   (i) Victor, Aurelius, *De Caesaribus*, translated by H W Bird (Liverpool University Press, 1994); (ii) Polemius Silvius, *Monumenta, Germaniae Historica, Chronica Minora*, Vol. 1 (ed. Mommsen, 1892). Latin.
3   (i) Victor, Aurelius, op. cit.; (ii) *Panegyrici Latini, In Praise of Later Roman Emperors*, translated by C E V Nixon and B S Rodgers (University of California Press, 1994).
4   Inscriptions throughout this chapter have been obtained by computer searches:
    (i) Epigraphische Datenbank Heidelberg:
    www.uni-heidelberg.de/institute/sonst/adw/edh/;
    (ii) Frankfurt Latin Inscriptions:
    www.rz.uni-frankfurt.de/~clauss/index-e.html.
    Also: Corpus Inscriptionum Latinarum (CIL), Prussian Academy. Latin; Peachkin, M, *Roman Imperial Titulature and Chronology* (Gieben, 1990).
5   Homo, L P, *Essai sur le Règne de l'Empereur Aurélian* (270–275) (a Fontemoing, 1904). French.
6   (i) For references to the mint master Sabinus, see Chapter VI, note 7; (ii) Casey, P J, *Roman Coinage in Britain* (Shire Archaeology Press, 1980); (iii) coins inspected by the author at the British Museum; (iv) 'Virtual Catalog of Roman Coins':
    http://artemis.austincollege.edu/acad/cml/rcape/vcrc/coin-info.html.
7   Justinian's Codex can be found at: www.theLatinLibrary.com. Latin.
8   (i) Zumptio, C T, *Annales Romani*, 3rd edn (Berolini, 1862). Latin; (ii) *Prosopographia Imperii Romani* ('PIR', 2nd edn, 1933). Latin; (iii) *Dictionary of Greek and Roman Biography and Mythology*, Vol. I, ed. W Smith (J Walton, 1870).

9   Rea, J P (ed.), *The Oxyrhynchus Papyri* (London), Vol. XL, 1972.
10 (i) Salzman, M R, *On Roman Time – The Codex Calendar of 354* (University of California Press, 1990); (ii) Chronicler of 354: *Monumenta, Germaniae Historica. Chronica Minora*, Vol. 1 (ed. Mommsen, 1892). Latin.
11 Chronicler of 354, op. cit.
12 See Note 6 for coin evidence of Aurelian's religion.
13 'Baalbek', Microsoft® Encarta© 1994.
14 Salzman, M R, op. cit.
15 Potter, D S, *Prophecy and History in the Crisis of the Roman Empire* (Clarendon Press, 1990).
16 (i) Eusebius, *The History of the Church*, translated by G A Williamson (Penguin, 1965; reprinted 1989), Chapter 7; (ii) St Augustine (Latin text at: www.theLatinLibrary.com; (iii) Lactantius, *On the Deaths of the Persecutors*, translated by W Fletcher (Translations in the Library of Nicene and Post-Nicene Fathers: www.ccel.org/fathers2/).
17 'Dionysius, Saint', 'Felix I, Saint', 'Eutychian, Saint', 'Gaius, Saint' in Encyclopaedia Britannica© CD 2000 Deluxe Edition, 1999–2000.
18 Kienast, D, *Römische Kaiser – Tabelle* (Wissenschaftliche Buchgesellschaft, 1992) and references therein.
19 Francis Bacon (Latin text at: www.theLatinLibrary.com).
20 Gibbon, E, *The Decline and Fall of the Roman Empire*, Vol. I, Chapter XXI (Everyman's Library, 1910; 1980 reprint).
21 See Note 4.
22 Daguet, Anne, 'L Domitius Aurelianus Perpetuus Imperator', *Antiquités Africaines*, 28: 173–86 (1992). French.
23 Eusebius, *The Oration of Constantine* (no translator given; Translations in the Library of Nicene and Post-Nicene Fathers: www.ccel.org/fathers2/npnf2-01/toc.htm).
24 Julian, Vol II, *The Caesars*, translated by W C Wright (Loeb, Harvard University Press, 1913; reprinted 1969).
25 (i) 'Valentine, Saint' in *Encyclopaedia Britannica*© CD 2000 Deluxe Edition, 1999–2000; (ii) City of Terni: www.sanvalentinoeventi.com/santo eng.asp.

CHAPTER IX

Interregnum and Probus

Interregnum[1]

The Roman empire might have been restored, but it was still fragile. The premature death of Aurelian had removed his iron grip that had so terrified the barbarians, and they began to consider fresh plans to plunder the increasingly prosperous provinces. A new emperor would have his hands full, consolidating his predecessor's achievements.

When Gallienus had been assassinated in 268, the conspirators had already arranged for a successor, Claudius, to take immediate charge. However, the murder of Aurelian had occurred unexpectedly, and no one had given a thought to the succession. Aurelian lacked a son who might have enabled an obvious dynastic choice to be made, while the most plausible successor generals, such as Probus, were loyally at their stations on the Rhine, the Euphrates or other remote frontiers. While there was no emperor a period called an Interregnum was declared, hitherto known only once in imperial times, after the murder of the hated emperor Domitian in 96, but really a throwback to the days of the Roman Republic. The Interregnum (literally, 'between rulers') defined a period when the Senate ruled, usually in circumstances in which the Republic's two annual consuls had both died in office.

The existence of the Interregnum, attested by four Latin historians, is confirmed by coinage issued at the time. However these, and the evidence of papyri, also suggest that the period of rule by the Senate probably did not exceed eight to ten weeks, although the Latin writers suggest six to eight months. It has even been suggested that this interval was the minimum required to assemble the views of the far-flung Roman generals about the successor, and that other delays evidenced by coinage and papyri simply reflect the time taken for news to reach distant mints and scribes; in other words, that there was no real period of senatorial control except by default. Now that he was safely dead, the Senate was quite happy to praise the fallen emperor, and Severina, his widow, was acknowledged as empress at Alexandria with her own coins for about a year after Aurelian's death, according to the evidence of the coins

145

themselves. There were virtually no changes in the Roman governors during the Interregnum.

So shocked was the majority of the Roman army by the murderous action of a handful of its officers that the legionaries invited the dis-believing Senate to select its own candidate as emperor. Considering that the Senate had long had its wishes ignored, and knowing that any appointment that it made was likely be overthrown by the army, the senators cautiously passed the buck back to the legions. Again the Senate was consulted by the army and finally the senators decided to acclaim one of their own number, an eminent 75-year-old Italian, M Claudius Tacitus, whose principal reputation was that he claimed to be a descendant of the illustrious 1st/2nd-century historian of the same name. The present Tacitus was probably the senator who had been made consul in 273 by Aurelian, consistent with the late emperor's policy of veneration of worthy members of the Senate. The story goes that Tacitus had retired to his villa in Campania when he learned that he was for the hot seat, but was recalled by the Senate on some pretext and virtually shouted into power by the acclamations of the other senators. The army accepted the choice in November or December 275.

Modern historians have doubted whether Tacitus was quite the blameless old man that the accounts describe. It has been suggested that he was another Danubian general, perhaps retired, and probably a lot younger than 75, as would be appropriate for the emergencies of the time. He might have been an army contemporary of Aurelian, who was 61 at the time of his death. However, the coins of Tacitus certainly appear to depict an elderly statesman. The Greek writers Zosimus and Zonaras also agree that Tacitus was appointed by the army, not by the Senate. The ancient descriptions of Tacitus as 'a kind man' with 'outstanding morals' may well be correct.

The first actions of Tacitus were to deify Aurelian and to make arrange-ments for the commemoration of the late emperor with statues and other monuments. A curious enactment of Tacitus is recorded in the 'Augustan Histories': it became a capital offence to manufacture certain alloys of precious metals. This presumably relates to further difficulties with the coinage or even with superior-grade forgeries. Then he hastened to the armies in Thrace to wreak vengeance on Aurelian's assassins who, we learn, were tortured to death 'good and bad alike' with special treatment for Mucapor, the assassin who struck the blow. However, some appear to have escaped, as we learn that the next emperor, Probus, also took action against the surviving murderers of Aurelian. Then it was time to deal with new barbarian inroads.

The appointment of Tacitus may well have been hastened by alarming reports from the Rhine that Franks, Alamanni, Lugii and other tribesmen had breached the defences of Gaul, no doubt in the hope of profiting from the confusion after Aurelian's death. The raiders seized some sixty towns that lacked walls, and wrecked the province's prosperity, but most cities in Gaul now had fortifications capable of repelling sudden barbarian invasions. We may suppose though that many of the province's inhabitants would have yearned for the return of a new Postumus.

More serious were the reports of disturbances by the Heruli tribesmen who had poured out of the Sea of Azov in 275–276. These barbarians claimed that they had been recruited by Aurelian to aid the latter's campaign against Persia. When they arrived – no Aurelian and no pay; so, being less-than-noble savages, they decided to plunder instead the assembly area, the province of Pontus in Asia Minor. They over-ran many cities and some had reached as far south as Cilicia. Tacitus and his legions were conveniently close; when they arrived in Asia Minor the emperor was able to buy off many of the marauders simply by paying them the fee agreed by Aurelian. Those who did not retire were squelched by the Romans, acting predominantly under the command of the praetorian prefect Florian (276). For this Tacitus received the title 'Gothicus Maximus'.

After a reign of just six months, Tacitus died in 276 at Tyana in the eastern province of Cappadocia, probably in June according to the evidence of papyri. The accounts of his death are contradictory. He may have died of natural causes or a fever; perhaps it was true that he was already 75 years old. Alternatively he may have been murdered, possibly by assassins who had already killed a relative whom Tacitus had appointed governor of Syria, and who may have feared his retaliation. Whatever the circumstances, he died lamented by the Senate, although he had not restored their military commands – and once again there was no prearranged plan for a successor. An unusual feature of the reign of Tacitus, which casts doubt on the idea that he was an appointee of the Senate, is that after death he was not deified. On the other hand, his name was not erased from monuments either. A puzzling combination.

His praetorian prefect Florian, perhaps also his brother or half-brother, present in Cappadocia with the late emperor, assumed the title of emperor, although without seeking the permission of the Senate. He was, however, recognised by that body and coins show that his rule was accepted by Europe and Africa. Florian then finished off the war against the Heruli.

However, Florian faced a formidable opponent in the East. Aurelian's old general, Probus, had been appointed commander of the Roman East by Tacitus and was supported by all his legions. Probus must have seen no reason to recognise Florian, who had simply appointed himself emperor, and Probus was himself invested with the purple by his own troops around June 276. Florian had to retire to Cilicia when he learned of this news, and the two armies confronted each other at Tarsus. Probus was probably the better general and would certainly have possessed the superior reputation with both armies. He manoeuvred his eastern-trained troops around until those of Florian, who had mostly been recruited from Europe, and were equally heavily armoured, wilted in the heat of the Middle-East sun. The western soldiers then rebelled against Florian and surrendered with very little bloodshed. Florian himself may have been murdered by his own men, as a preliminary to the surrender, or may have been seized by Probus' troops, held while they sought their emperor's decision and then killed by his former soldiers after Probus had given the command. This left Probus as sole emperor (September 276).

Probus the Upright (276–282)

Marcus Aurelius Equitius Probus was born on 19 August[2] around 232[3] at Sirmium in Lower Pannonia, and was therefore another Danubian. His father may have been the farmer of a smallholding or a military officer. The 'Augustan Histories'[4] describe his earlier career: as tribune he had crossed the Danube during the 'Sarmatian War' and was rewarded for his exploits. The emperor Valerian appointed him as the first young commander of the Third Legion 'The Fortunate', although no such legion is known to have existed. Gallienus made Probus commander of the armies in Illyricum. Under Aurelian, Probus became commander of the 10th Legion ('the Bravest of his Army'); again, this statement is probably inaccurate. We know from other sources that Probus had certainly been favoured by Aurelian, who put him in charge of armies first in Egypt, where he defeated Zenobia's intrusion, and then on the Rhine. It is likely that his appointment to the command of the east had been made by Aurelian, to whom he was always a valuable lieutenant. Probus, we are told, dissuaded Aurelian from some of his cruelties. Finally Tacitus appointed Probus as military commander of the entire Eastern Command.

While the precise accuracy of some of these statements is dubious, there is no doubt that it reflects an illustrious career. Probus had evidently acquired an excellent reputation as a Roman army general – more importantly, perhaps, as a loyal Roman army general. Probus was also highly regarded by his soldiers, especially because he retained little of their plunder for himself.

When Tacitus died unexpectedly, there was surely much discussion among the soldiers about his likely successor. 'What we want,' shouted one of Probus' officers, 'is an emperor who will be strong, just, modest, merciful and upright [probus]'. At once the superstitious troops assembled together observed the omen and took up the cry: 'We want Probus!' Their general duly allowed himself to be invested with the purple. He claimed to be the former emperor's appointed successor, rather than Florian. The truth of this claim is unknown.

After the defeat and death of Florian, recorded above, the Senate was happy to accept Probus as the new emperor in late 276. Probus in turn was careful always to show the Senate proper respect or, at least, a show of proper respect, a policy which was not only wise but also endeared him to later Latin historians. He took his first consulship in the year 277. According to his biography in the 'Augustan Histories', Probus finally settled accounts with those assassins of Aurelian still surviving by the dubious expedient of inviting them all to a banquet and then retiring to an upstairs room from which he gave the signal for guards to storm in and massacre the banqueteers. If this story is true, then the conspiracy against Aurelian must have been better organised than otherwise supposed, or there were a very large number of names on Aurelian's alleged death list. It seems strange, too, that those meeting at the banquet could not recognise one another and thereby receive a premonition of the doom awaiting them. The same source claims that Probus also avenged himself against the killers of Tacitus, but pardoned all the former supporters of Florian. Zonaras confirms that Probus rounded up the assassins of both Aurelian and Tacitus in disgrace, and then killed them all. We may assume that the new imperial ruler felt it prudent to set a severe example against those who murdered incumbent emperors.

It seems likely that Probus continued to mop up any of the barbarians still in Asia Minor after the attentions of Tacitus and Florian. He was awarded the title of 'Gothicus Maximus' in 277. Now that he was in command of the whole empire, Probus lost no time in marshalling a vast army and leading it against the Franks and Alamanni in Gaul, whom Tacitus had been forced to ignore while he acted against the invaders in Asia Minor. Gaul had been devastated and was still in turmoil with parties of barbarians plundering as they pleased and with numerous towns fallen to them. The intruders were withdrawing laden with their loot, but Probus sent his generals and his legions off in hot pursuit (277–278).

The destruction wreaked by the barbarians had ensured that there was little food to be found for citizens, invaders and legions alike. Yet in the midst of famine Probus enjoyed a miracle. A whirlwind pulled down rain and grain – and the latter was found to be wholly edible after cooking into loaves. The latest incursions by the Franks were checked and the Romans captured Semno, the chief of the Lugii, and his son after a campaign lasting about a year. The Franks were permitted to depart freely once they had released their captives and plunder. Probus personally commanded the legions that crushed the Alamanni and he introduced a general system of reward in Gaul: one gold coin, an aureus, for every barbarian head brought in.

Meanwhile other German tribesmen, Burgundians and Vandals, poured through Raetia to the aid of the Franks in huge numbers, much larger than the forces that Probus could muster. The emperor manoeuvred skilfully. With both sides facing each other across a river, the Roman legions provoked the barbarians to cross over in small detachments, each of which was destroyed one after another. The large remnant sued for peace and offered to return their plunder in order to recover those captives that the Romans now held. However, the tribesmen then failed to return their own prisoners to the Romans, and an outraged Probus attacked and destroyed them during their retreat with a pitched battle that resulted in the submission of nine enemy chieftains and their leader Igillus, the taking of barbarian hostages and the grant of 16,000 German soldiers absorbed into the Roman army. For obvious reasons, the latter were dispersed well away from the Rhine. Probus commented 'the Roman is pleased to be experiencing, not seeing, barbarian auxiliary troops'.

Probus had now restored all the Rhine and upper Danube, for which the emperor was granted the title 'Germanicus Maximus'. He and his generals had expelled the Franks from northern Gaul, the Alamanni from central Gaul and the Burgundians and Vandals from Raetia and Illyricum. After remarkable successes in battle, the restoration of Gaul was probably Probus' single finest achievement. The emperor followed up his success by the creation of new forts ('limes') east of the Rhine, probably as part of a trip-wire system against new barbarian attacks. He advanced as far as the Elbe river and planned to follow up his successes with the conquest of all of Germany but, as the 'Augustan Histories' correctly inform us, 'the time was not ripe'.

Vandals or Sarmatians again invaded Illyricum in 278. Probus crushed that attack and recovered stolen property, earning the title 'Restitutor Illurici'. Some of the new invaders were settled in Britain. As Probus and his legions continued their march into Thrace, their reputation alone was sufficient to frighten the Getae tribe into submission.

Probus in the east

Aurelian had left unfinished business with Persia. It may be recalled that he had planned to accompany a large army on a punitive expedition to deal with the Sassanid monarchy, and perhaps to recover the lost Roman province of Mesopotamia. It is unclear who occupied the province at this time. Tacitus and Probus had so far been too preoccupied with barbarian invasions to continue where Aurelian had left off, but the time now seemed to be right to make another attempt. In 279, then, Probus and his legions marched off towards the east where, to complicate matters, a usurper had arisen.

The story of the usurper in these turbulent times illustrates the circumstances that forced their hands. Saturninus, a Moor and one-time close friend of Probus, was at this time the governor of Syria with, apparently, influence in Egypt. After a riot had occurred in that sensitive corn-producing province, he was proclaimed emperor at Antioch in Syria around 278 by his own troops and was also recognised by Egypt. Saturninus took up the purple reasoning that, whatever happened, his life was probably forfeit. As the formidable Probus and his huge armies, the legions of an empire, approached, the mutineers clearly recognised their folly and promptly murdered their own appointee.

Another problem was that a community of brigands had installed itself in a mountain fortress, the town of Cremna, north of Lycia within the region of Isauria in southern Asia Minor. Again Zosimus gives us the details. The brigand leader Lydius, who had been robbing the provinces of Pamphylia and Lycia, withdrew to Cremna as Probus approached. The Romans set up a siege, and Lydius was forced to raze buildings in the centre of his walled town to make space for crops in order to feed the population. Still there were too many inhabitants, so their leader ejected all those whom he deemed to be useless. However, the Romans promptly herded them back into Cremna whereupon Lydius simply threw them off the city walls out into the surrounding precipices. Then he made a tunnel, so as to make sorties for food, but the besiegers discovered it and blocked it up. Now Lydius tried to eke out his supplies by giving orders to kill all those not necessary for his survival. Unsurprisingly, this was not well received by the brigands remaining and one of his own highly skilled archers defected to the Romans. Knowing the habits of his leader, he was able to arrange with his new allies that they provide him with a Roman long-range, arrow-discharging machine, the Scorpion. Then he shot Lydius. The murderous bandit died, telling his remaining supporters never to surrender, but they gave up shortly thereafter. Thus Isauria was freed from one of its worst predators (279). Probus made sure by settling some of his veterans at a new colony in the area. The 'Augustan Histories' tell us that Probus dealt with an Isaurian brigand leader, Palfuerius, who may or may not be identified with Lydius.

Still Probus marched east towards Syria. A further distraction was an invasion of southern Egypt by the Blemmyes tribesmen, resurgent after suppression by Aurelian, and a revolt by the town of Ptolemais on the Nile, deep within Egypt, but Probus' local governor was able to suppress them. The emperor himself reached Antioch in Syria in 280.

With these difficulties all along his march, Probus seems to have lost enthusiasm for a war with the militarily powerful Persian kingdom. However the Persians, too, were in disarray. Their unspeakable king Shapur had died and finally been replaced after several civil wars by Bahram II. While the new monarch tried to consolidate his power, it was possible for an uncertain emperor to create a favourable truce. This was arranged, and coins issued at this time show Probus as 'Persicus Maximus'. The emperor hurried back to Europe, no doubt fearing what he might find there.

151

Revolt in Gaul

Probus' fears were realised. In his absence there had arisen two mutinies. Bonosus, one-time commander of the Roman fleet on the Rhine, had previously been relieved of his command by Probus after he had allowed some barbarians to burn his boats. Bonosus had seized the chance to proclaim himself emperor (280) while Probus was in the east. In the same year Proculus was acclaimed at Colonia Agrippinensium (Cologne) as another emperor by the troops on the Rhine. He appears to have had plans to set up another breakaway Gallic–Roman empire claiming Britain, Gaul and Spain. The governor of Britain also rebelled. It is possible that severe disturbances had continued in Gaul even after Probus had departed, caused by a ruined economy, barbarians and a general breakdown of law and order. The result was that local solutions were being sought by the citizens and army, and Proculus is credited by the 'Augustan Histories' with having defeated a fresh incursion by the Alamanni.

As Probus and his army passed through Thrace, some 100,000 Basternae tribesmen, loyal to Rome and perhaps fleeing from barbarian pressure behind, were settled within the Roman frontier near the mouth of the Danube or in Thrace. Many Franks were also settled, but once Probus had departed the Franks began to build ships and then to plunder the coasts of Greece, Sicily and north Africa before returning home with few casualties.

As had been the case with the pretender Saturninus, both rebel usurpers found their support evaporating as the real emperor drew close. One died by betrayal, another by suicide and there were only skirmishes with Probus' legions. The rebellion in Britain was quashed by one of Probus' generals, who had recommended the rebel for his post and gladly seized the opportunity to make amends.

The emperor enjoyed a magnificent Triumph in Rome towards the end of 281, noted for the numbers and varieties of conquered peoples represented in it. The highlight was a spectacular hunt for wild beasts in an artificial forest created in the Circus, when the spectators were allowed to plunge in and grab what they wanted from ostriches, stags, boars, deer, sheep and other animals. Three hundred gladiators, taken from barbarian prisoners, fought to the death and it must have been at about this time that eighty gladiators conspired to break out; they killed their guards, set off on a trail of robbery during which they were joined by other fugitives, and were finally rounded up by soldiers sent after them.

Probus had proved to be as successful and energetic as his mentor Aurelian. However, there was economic dislocation everywhere, and a sign of the times was that the great city of Athens reconstructed its walls in 280 well within the earlier perimeter, and using rubble from the older, larger wall that had been wrecked by the barbarian invasions of 267–268. Indeed, archaeology shows that most of the walls that now surrounded

Roman towns were built during the reign of Probus, presumably at his urging. Aurelian's huge wall surrounding Rome was also completed. With peace at last to hand Probus might perhaps have tried to improve on the economic reforms of his illustrious predecessor, but he had not seized any real wealth as the majority of his victims had been barbarians. Further, such gold as he had managed to confiscate had largely been spent on his costly Triumph. Probus continued to issue the reformed coinage of Aurelian, and his coins attest the fact that, like his predecessor, the new emperor was a Sun-worshipper. To replenish the imperial treasury significantly, he would need to overcome the Persians.

A sign of the emperor's insecurity may be revealed in the number of consulships he took for himself. Out of six successive years when he might have been consul, years 277 to 282 inclusive, he was consul five times. Probus also tried to encourage viticulture by easing some protectionist laws dating back more than 180 years, to the emperor Domitian, concerning the extent and growing of vineyards outside Italy. Aurelian had previously promoted similar reforms within Italy. The net result was to raise prosperity in many regions capable of growing the grape.

Probus set about assembling another army to tackle Persia in 282, either for the simple purpose of recovering Mesopotamia or for the broader economic reason speculated above. However the armies rebelled.

The reason for the outbreak of fresh mutinies among the army in 282 is not entirely clear. Some modern historians have conjectured that the underlying problem was that the armies had fought too hard for too long. As a typical army term was twenty years, some of the troops must have been in almost continuous service for Aurelian and Probus in repelling interminable hordes of barbarians, restoring the empire and on the verge, at least, of several bloody civil wars. Moreover, deaths among the general population caused by the terrible and persistent plague, or by barbarian incursions, must have reduced the number of potential army recruits, requiring existing soldiers to serve for longer terms. The Latin writers, however, give an entirely different explanation. Probus was a stern disciplinarian who would never allow the soldiers to be idle, as he feared that that was when they dreamed of rebellion. He put one of his armies to work on a grand land reclamation project near his home town, Sirmium, in Pannonia, a thankless task that would earn the soldiers none of the booty that they sought from successful battles; a strange task, too, if the army was on its way to fight in Persia. When he made a speech to the effect that soon he hoped that there would be no more need for soldiers, it was the last straw.

The army in Raetia, close to Pannonia, rebelled and put up its commander, Carus, as the new emperor around August 282. When Probus sent a detachment of his troops to suppress the rebellion, they deserted to join Carus. Shortly afterwards, the soldiers working on the land reclamation project rioted and chased the luckless Probus into a large, iron watch tower. The soldiers burst in and killed him (September 282).

Such was the end of one of Rome's finest generals who had also made an outstanding emperor. There is a little mystery about the date of his death, as a salutation in a recently discovered papyrus suggests that he enjoyed an eighth year. The years of his reign are traditionally stated as 276–282 (seven years), and the 'eighth' year might be due simply to a clerical error on the part of the scribe. The succeeding Roman writers made little attempt to disguise the panegyrical nature of their accounts of his reign, but even a modern historian may admit that, if it had required an Aurelian to restore the empire, it had taken a Probus to defend it against the barbarians. The emperor Julian[5] reckoned that Probus had recovered no fewer than seventy cities and summarised him as a good administrator who failed to handle the legions with sufficient tact. Probus was described by Victor as a 'Second Hannibal'. He possessed great knowledge of warfare, trained recruits well and, like Hannibal, used idle soldiers to plant vineyards. Eutropius claimed that the emperor was an ardent, energetic and fair ruler, the equal of Aurelian in military skills and the superior by virtue of his gracious nature. Zosimus describes Probus as 'brilliant and just' shortly before a gap appears in the surviving text.

The modern view is that Probus made a severe error in accelerating the settlement of huge numbers of barbarians within the Roman frontiers. Some of them had promptly rioted. Inscriptions confirm that Probus was deified, although the written evidence is patchy and his relations with the Senate at Rome may not have been so cosy as his panegyrists suggest. Fourteen senators were ambiguously 'missos'[6] after an uprising in the Circus Maximus (the word may mean dismissed or put to death) and the 'Augustan Histories' express doubt about his deification. His salutation, like that of Aurelian himself, as 'Restitutor Orbis' had been well deserved. Other hopes expressed on his coinage such as 'Concordia Militum' (harmony of the soldiers) and 'Felicia Tempora' (felicitous times) remained only dreams.

Carus and sons (282–285)

Carus was Probus' praetorian prefect and, in an age that relied heavily on Danubian generals, probably came originally from Narbo in Gaul. He always claimed to have played no part in the murder of Probus – whom he had deified at once, and he punished the assassins – and also protested, like several others, that he had not sought the purple. As with earlier praetorian prefects, he may well have had legal training and certainly the edicts that he decreed showed a concern for legal niceties. However, he broke with tradition, in a manner that raised eyebrows, by not seeking ratification from the Senate for his appointment as emperor. This had always been a formality anyway, but Carus dispensed even with that token pretence by curtly announcing to the Senate through a letter 'I am emperor'. The Senate accepted the decision.

Like so many of his predecessors Probus had died without sons, leaving the question of succession wide open again. Carus, however, not only had two sons, Carinus and Numerian, but both were already old enough to play an active role in command of the empire. This would be certain to create difficulties for any new pretender to the throne – not only would he have to overthrow Carus, but he would have to deal with the sons too.

Carus' first task was to initiate himself with the blood of barbarians. Knowledge of the death of Probus may have provided the opportunity for which the barbarians had been waiting. Once again, there had been an invasion into Pannonia from across the Danube, this time by Quadi and Sarmatian tribesmen. Luckily his own army and the former legions of Probus were conveniently to hand, and the incursion was smashed with 16,000 tribesmen counted dead and 20,000, of both sexes, captured. Coin inscriptions confirm the victory. It appears that the tribal migration had been motivated by a search for new lands if whole families were in movement.

Now, at last, it might be possible to implement the grand strategy of Aurelian and Probus for a war with Persia. Carus began by taking the precaution of guarding his rear with the appointment of his elder son Carinus as governor of the western empire. Any usurper here would have to contend with Carus' deputy, whose loyalty need not be questioned. We may remark, in passing, how unfortunate Aurelian and Probus had been never to be able to rely on a similar lieutenant when they set out on their remote campaigns. Carus and his younger son Numerian departed together with the bulk of the Roman armies for the east.

Persia was still suffering from internal dissensions within her monarchy. Three different kings, Hormizd, Bahram I and Bahram II, had come and gone since the death of the infamous Shapur, while civil war had broken out in 282 between Bahram III (276–293) and Narses, who was Shapur's last surviving son and the Sassanid king of Armenia. It was at this opportune moment that Carus struck the Persians and he was able to recover the lost Roman province of Mesopotamia, achieving a victory over the Persians in 283 and even capturing their cities of Coche and Ctesiphon on opposite banks of the Tigris river. At long, long last the Roman empire had been restored to the extent bequeathed to it by Septimius Severus in 211, if we overlook the voluntary abandonment of Dacia by Aurelian and the uncertain status of the Agri Decumantes at this time. Carus received the title of 'Persicus Maximus'.

Carus had intended to penetrate deeper into Persian territory, although oracles consulted previously had informed him that he would be allowed to reach Ctesiphon after his victory, but could go no farther. He was still with his army, although ill, when a violent thunderstorm overtook the camp. His body was found in the emperor's tent after a flash of lightning; apparently he had been struck by the bolt from the heavens and one can readily guess the mileage that the Roman soothsayers got out of this event. Suffice it to say that Numerian, who was of an unwarlike disposition although apparently a good poet, suffered a minor defeat at the hands of the Persians and then chose to pack up the camp and take home the bulk of the army, excluding the necessary garrisons.

The modern suspicion is that Carus was murdered as step one of an elaborate plot to overthrow the whole dynasty. This seems unlikely; why not kill Numerian too and proclaim a revolt? However, matters were to become more complicated. During the long trek back to Europe, Numerian suffered from an eye infection so that he had to be kept hidden within a tent protected from wind movements. At some point on the way home, he died (284). Aper, the praetorian prefect and also Carus' son-in-law, continued to hide the body until the stench that arose could not be disguised. The general Diocles led the investigation. Aper was already rumoured to have been involved with the death of Carus and now appeared to have killed Numerian, and Diocles ended an impassioned speech to the soldiers by stabbing Aper, killing him. Then the army appointed Diocles as the new emperor, after which he changed his name to Diocletian. Diocletian claimed to have avenged Carus' son, but the name of Numerian was later erased from public monuments. Was the murder of Numerian and of an innocent Aper, who may have concealed the body simply to avert the rebellion that actually did occur until Carinus could join him, step two of Diocletian's scheme? Probably we shall never know.

Carinus had already dealt with one barbarian invasion across the Rhine and put Britain in order while his father was in the east. After news of the mutiny reached him, he at once marched his troops eastwards from Gaul across the north of Italy and into Illyricum, easily knocking over a rebel, one Julianus, en route near Verona. Julianus appears to have made his revolt in favour of Diocletian, to whom he appealed for aid. The large army of Carinus prepared to engage Diocletian's weaker forces near Margus in the province of Moesia. However Carinus' personal traits of luxurious living and viciousness endeared him to few and, when it became apparent that his loyal soldiers were winning the battle with the returning armies from the east, the emperor was assassinated by one of his own officers – allegedly one whose wife Carinus had seduced. This left Diocletian as sole ruler of the Roman world (285).

Carus and his two sons had enjoyed only two full years of uninter-rupted rule before dying or being challenged, yet Carus had finally finished the task that had been left incomplete by the assassinated Aurelian. An impressive result for so short a reign. Carus and Numerian would later be deified, attested by coins; Carinus appears not to have been so honoured. Years later, the emperor Julian felt disinclined to invite any of the three to his imaginary 'Banquet of the Caesars'.

Conclusion

Diocletian (284–305) showed his statesmanship after his victory over Carinus by an action unique in previous Roman history: he offered a general amnesty to all those who had supported Carus and Carinus even to the extent of permitting them to retain their existing ranks and appointments. He also arranged for the reconstruction of the Roman Senate building that had been wrecked by a devastating fire in 283, which had destroyed much of Rome. The building that still stands in the ancient Forum at Rome is his replacement. The newly restored and consolidated Roman empire enjoyed an almost unbroken peace, troubled only slightly by barbarian incursions that were ruthlessly suppressed, and at the end of twenty years Diocletian performed another action unique among all the emperors of Rome: he retired voluntarily in favour of his designated successor. After his death, the Senate proudly deified Diocletian, an act that was also unparalleled – the deification of a private citizen. We may leave the Danubian generals of the 3rd century with the knowledge that the Roman empire had been as fully restored as it could be.

NOTES

1   (i) Principal original sources (see Chapter IV, Note 1); (ii) General source: Dodgeon, M H, *The Roman Eastern Frontier and the Persian Wars, AD 226–363: A Documentary History* (ed. S N C Lieu, Routledge, 1993).
2   Chronicler of 354: *Monumenta, Germaniae Historica. Chronica Minora*, Vol. 1 (ed. Mommsen, 1892). Latin.
3   *Prosopographia Imperii Romani* ('PIR', 2nd edn, 1933). Latin.
4   Abbreviated version from *Scriptores Historiae Augustae*, Vol. III, Probus (see Chapter IV, Note 1).
5   Julian, Vol. II, *The Caesars*, translated by W C Wright (Loeb, Harvard University Press, 1913; reprinted 1969).
6   Chronicler of 354, op. cit.

CHAPTER X
The Legacy of the Danubian Emperors

Permanent damage caused during the 3rd century

Notwithstanding the revulsion with which his name was held by later Roman writers, the emperor Gallienus had at least managed to prevent the complete disintegration of the Roman empire. He had personally taken the field to withstand barbarian attacks, even though he had not been able to prevent the secession of large parts of the empire from his rule, and his reputation has been largely restored by modern historians.

Yet it had taken the actions of three super-human Danubian generals to stem the tide of anarchy, civil strife and barbarian invasions, each personally leading battle-hardened legions recruited largely from the Balkan areas.

- Claudius had smashed the Gothic barbarians thoroughly when their ravages seemed to be unstoppable, but his premature death by plague had prevented him from following up his success.
- Aurelian had similarly crushed all barbarian intruders and re-united the entire empire under his rule. He had also set in motion the economic reforms needed to restore the devastated Roman economy.
- Probus, Aurelian's loyal general and later emperor in his own right, had maintained his reputation as a destroyer of barbarians while also consolidating the fragile, newly restored empire. He had in addition settled an honourable peace with Persia.

These three rulers truly deserved the title of 'Restorer of the World' (formally awarded only to Aurelian and Probus) and their actions had checked serious barbarian incursions for decades. They had fostered a climate of stability, so important for the restoration of economic confidence, creating the background in which the administrative skills of Diocletian, also a Danubian general, could flourish.

Yet even these three supermen could not undo all the damage caused by the chaos of the mid 3rd century.

1. Poor discipline of the Roman legions

It had become very difficult for even an Aurelian or a Probus to impose strict discipline on the troops, and the latter had lost his life in the attempt. The army was now drawn primarily from the provinces and from the barbarians, so it had little commitment to the concept of supporting Rome. Few Italians, still fewer Romans, now served with the legions. The loyalty of the troops was generally bought with large handouts.

The new emperor Diocletian would be the first of some two dozen of his predecessors – and that tally excludes pretenders to the purple – to have died of natural old age since Septimius Severus one hundred years previously. Indeed, if we except the premature death from plague of Claudius in 270, and the doubtful causes of death of Tacitus, Carus and Numerian, Diocletian was the first of these two dozen not to have died violently. However, Diocletian found it necessary to make a huge increase in the size of the Roman army, perhaps by as much as 50%, and this inevitably led to a fresh decline in the standard of the recruits. The Latin historian Aurelius Victor, writing in 360, showed strong antipathy towards the contemporary Roman army, which he blamed for most of the troubles of his and recent times.[1]

In passing, we find that in later years Aurelian's elite light Dalmatian and Moorish cavalry no longer serve as part of the emperor's main mobile army, but have been stationed on the Danube and Euphrates frontiers. The originator of this change is unknown. Ultimately the Roman clibanarii (heavy-armoured cavalry) were a flop. The armour was far too stiff for manoeuvrability, was also far too hot for use against the similarly-attired Persians, and a mass cavalry charge could easily be countered by tripping up the horses or by slashing at the animal. The unseated rider could scarcely move! The named units of clibanarii known to have existed at the end of the 4th century are believed to have comprised lightly armoured cavalry units only.[2]

2. Economic crisis

The need to fund the army had caused heavy taxation and the gross debasement of the coinage, resulting in severe inflation. This phenomenon was well recognised, but little understood at the time. It left an economic legacy that would baffle even Diocletian.

The discovery in later ages of many coin hoards buried during the 3rd century reveals the general insecurity of the times and the need to store the few old coins, with a high proportion of silver or gold, that still possessed real intrinsic value. However, hoarding tended to make everyone less well off, by restricting the free circulation of precious metals.

Even the number of burial inscriptions fell steeply during this period of disorder, as evidenced by surviving examples. The trend was not reversed until the accession of Diocletian.

3. Loss of rights

The Romans had for centuries understood that in national emergencies it was necessary to appoint a dictator who would take severe steps as he thought appropriate – and for which he could not later be held accountable – but military necessity had turned every emperor into an outright dictator with the absolute right to pass laws, make civil and military appointments and command armies. Thus the old Roman spirit of seeking public office for personal honour and public benefit had all but died out. The Senate itself was largely abandoned by those qualified to sit in it as it possessed virtually no real power. Moreover, the fiction by which the emperor referred to himself as 'Princeps' (leading citizen) was vanishing. The emperor had become a sovereign in all but name, and it is now customary to refer to the empire during and after the time of Diocletian as a 'Dominate' (ruled by a lord) where previously it had been a 'Principate'.

4. Walled cities

Another sign of the insecurity of the times was the number of towns and cities that now possessed their own surrounding walls for defence. Rome herself had to be similarly protected during Aurelian's reign. The walls were built as quickly as possible from any materials that lay to hand; even tombstones were employed as part of the basic structure. The new walls generally enclosed a lesser area than the original town. This may partly have been for convenience in building the fortifications, but also reflected a steep decline in the Roman population. The smaller cities were cramped, and had no room for large monuments. The construction of an inner city wall at Athens has already been described.

5. Population decline

The population of the Roman world had fallen markedly as a natural consequence of the catastrophes of the 3rd century. Wars, an endemic plague that had lasted for twenty years, causing at one point 7,000 deaths each day at Rome, and general insecurity, which has long been known to reduce birth rates, had all taken their toll. One interesting by-product from the disturbances in Gaul was that many wealthy landowners sold up their estates and fled to the relatively safer province of Britain, where they established the large villas whose remains survive to this day.

161

6. Collapse of agriculture and of trade

The lands had been ravaged and the population killed or fled. Inevitably there was less land under cultivation, fewer farm hands and fewer mouths to feed. One solution to the shortage of unskilled agricultural labour was to ask cities to send out their idle occupants. The luxury of bread and circuses for the unemployed could no longer be afforded by most towns. Equally, there were fewer markets in which to sell goods. Manufacturers found that their distant markets were inaccessible, due to dangerous communications, or the local people too poor to afford the wares. The glass and pottery industries are known to have been very hard hit in the mid 3rd century.

The consequence was that the emperors themselves had increasingly to sponsor their own industries, particularly for military goods, and this created unfair competition for any would-be entrepreneurs trying to start their own businesses.

7. Loss of skills

The most intractable problem was the loss of basic skills. The armies themselves had lost large numbers of men in the interminable civil wars, although there was an increasing tendency for the legions on both sides to count their numbers first and for the weaker to murder their own emperor before he led them into a hopeless battle. Worse still was the loss of skilled artisans who had died or been killed, and simply could not be replaced.

The advanced Greek sciences and philosophies virtually dried up in the mid 3rd century. The last great exponent of pagan philosophy, the Egyptian-Greek Plotinus (205–270), who taught at Rome from 245 after an apprenticeship in Alexandria, produced late in life several books intended to explain the workings of the universe and especially to explain the concept of evil. The writer Porphyry, who was his pupil, attempted to popularise the Neoplatonism of Plotinus, but it soon fell into disuse. The cultured emperor Gallienus, however, had been much impressed by the philosopher's work.

The extent and standard of art, as measured by sculptures, books and paintings, and of public buildings, declined markedly over this period, while the later emperor Constantine the Great would celebrate his victory over Maxentius (312) with a standard triumphal arch in Rome, for which some of the sculptures had to be removed from a 2nd-century monument. Constantine's arch still stands next to the famous Colosseum. However, mosaics remained of good quality, as can be seen even in Britain, and the standard of engravature on Aurelian's new coins had much improved. There are virtually no original written works excepting novels, most notably the lengthy 'Aethiopica' by the Greek author Heliodorus. There

162

are also no major poets and no useful histories, save that of Dexippus, known from the mid 3rd century. Fragments of the lesser Latin poets Reposianus and Nemesianus have survived from 280–290.

8. Serfdom

Some of the few remaining wealthy landowners within the empire, such as those in the undisturbed provinces of north Africa, were in the happy position of being able to purchase large chunks of devastated farmland at knockdown prices from those who had fled. At the same time, the later emperors issued many ordinances to force surplus city dwellers onto the land, to which they were bound by other laws that obliged sons to take up the occupations of their fathers.

The embattled emperors depended heavily on land taxes to pay their armies, and connived – by the passage of legislation – at an arrangement with the landowners whereby the freemen, the clients, on the giant new estates were tied to the land, unable to leave. Thus they became serfs in a system recognisable as the forerunner of the medieval feudal system. Another part of the deal between landlord and emperor was that the estates should provide conscripts for the armies, and this burden also fell on the former clients. The net effect of these changes was that the flight from the land had been arrested, areas under cultivation increased – and the clients had become serfs. This section of the Roman community had involuntarily given up its freedom in order to avoid enslavement by the barbarians.

9. Settlement of barbarians within the empire

One solution to make good the population loss in the shattered areas was to settle captured barbarian tribesmen within the areas that they had devastated, providing a robust new work force and enabling them to make good the damage they had caused. This was always a dubious policy, as was recognised even by contemporary writers. Many tribesmen were glad of the chance to contribute to Roman civilisation, with the attendant benefits for themselves, while the Roman army found them a useful source for hardy recruits. However, some of the barbarians went through the motions of settlement before using their new territory as a convenient base from which to plunder their neighbours. The loyalty of the newly settled tribes must always have been uncertain; less so when the new settlers were themselves fleeing from more violent barbarians in their rear.

10. Degeneration of language

While the empire had remained a strong, cohesive unit, its standard of Latin had remained remarkably homogeneous in all the provinces, as evidenced by surviving inscriptions. The invasions of the mid 3rd century, and the separation of the breakaway Roman empires, caused the degeneration of the Latin speech and grammar into regional accents and variations. In later centuries, these variants would form the foundation of the modern Romance (Latin-derived) languages, French, Italian, Spanish and Portuguese.

11. Failure of the pagan religions and philosophy

Worship of the emperor, or of his 'genius', was never very convincing and adoption of the title of 'Dominus et Deus' did not save any of the bearers (Aurelian, Probus and Carus) from assassination.

Sun-worship ultimately offered nothing to humanity struggling under the burdens of barbarian invasions, plague and oppressive taxation. It implied no rules of behaviour and failed to explain the only-too-obvious struggle between good and evil. Philosophy was also a disappointment; a policy of ascension from the Body to the Soul to the Divine Mind to a god-like state (the 'One') by yearning and self-contemplation had little appeal or even challenge. Neither could stand up against the fast-rising movement of Christianity that offered so much more: salvation by Grace and immortality of the soul coupled with strict rules for conduct towards your neighbour and God.

The final legacy

The most enduring achievement of our Danubian supermen may therefore be simply that they allowed the empire to survive; to survive long enough for Christianity to become widespread even among the barbarians and thereby, in Gibbon's words, '[Christianity] broke the violence of the fall [of the Roman empire], and mollified the ferocious temper of the conquerors'. Ironically, none of our supermen showed much enthusiasm for Christianity.

Aftermath

This book ends properly with the ascent of Diocletian and the united empire free, temporarily, from internal pretenders and external enemies. However, the sequel might as well be stated.[3]

The new emperor, Diocletian, was yet another former Danubian general who was to prove to be as outstanding an administrator as his predecessors had been military exponents. Diocletian realised early on that the empire simply could not any longer be handled by one man; whenever he was in any one part of it pretenders arose or barbarians invaded in another. Carausius, given a fleet to combat the pirate menace in the North Sea, had fled with it in 286 to Britain. The Bagaudae tribe had rebelled once the former emperor Carinus had left Gaul, and barbarians had invaded in 286. Therefore he divided the empire into two (286), appointing an old army friend and general, Maximian, as his co-emperor in the west; Diocletian took the wealthier east. Both in turn appointed successors as emperors-designate, known as caesars, to provide a system of rule known as the Tetrarchy (293). It meant that the most capable generals were assured a share of the imperial power, while the presence of effectively four rulers enabled a much closer guarding of the frontiers and posed an almost insuperable problem to any usurpers. The tetrarchs built magnificent palaces for themselves in their self-selected capitals of government. They also launched a savage new attack (303–304) on the fast-growing Christian Church that would prove to be both the last and also the fiercest of all the Church's persecutions, and would persist in the eastern empire until 311.

Diocletian raised the manpower of the army from some 300,000–400,000 in the time of Severus to more than half-a-million men under arms, and again favoured the concept of a frontier defence where barbarians were to be checked at the empire's perimeter and not within it. He continued the separation of the frontier garrisons, comprising mostly ex-barbarian soldiers, from the mobile 'rapid-response' units of infantry and cavalry that were generally made up from conscripts from the empire reinforced with barbarian special troops. This rapid expansion of the army must have caused a deterioration in the quality of the recruits.

Diocletian also reorganised the provinces into 'dioceses' for better management and defence. The number of provinces within each diocese was approximately doubled from the original total, with extra provincial governors and their administrations, partly with a view to making rebellion harder for would-be usurpers. Each provincial governor now commanded about half the number of soldiers that he might have called upon to support a rebellion before the division of the provinces.

The Tetrarchy also had the effect that the numbers of senior administrative staff were perhaps quadrupled, the dioceses doubled the number of civil servants and the army had also been greatly increased. All had to be paid for; taxation was changed from an erratic collection when needed to a regular levy. Aurelius Victor claims that the new tax burden to pay for all this had been fair as first imposed by Diocletian, but that later emperors became greedy.[4] The Christian writer Lactantius, a contemporary of Diocletian, paints a grim picture of the cost of the new bureaucracy and armies.[5]

Diocletian tried again to reform the currency after Aurelian's partial success in the 270s.[6] He re-minted the gold coin at sixty to a Roman pound of gold and a high-grade silver coin was issued at ninety-six to the pound weight of silver. The old antoninianus was standardised at 3% silver content, including face wash, and about 10 grams weight. The name of the new coin is unknown; it is today referred to as a 'follis'. Again the silver content of the follis drifted down over succeeding years to about 1.5% silver before Constantine the Great introduced new reforms. Diocletian also took giant steps to improve the economy, but his attempts to control inflation by mandate (prices were not allowed to rise – by order) proved to be a failure despite the most stringent penalties.

On Rome's eastern front, Diocletian established numerous fortresses to watch over the Persians. Their new king, Narses (293–302), tried to renew hostilities against Rome with the invasion of Mesopotamia and Armenia in 296, followed by an incursion into Syria. The nearest tetrarch, Galerius, lost a battle in 297, but the new forts held steady and Galerius heavily defeated Narses in the following year, seizing the Persian ruler's family and harem. Diocletian was able to dictate terms to Narses, resulting in a pact in 299 that ended some fifty years of hostility between the two kingdoms and enabled trade to resume. The peace lasted for forty years.

After twenty years of rule Diocletian committed the unique act of resigning as emperor, and forced his reluctant colleague to do the same, so that the caesars now stepped into power and appointed in turn their successors. Unfortunately, squabbles began as to the appointments, another dreary cycle of civil wars began and finally the empire was re-united (324) under the sole reign of Constantine, who was joint or sole emperor between 306 and 337.

The individual rule of Constantine ushered in a new era, variously described as 'the Police State', 'the beginning of the Middle Ages' or 'the end of the Roman empire'. At first the new emperor was an ardent adherent to the Sun-god, and Sol Invictus appears on his coins as late as 318. However Constantine attributed his military victories in the civil war of 312 to a vision of Christianity, made it the official religion and received the title 'The Great', bestowed by a grateful Church. He created what we would today recognise as a medieval court, which he moved from Rome to a new capital on the Bosporus that he named modestly 'Constanti-nople'. The new capital was furnished by removing valuables from other parts of the empire, and particularly from pagan temples, and it possessed its own Senate so that the ancient centre of power in Rome was greatly diminished. At the same time, all power was concentrated completely into the hands of the emperor, who served as head of state and head of the Church. Constantine was a king in all but name.

Because Christianity was now the official Roman religion, Constantine was in the happy position of being able to grab gold from the richly ornamented pagan temples in order to institute another revision of the currency. He introduced the new 'solidus', a gold coin minted at seventy-two to a pound weight of gold, and this high quality coin would be retained as the standard gold issue for centuries to come – well into the Middle Ages. He also minted a new, high-quality silver coin at ninety-six to the pound weight. However, the follis continued to deteriorate and its production had largely ended by 353. Simple silver-less coins of base metals still provided the small change for day-to-day transactions.

Constantine extended Diocletian's laws creating hereditary classes of citizens so that members could not move into any of the (many) occupations, such as the clergy, that were exempt from taxes. They could not even join the army. These changes resulted in widespread, overt hostility to the rule of the state. He also formalised the distinction between the frontier army and the better-paid mobile army, a decision that Zosimus would claim in the next century to have been ultimately responsible for the collapse of the Roman empire. Worse, increasing use was made of barbarians within the army at all levels up to the top officers, while higher levels of immigration were permitted. The size of the legion, which had remained fairly constant at some 5,000 men for centuries, was reduced to 1,000 infantry and/or cavalry for flexibility of deployment. There were accordingly far more legions than before.

The relative freedom from external enemies and civil wars allowed a final flourishing of Roman art in the middle of the 4th century. For a while pagan and Christian cultures coexisted comfortably in a nominally Christian empire, and this was when several historical works and the illustrated Calendar of 354 were produced. The latter shows that the birthdays of several of the 'good' emperors were still officially celebrated as public holidays, with circus races in their honour.[7] Present in the list are the birthdays of Augustus, the first true emperor, Trajan, Hadrian, the Antonine emperors, Severus and, more recently, Claudius II Gothicus, Aurelian and Probus, followed by Constantine and his successors. Remarkable omissions from the feast days are the names of Diocletian, Carus and his sons, Valerian and Tacitus. Less remarkable are the omissions of the despised Commodus, Caracalla and Gallienus. The immediate successors of Augustus are also absent. The list of feast days includes the celebration of several pagan gods, including Sol Invictus, but lacks the celebration of the pagan god Mithras, still very popular but significantly never adopted by an emperor. Christian feast days are not yet commemorated.

There was a brief pagan revival under the last non-Christian emperor Julian (361–363) who, wisely, contented himself with encouraging pagan rituals rather than active persecution of Christians. While still a general, Julian had crossed the Rhine in 359 to harass the Alamanni after repelling their earlier invasion. In the east, the Persians again became aggressive under the rule of a new Shapur II. Between 337 and 350 Shapur made three raids into Mesopotamia, and in 359 the Persians made a full-scale invasion, seizing several of the key fortress-cities. Julian moved his armies to the east, but died in action; his Christian successor Jovian abandoned the Roman conquests so hard won by Galerius in 298.

Again the empire had to be divided for defence, and the last strong emperor of the western empire, Valentinian, not only repelled a barbarian invasion but decided on a policy that had not been seen for generations. He carried the war back into the barbarians' territory across the Rhine and ravaged their lands intermittently for the next seven years. This strategy was undoubtedly made possible by the fact that Valentinian had appointed his loyal younger brother, Valens, as emperor in the east, so that Valentinian could safely deploy the great part of his army for reprisals. However Valentinian died of apoplexy at the height of his triumph over the German tribesmen, and in the east Valens and his legions were overrun by the resurgent Goths – who had been allowed to settle within the Roman frontier – at the battle of Adrianople in 378. The army was almost wiped out after a dust storm blew into their faces and Valens was never seen again.

The victorious barbarians swarmed over Thrace but were unable to break into its walled cities. The new emperors of west and east, respectively Gratian and Theodosius, settled the Goths within the Roman frontier and recruited heavily from them to replace the vanished legions. Yet the barbarians served under their own chieftains and could be persuaded to adopt Roman military tactics only with difficulty, while they were also reluctant to wear their heavy Roman armour. Even the famous Roman curved, rectangular shield gave way to a lighter, circular type. The imposition of strict discipline on Roman armies had become troublesome from the early 3rd century with their propensity to make and unmake emperors; now it would be well-nigh impossible. Although neither the bravery nor, surprisingly, the loyalty to Rome of the new recruits could be criticised, the fact remains that by the end of the 4th century the 'Roman' army largely amounted to just another barbarian force. Less surprisingly, the new army was not successful against the numerically superior waves of other barbarians pouring in across the frontiers.[8]

As the situation deteriorated, the increasingly Christian rulers and leaders of the empire took firmer steps to prevent its superstitious population from reverting to pagan worship in the hope of averting the barbarian onslaught. The use of public funds to pay for pagan ceremonies was halted in 384. In 389 all pagan festivals were stopped, except those deemed to be innocuous, such as the celebration of 'Roma Aeterna'. Six years later, all pagan holidays were removed from the calendar but the games that formerly celebrated them were allowed to continue, although the gladiatorial schools were closed in 399.[9] The barbarian army, however, remained predominantly pagan.

The first intimation of the end of empire came in 405–406 when swarms of tribesmen crossed the frozen Rhine and devastated Gaul. The Goths under their chieftain Alaric again rebelled, crossed the Alps and finally sacked Rome herself in 410. The last stupendous achievement by a western Roman general, Aetius, was to ally with the Goths in Gaul to inflict a decisive defeat on the fearsome Attila and his Huns (451) – the only time that Attila was ever defeated and a crucial victory which held the west for civilisation.

Thereafter the end came swiftly, and the last Roman emperor of the west was deposed by a Gothic king ruling from Gaul in 476. This is the date traditionally given for the fall of Rome. A lot of nonsense has been written about the reasons for the fall of Rome; Gibbon famously attributed the fall to the triumph of the barbarians and Christianity. It would be fairer to argue that the Church had defended and salvaged Roman culture. Modern historians have imputed a huge number of reasons, while some have even denied that anything unusual happened at all, arguing that Constantine's medieval court merely progressed to a German medieval court. It is unlikely that it felt that way to the citizens of Italy. The truth is that Rome's barbarian armies could not withstand the larger numbers of barbarians from across the frontiers.

By now the Roman empire had been divided permanently into two. In the east a series of dynastic emperors ruled from Constantinople over what was effectively a Greek dominion, in speech and in culture, later called the Byzantine empire. The Christian Byzantines withstood the onslaught of Islam from the east for centuries, with the intermittent help, or hindrance, of the Crusaders. The last Roman emperor Constantine XIII died in action at Constantinople when that great city fell in 1453 to the Turks, who were aided by gunpowder and cannon provided by rogue western traders. It was Gibbon who defined the thousand-year period between the fall of Rome and the fall of Constantinople as the 'Middle Ages'.

Aurelian's original wall had not made a full circuit of the city, and this was completed in 402/3 under the emperor Honorius.[10] It was rebuilt, perhaps after the earthquake of 502, by Theodoric the Goth as part of the general Gothic rebuilding programme in Rome. However, in the east the powerful, 6th-century Byzantine emperor Justinian coveted Italy and Rome, and sent his best general Belisarius to recapture both. The city was taken and retaken at least three times. In 536 Belisarius overhauled the walls for defence against the Goths, but the Byzantines were ejected. Ten years later, having been damaged by the departing Goths, the walls were again repaired by Belisarius. The last recorded races were run at the Circus Maximus in 549. Once more the walls were repaired in the 8th and 9th centuries, against threats from sea-going Arabs and the intruding Lombard peoples, by the Christian popes who now provided virtually the only stable government in Rome. After St Peter's Basilica had been looted by the Arabs in 846, the old wall was extended to provide protection to the Vatican (848–852).

The legacy that the fallen Roman empire left to its European successors comprised Christianity and Roman Law. The latter was finally written down in definitive form as a Digest under the great emperor Justinian (527–565)[11], and was separately abridged by the Gothic kings for re-use in Italy around 500. It was the rediscovery of a copy of Justinian's Digest in north Italy about the year 1100 that invigorated the readoption of Roman Law within Europe. Roman Law is currently the basis of most European law, but not in England where Saxon Law prevailed and was passed on to the majority of countries of the British empire, including north America.

Christianity, with its central tenet of 'love thine neighbour', had a strong civilising effect on the conquering barbarians that overthrew the western empire. The Goths, for example, had already largely adopted the religion by the time they settled in Gaul. Later medieval nobles would create 'rules of war' incorporating Christian elements into the age of chivalry and heraldry, providing a strong influence to tame actions even in this field.

And what was the legacy of the barbarians? What do you do when you have stolen everything from the civilised peoples of the Roman world, ruined their lands, destroyed their buildings and given nothing back? You have to start fending for yourself, that's what. In the former province of Britain, the invading Anglo-Saxons built their mud huts amid the ruins of the greatest civilisation that the ancient world had ever known. The structures of Rome and other cities were deliberately knocked down to furnish building materials for churches or farmsteads. Europe entered the Dark Ages.

Finally, what of the Sibylline Books? The last known consultation by the Senate of the genuine Sibylline Books was in 363, during the reign of the pagan emperor Julian. Shortly after the barbarians reached north Italy, following their mass invasion across the Rhine in 405–406, the Christian emperor of the west, Honorius, ordered that the books be burned by his general Stilicho. They have never been seen again.

Conclusions

'Those who do not remember the past are condemned to repeat it' (G Santayana, philosopher, 1863–1952).

The barbarians had overthrown the western Roman empire, but they could offer nothing to replace it. The Saxons who violently invaded Britain in the 5th century, destroying the remnants of Romano–British society, dwelt in hovels while they watched the collapse of great, but unmaintained, Roman buildings and aqueducts. The 'Dark Ages' lasted for hundreds of years, say from 500 to about 1100 in the more distant parts of Europe. When Gibbon finished his *Decline and Fall* at the end of the 18th century, many parts of the world were still unexplored. Gibbon therefore considered whether a new race of barbarians, hitherto unknown, could undo the civilisation in Europe in the same way that Roman society had been ruined. He reasoned that technological developments in Europe, predominantly in weapons, ensured that no undiscovered race of barbarians could conquer Europe without first learning how to master the same or equivalent technologies. In other words, the barbarians would first have to become civilised before they could encompass the downfall of European civilisation. One wonders what Gibbon would have to say about a western civilisation that sells sophisticated armaments to (relatively) barbarian potential enemies.

The second great lesson from the decline of the Roman empire is the importance of ensuring that soldiers and their generals are subject to proper control by their masters. The English civil war occurred nearly as soon as a general had a professional army to do his bidding, while rebellions in south America have been almost endemic. The only long-term solution appears to be to ensure that soldiers are drawn from the society they are supposed to defend, so that they are subject to peer pressure.

The third great lesson comes from the middle of the 3rd century AD. Populations will take steps to find local solutions to pressing problems if the central authority will not act. Both the western and the eastern parts of the Roman empire created their own governments, under Postumus in the west and Macrianus or Odaenathus in the east, when the acknowledged emperor failed to respond to invasions in these territories. The emperor, Gallienus, was perceived to be more interested in the suppression of invasions or rebellions elsewhere than in protecting the peoples of the west and east. He was actually removing their frontier troops, reducing their protection. Today the same phenomenon of finding local solutions can be seen in the trend for larger countries to split, such as has occurred with Yugoslavia and Czechoslovakia. At a different level, the perceived failure of the police to respond to residents' concerns has led to the increasing appearance of vigilante groups in Britain and the USA.

Postscript – the Triumph of the Barbarians[12]

It is not generally recognised today just how catastrophic for the future of civilisation was the final collapse of the Roman empire in the west. Contrary to general belief, it is prolonged periods of stability that result in the greatest human advancement, not the pressure of wars. Economic prosperity advances on all fronts when ordinary people can prepare long-range plans or can enjoy the luxury of leisured thought about life's problems. The economic prosperity of Britain, and the huge scientific advances of the 19th century, were greatly dependent upon the long period of unbroken peace under Queen Victoria.

The 'Pax Romana' had created for about four centuries a settled condition – for most of the empire's population – in which trade could flourish to the advantage of all, and new inventions could spread rapidly. The propagation of Christianity was perhaps the empire's greatest achievement. When the barbarians marched in for the last time, trade collapsed and non-military inventions died.

The names of some of the invading tribes still echo through the ages, as by-words for death and destruction – the Vandals and the Huns. The reputation of those old Roman foes, the Goths, has fared better. According to one of their own chieftains, he entered the remnant of the empire as a would-be plunderer, but recognised in time the value and the achievement of what he would destroy. And thus he stayed his hand. By now, constant contact between Romans and Goths had largely civilised the latter anyway, and many had converted to Christianity. Gothic kings ruled Rome herself after the last emperor had been deposed, and today we associate the Gothic name more with architecture than with pillage.

Even so, the areas controlled by the Goths were as uncertain of their futures as those held by the other barbarians, while the eastern Roman empire lapsed into introspection and lethargy. Much Roman literature was lost, as were many Roman inventions from the old, great empire. Worst of all was the loss of economic efficiency with the collapse of overseas markets. Pottery and glassware were still manufactured, but were no longer of the old high standard, nor were they widely distributed. Glass would no longer appear in window frames. Tribes on the periphery of the empire would abandon even those advanced farming techniques that the Romans had taught them.

The collapse of trade routes and safe lines of communication greatly reduced the scale of building in brick or stone. The necessary raw materials simply could not be moved from quarries to building sites. In Rome herself, older monuments and buildings were knocked down to provide materials for new churches and new dwellings. The creation of the fine old country villa, with baths, mosaics and underfloor heating, ended and would not be seen again until the 19th century. The generally good hygiene practices of the Romans, engendered by flowing (piped) drinking and washing water, public baths and good medical treatment, had also gone, as had the plentiful supply of food known to be necessary to create resistance to illness.

The great public records were upheld no longer, and literacy was no longer widespread. In the general collapse of law and order, the Roman attempts at early police and fire-fighting forces were seen no more. Roman roads and viaducts (for conveying fresh water) were allowed to disintegrate, where previously they had been regularly maintained. Again, it was not until the 19th century that these deficiencies were made good again.

And what of the loss of inventions? When I was a child, I was taught that the magnetic compass was a Chinese invention imported to Europe in the Middle Ages. In more recent years, though, marine archaeology on the wrecks of Roman ships in the Mediterranean has discovered that each ship has a lump of rusted iron next to the steersman's post. The Romans had the magnetic compass. The barbarians lost it. A similar fate befell the secrets of Roman concrete and mortar. The mortar in Hadrian's wall had to be chemically analysed recently in order to discover the secret of its extraordinary longevity. The Romans produced a concrete that could even be used underwater.

The Baths of Caracalla at Rome were one of the wonders of the medieval world. No one could understand how the long, unsupported concrete beams could stand up under their own weight. In the end, they collapsed. Subsequent investigation showed that the beams were made of iron-reinforced concrete. When the iron finally rusted, the concrete beams fell down. Today we use steel-reinforced concrete for much the same kind of purpose.

The Romans used water for power, as in water mills and various hydraulic machines. They employed springs in their carriages, again confirmed only from some very recent archaeological finds in Germany. This technique had also to be re-discovered centuries later. The carriages were used on the impressive network of well constructed Roman roads. Even Roman surveyors used methods subsequently forgotten and re-discovered, and they drew accurate maps. The Romans did not believe that the world was flat.

It is surprising to discover that the Romans never invented the printing press. They had advanced as far as putting several inked seals onto a wooden bar so as to make multiple official stamps on documents, but there is no evidence of printing. Despite their high levels of literacy, they never found it necessary to put individual letters, instead of seals, onto their wooden bar. When slave labour is cheap, the need for labour-saving devices becomes greatly reduced. Anyone who wanted a copy of a book simply asked their slave to copy the original.

The barbarians are sometimes credited with bringing an end to slavery in the Roman empire, but the Christian empire was improving the lot of the declining number of slaves and had already terminated gladiatorial contests. Europe did not recover the state of civilisation enjoyed by the Roman peoples until the 19th century. Even today, many parts of the world remain more backward than the Roman era. *That* was the achievement of the barbarians.

NOTES

1   Victor, Aurelius, *De Caesaribus*, translated by H W Bird (Liverpool University Press, 1994).
2   Eadie, J W, 'Development of Roman Mailed Cavalry', *Journal of Roman Studies*, 57: 161–73 (1967).
3   Main sources: (i) Blockley, R C, *The Fragmentary Classicising Historians of the Later Roman Empire* (Francis Cairns at Liverpool University, 1983); (ii) Carey, M and Scullard, H H, *A History of Rome*, 3rd edn (Macmillan, 1979, reprinted 1986); (iii) Gibbon, E, *The Decline and Fall of the Roman Empire*, Vol. IV, Chapter XXXVIII (Everyman's Library, 1910, 1980 reprint); (iv) Jones, A H M, *The Later Roman Empire*, Vols 1 & 2 (Blackwell & Mott, 1964; reprinted Johns Hopkins paperbacks, 1986).
4   Victor, Aurelius, op. cit.
5   Lactantius, *On the Deaths of the Persecutors*, translated by W Fletcher (Translations in the Library of Nicene and Post-Nicene Fathers: www.ccel.org/fathers2/).
6   Casey, P J, *Roman Coinage in Britain* (Shire Archaeology Press, 1980).
7   Chronicler of 354, *Monumenta, Germaniae Historica. Chronica Minora*, Vol. 1 (ed. Mommsen, 1892). Latin.
8   Ferrill, A, *The Fall of the Roman Empire* (Thames & Hudson, 1986).
9   Salzman, M R, *On Roman Time – The Codex Calendar of 354* (University of California Press, 1990).
10   Richmond, I A, *The City Walls of Imperial Rome* (Clarendon Press, 1930).
11   Justinian, *Digest of*, Vols I–III, eds Mommsen, Krueger and Watson (University of Pennsylvania Press, 1985).
12   Greene, K, *The Archaeology of the Roman Economy* (Batsford, 1986).

APPENDIX A
Key Dates[1]

All dates AD unless otherwise indicated. Many dates between 235 and 285 are approximate only.

Date	Event
753 BC	Traditional date of founding of Rome
ca. 650 BC	Etruscans at Rome
510 BC	Etruscan kings expelled from Rome
390 BC	Barbarians from Gaul sack Rome
343 BC	Beginning of Samnite wars
290 BC	End of 3rd Samnite war. Rome expands into southern Italy
268 BC	First silver coins minted by Rome
263–146 BC	Wars with Carthage and other Mediterranean powers
91–88 BC	Social wars in Italy
88–31 BC	Intermittent civil wars. Conquest of Gaul and the East
31 BC	Octavius (Augustus) becomes first emperor
AD 14	Tiberius succeeds Augustus
43	Conquest of Britain
96–180	Golden age of the Roman empire (includes the Antonine emperors)
193	Septimius Severus emperor. Expansion in East. Consolidation of empire
211	Caracalla emperor. Debased antoninianus issued soon after
212	Caracalla makes all free men in empire full Roman citizens
ca. May 214	Claudius, the future emperor, born
ca. Sept. 214	Aurelian, the future emperor, born
217	Caracalla murdered. Macrinus emperor
218	Macrinus murdered. Elagabalus emperor
222	Elagabalus murdered. Severus Alexander emperor
223	Revolt of Ardashir in kingdom of Parthia
226/7	Ardashir king in Parthia

230	Persians invade Roman Mesopotamia
ca Aug. 232	Probus, the future emperor, born
ca 233	Aurelian joins Roman army
235	Alexander murdered. Maximinus emperor
237–8	Persians again attack Mesopotamia and capture several cities
238	Rebellions in Africa and Rome against Maximinus. Maximinus murdered, as are the Senate's emperors. Gordian III emperor
241	Shapur I ruler in Persia. Instigates attacks on Roman provinces
243	Romans defeat Persians
244	Gordian III murdered. Philip emperor
248	Millennium Games in Rome celebrate 1,000 years of existence
249	Decius defeats and kills Philip. Decius emperor
250	Approximate date of start of plague in Roman empire. Decius requires sacrifices to Roman gods by all citizens
251	Decius killed in action against Goths. Gallus emperor
252–3	Persians raid eastern provinces and capture Antioch
253	Aemilian defeats Gallus and becomes emperor
253	Valerian, general of Gallus, overthrows Aemilian and becomes emperor. His son, Gallienus, is made joint emperor
253	Goths invade Balkans
254–8	Gallienus defends Gaul and Rhine frontier against barbarians
257	Valerian issues edict against Christians
ca. May 257	Aurelian possibly Consul Suffectus
257–8?	Goths mount naval invasion of Balkans and Asia Minor
ca 258	Aurelian marries Ulpia Severina
260	Persians under Shapur invade Mesopotamia. Valerian taken prisoner by Shapur. Gallienus sole emperor. Gallienus issues edict of toleration for Christianity. Proliferation of pretenders and rebellions against Gallienus: (i) Postumus defects to create Independent Gallic Empire with Gaul, Britain and Spain (ii) Macrianus rebels in east, defeats Persians and holds Syria, part of Asia Minor and Egypt (iii) Several other rebellions
261 (or 263)	Agri Decumantes overrun by Alamanni
261	Gallienus defeats Macrianus and son
ca. 261	Gallienus appoints Odaenathus, king of Palmyra, to

	defend the Roman east. Odaenathus overthrows last son of Macrianus
262–4	Invasion of Balkans and Asia Minor by Goths. Sack of Temple of Artemis (Diana) at Ephesus. Gallienus defeats Goths
262–7	Odaenathus crushes Persians, recaptures Mesopotamia. Postumus defeats barbarians on Rhine
264	Triumph of Gallienus at Rome
264–8	Gallienus reforms Roman cavalry
267 or 268	Odaenathus murdered in palace plot. His wife Zenobia succeeds in the name of their son Vaballathus
267/8	Goths and Heruli sea-borne invasion of Balkans and Asia Minor. Athens destroyed
268	Goths crushed by Gallienus at Battle of Nish. Revolt of Aureolus
ca. Aug. 268	Gallienus murdered. Claudius II emperor
268	Postumus, emperor of Independent Gallic Empire, murdered. Succeeded briefly by Marius, then by Victorinus
ca. 268	Spain reverts to central rule
ca. 268/9	Zenobia captures Antioch for Palmyra
269	Claudius defeats Alamanni near Lake Garda. Goths invade Balkans
269/270	Claudius destroys Goths at Naissus. 'Gothicus Max.'
270	Zenobia occupies Arabia and Egypt
July/Aug. 270	Claudius dies of plague. Quintillus declared emperor by Senate
ca. Sept. 270	Aurelian declared emperor by army
autumn 270	Quintillus commits suicide. Aurelian back-dates accession to August
ca. Sept. 270	Aurelian defeats Juthungi on Danube
ca. Sept. 270?	Aurelian accepted by Senate as emperor.
ca. Oct. 270	Aurelian makes peace with Vandals. 'Sarmaticus Max.'
winter 270/1	Invasion of north Italy by Alamanni
ca. 270–1	The twenty-year plague finally fades away
Jan. 271	Aurelian takes first consulship
spring 271	Aurelian defeated by Alamanni at Placentia. Riots in Rome. Rebellions by generals. Aurelian defeats Alamanni in three major battles in north Italy. 'Germanicus Max.' Aurelian in Rome. Suppression of civil disorders. Victorinus of Independent Gallic Empire murdered. Tetricus becomes emperor.

	Palmyrene troops occupy Asia Minor
271	Wall surrounding Rome begun (work finished during reign of Probus)
autumn 271	Aurelian sets out to east. Defeats Goths in Balkans, creating enduring peace. 'Gothicus Max.'
	Roman province of Dacia probably evacuated (or 272 or 273)
spring 272	Zenobia/Vaballathus declare themselves as Augusta and Augustus
May/June 272	The general Probus recovers Egypt for Aurelian
May/June 272	Aurelian defeats Zenobia at the Battle of Immae, nr. Antioch
ca. June 272	Aurelian defeats Zenobia at the Battle of Emesa
summer 272	Aurelian besieges Zenobia at Palmyra
summer(?) 272	Death of Persian ruler Shapur I
autumn 272	Palmyra falls. Aurelian makes punitive expedition to Persia. 'Restitutor Orientis', 'Arabicus Max.', 'Palmyrenicus Max.', 'Parthicus Max.', 'Persicus Max.'
272/273	Carpi tribe defeated by Aurelian on middle Danube. 'Carpicus Max.' Possibly 'Dacicus Max.'
early 273	Revolt at Palmyra. Aurelian destroys the city
mid 273	Rebellion by Firmus in Egypt. Aurelian defeats Firmus and recovers Egypt
winter 273/4	Aurelian defeats Tetricus in Gaul
Jan. 274	Aurelian consul for second time
Feb. 274	Gallic mints produce coins for Aurelian. Britain submits voluntarily to Aurelian. 'Britannicus Max.'
274	Triumph of Aurelian at Rome. 'Restitutor Orbis'. Temple of Sun dedicated at Rome.
	Aurelian's legal and monetary reforms at Rome. Improved coinage issued. Increased handouts of food to Roman population
274–5	Aurelian defeats barbarians who have invaded province of Raetia. Aurelian suppresses rebellion at Lugdunum, Gaul
Jan. 275	Aurelian consul for third time
early 275	Aurelian restores fortifications between Rhine and Danube
summer 275	Aurelian sets out with army for Persia. Barbarians crushed in Balkans
Sept./Oct. 275	Aurelian murdered en route. Interregnum – no appointed successor emperor
Nov./Dec. 275	End of Interregnum. Tacitus declared emperor

winter 275/6	Heruli invade Asia Minor. Franks and Alamanni invade Gaul
276	Tacitus defeats Heruli. 'Gothicus Max.' Bahram III becomes ruler of Persians
ca. June 276	Tacitus dies (or murdered). Florian succeeds. Probus declared emperor by army
Sept. 276	Probus defeats and kills Florian
late 276	Probus defeats Goths in Asia Minor. 'Gothicus Max.'
277	Probus takes first of five consulships
277–8	Probus defeats all barbarians in Gaul. 'Germanicus Max.'
278	Probus defeats Vandals/Sarmatians in Illyricum. 'Restitutor Illurici'
279	Probus moves to east. Brigand Lydius overthrown. Usurper Saturninus overthrown
280	Probus at Antioch. Peace with Persians. 'Persicus Max.'
280–1	Revolts of Bonosus and Proculus in Gaul, and of governor of Britain. All overthrown by Probus
autumn 281	Triumph of Probus at Rome
282	Probus sets out for Persia. Civil war in Persia/Armenia between Bahram III and Narses
Aug. 282	Carus rebels in Raetia
Sept. 282	Probus murdered. Carus becomes emperor. Sons Carinus and Numerian appointed joint emperors
282	Carus and Numerian move to Persia
283	Carus defeats Persians, recovers all of Mesopotamia. 'Persicus Max.' Death of Carus. Succeeded by Carinus and Numerian
284	Death of Numerian. Diocles (Diocletian) declares himself emperor
285	Diocletian defeats Carinus in Balkans. Diocletian now sole emperor
286	Maximian joint emperor
293	Diocletian introduces 'Tetrarchy' system to create new emperors. Death of Persian ruler Bahram III
305	Abdication of Diocletian and Maximian
306	Constantine becomes emperor
324	Constantine reunites empire by defeating last of surviving joint emperors. Constantine declares Christianity to be the State religion
337	Death of Constantine. Three sons divide the empire

179

361–3	The new emperor Julian revives paganism. As state religion, it does not survive his death
378	Battle of Adrianople. The emperor Valens is killed in action against the Ostro-Goths. Barbarians heavily recruited to replace legionary losses
405–6	Mass invasion of Gaul by Visi-Goths who cross the frozen Rhine
410	Rome sacked by Visi-Goths
451	Goths and Romans together defeat Attila the Hun
476	Gothic kings rule Rome directly from Gaul. Traditional date of the end of the Roman empire in the west. The eastern (Byzantine) empire survives, with capital at Constantinople
527–65	The Byzantine emperor Justinian recaptures Rome and much of Italy. Codification of Roman Law
1453	The Turks sack Constantinople. End of the Roman empire in the east. Scholars fleeing from Constantinople to Europe provide the seed to trigger the Italian Renaissance

NOTE

1 (i) Clinton, H F, *A Chronology of Rome and Constantinople* (Oxford University Press, 1853; reprinted 1911); (ii) *Dictionary of Greek and Roman Biography and Mythology*, ed. W Smith (J Walton, 1870), Vol. I; (iii) Carey, M and Scullard, H H, *A History of Rome*, 3rd edn (Macmillan 1979; reprinted 1986) – a more modern listing.

Consulships (Ordinarii) known from the Fasti[1]

Inscriptions found at Rome, or in Codex-Calendar of 354, listing all the Roman Consuls. Names in **bold type** denote emperors as consuls. Latin numerals (e.g. 'II') denote that the consul is taking another consulship after a previous one.

Year	Consul I	Consul II
253	Volusianus II	Valerius Maximus
254	**Valerian**	**Gallienus**
255	**Valerian III**	**Gallienus II**
256	L Valerius Maximus II	M Acilius Glabrio
257	**Valerian IV**	**Gallienus III**
258	M Nummius Tuscus	Mummius Bassus
259	Aemilianus (Dexter)	T Pomponius Bassus
260	P Cornelius Saecularis II	C Iunius Donatus II
261	**Gallienus IV**	L Petronius Taurus Volusianus
262	**Gallienus V**	Nummius Fausianus
263	Nummius (Ceionius)	Albinus II Dexter (or Maximus)
264	**Gallienus VI**	Saturninus
265	Licinius Valerian II	Lucillus
266	**Gallienus VII**	Sabinillus
267	Paternus	Arc(h)esilaus
268	Paternus II	Marinianus
269	**Claudius**	Paternus
270	Flavius Antiochianus II	Virius Orfitus
271	**Aurelian**	Pomponius Bassus II
272	Quietus	Iunius Voldumnianus
273	Tacitus	Iulius Placidianus
274	**Aurelian II**	(C Iulius?) Capitolinus
275	**Aurelian III**	(T Nonius?) Marcellinus
276	**Tacitus II**	Aemilianus
277	**Probus**	Paulinus
278	**Probus II**	Virius Lupus

279	**Probus III**	Paternus II
280	Messalla	Gratus
281	**Probus IV**	C Iunius Tiberianus
282	**Probus V**	Victorinus
283	**Carus**	**Carinus**
284	**Carinus II**	**Numerian**
285	**Carinus III** (later **Diocletian II**)	C M Aurelius Aristobulus
286	M Iunius Maximus II	Vettius Aquilinus

The annual consulships were nominally taken together by consuls with equal power. By imperial times, it had become customary to have several pairs of consuls to fill out the year, the first pair giving their names to the year.

The ancient inscriptions, known as the Fasti, preserve for this period only the 'Consularii Ordinarii'. However, a 'Consul Suffectus' might be appointed to replace an ordinary consul who had died or was sick during his term of office. The 'Suffectus' appointment was reckoned to be of inferior prestige to the main consulship, but counted towards the number of times that a consul had held his position. There were also 'Ornamenta Consularia', honorary consulships which could also count towards the number of total consulships held. Because there remain no lists of such consuls, they can only be inferred. For example, the emperor Valerian took his first consulship in year 254, but his third in 255. Unless there is a mistake in the Fasti, he must have been 'Consul Suffectus' (he would hardly have awarded himself the inferior 'Ornamenta') in 254 as well.

NOTE

1   Bickerman, E J, *Chronology of the Ancient World*, revised edn (Thames & Hudson, 1980). Contains the lists of Roman consuls.

APPENDIX C
Concordance of place names[1]

Ancient Name	Modern Name
Abrittus	Nr. Razgrad (Bulgaria)
Adrianople	See Hadrianopolis
Agri Decumantes	Swabia (south-west Germany)
Alexandria	(Egypt)
Amida	Diyarbakir (Turkey; on the Tigris)
Anchialus	Pomorie, nr. Burgas (Bulgaria)
Ancyra	Ankara (Turkey)
Antioch	Antakya (Turkey)
Aquileia	(Italy)
Aquincum	Budapest (Hungary)
Ariminum	Rimini (Italy)
Armenia	(Middle East)
Asia Minor	Turkey
Athens	(Greece)
Augusta Treverorum	Trier (France)
Augustodunum	Autun (France)
Axomis	Axum or Aksum (Ethiopia)
Babylon (Nile)	Baboul, nr. Old Cairo (Egypt)
Batnae	Suruc (Turkey)
Bostra	Busra esh-Sham (Syria; border with Jordan)
Britannia	Britain
Burdigala	Bordeaux (France)
Byzantium	Istanbul (Turkey)
Caenophrurium	Corlu or Simekli (Turkey, n. of Bosporus)
Caesarea	(several; mostly in Turkey)
Caesena	Cesena (Italy)
Carrhae	Haran (Turkey)
Carthago	Carthage (Tunisia)
Catalaunum	Chalons-sur-Marne (France)
Chalcedon	Kadikoy (Turkey)
Coche	(Iraq)

183

Colonia Agrippinensium	Cologne (Germany)
Constantinople	Istanbul (Turkey)
Cremna	nr. Gurmegi (Turkey)
Cremona	(Italy)
Ctesiphon	Taysafun (Iraq)
Cularo	Grenoble (France)
Cumae	Cuma, n. of Naples (Italy)
Cyzicus	Bal Kiz (Turkey)
Dacia	Romania
Dap(h)ne	Beit-al-Maa, nr. Antioch (Turkey)
Doberus (river)	Strimon river (Greece/Bulgaria)
Emesa	Homs (Syria)
Ephesus	Selcuk (Turkey)
Etruria	Tuscany (Italy)
Fanum Fortunae	Fano (Italy)
Gaul	France
Grumentium	Grumento (Italy)
Hadrianopolis	Edirne (Turkey, n. of Bosporus)
Hatra	al-Hadr (Iraq)
Illyricum	(old) Yugoslavia
Immae	(Turkey)
Isauria	Mountaineous region embracing parts of provinces of Galatea, Cilicia and Pamphylia
Ister (river)	Danube river
Istrus	Istria (Romania, Black Sea coast)
Londinium	London (Britain)
Lugdunum	Lyons (France)
Maeotis ('lake')	Sea of Azov
Marcianopolis	Reka Devniya (Bulgaria)
Margum	Orasje, nr. Dubravacia (Yugoslavia)
Mediolanum	Milan (Italy)
Mesopotamia	(between Euphrates and Tigris, Syria/Iraq)
Metaurus (river)	Metauro river (Italy)
Misenum	Miseno (Italy)
Moguntiacum	Mainz (Germany)
Mt Haemus	Gt Balkan Mountains (Bulgaria)
Naissus	Nis (Yugoslavia)
Narbo	Narbonne (France)
Nestus (river)	Nesta river (Yugoslavia)
Nicaea	Iznik (Turkey)
Nicomedia	Izmit (Turkey)
Nicopolis ad Istrum	Nicupe (Bulgaria)
Nisibis	Nusaybin (Turkey/Syria border)
Orontes (river)	Nahr-el-Asi river (Turkey)

Ostia	Ostia (Italy)
Oxyrhynchus	(Egypt)
Palmyra	Tudmor (Syria)
Panticapeum	Kerch (Crimea)
Parthia	kingdom embracing Iran/Iraq/ s. Russia/Afghanistan
Perinthus/Heraclea	Marmaraereglisi (Turkey, n. of Bosporus)
Persepolis	(Iran)
Petra	Petra (Jordan)
Philippopolis (Thrace)	Plovdiv (Bulgaria)
Piraeus	Piraeus (Greece)
Pisae	Pisa (Italy)
Pisaurum	Pesaro (Italy)
Pityus	Pitzunda (Georgia, USSR)
Placentia	Piacenza (Italy)
Ptolemais	El-Manshah (Egypt)
Ravenna	(Italy)
Rhenus (river)	Rhine river
Rhesaena	Resulayn (Syria)
Roma	Rome (Italy)
Samosata	Samsat (Turkey)
Seleucia ad Tigrim	Tell Umar (nr. Baghdad, Iraq)
Serdica	Sofia (Bulgaria)
Sirmium	Sremska Mitrovica (Yugoslavia)
Siscia	Sisak (Yugoslavia)
Smyrna	Izmir (Turkey)
Tarentum	Tarento (s. Italy)
Tarraco	Tarragona (Spain)
Tarsus	(Turkey)
Thessalonika	Salonica (Greece)
Tibur	Tivoli (Italy)
Ticinum	Pavia (Italy)
Trapezus	Trabzon (Turkey)
Tripolis	Tarabulus or Tripoli (Lebanon)
Troy	Troy or Truva (Turkey)
Tyana	nr. Kemerhisar (Turkey)
Uzappa	Ksour Abd el-Melek (Tunisia)
Verona	Verona (Italy)
Zenobia	Nr. Tibni (Syria)

NOTE

1 *Dictionary of Greek and Roman Geography*, ed. W Smith, (John Murray, 1854), Vols I & II.

APPENDIX D

The Biography of Aurelian by Vopiscus

Author's new computer study

The 'Augustan Histories' are an account of the lives of the later Roman emperors, supposedly written by six separate authors of whom one was Vopiscus. However, the real authorship continues to fascinate classical scholars. Despite the authors' own claims that they wrote early in the 4th century, most modern historians prefer to accept Dessau's 1889 conclusion that the Histories were all written by one author late in the 4th century.

Marriott[1] examined the Latin text of all the alleged authors listed in the 'Augustan Histories', using a computer-assisted automatic analysis of average sentence length (i.e. mean number of words per sentence). The 'standard deviation' of these averages provides a measure of the range of each sentence length from their average length. He then compared the 'standard errors of the differences' (SEDs), which are calculated by comparison of their standard deviations, and found that the sentence lengths of each of the six authors were not significantly different. Considering also their grammatical similarities, he concluded that the six authors could be presumed to be the same, particularly as their sentence lengths were significantly different from late 4th-century authors. The following table summarises Marriott's results:

Table I

Author	Mean sentence length	Author	Mean sentence length
Spartianus	16.0	Capitolinus	16.5
Gallicanus	14.2	Lampridius	16.0
Pollio	16.6	Vopiscus	15.4
Augustan Histories average	16.1	Codex Theodosianus (control)	26.2
Anon De Rebus Bellicis (control)	21.7	A. Marcellinus (control)	ca. 36 (depends on book)

Marriott chose to include in the analysis of the 'Augustan Histories' not only each author's main text, but also the text of the many documents that they quoted verbatim, on the assumption that the documents were also forgeries by the one supposed author writing in the late 4th century. His controls were the Latin texts 'De Re Bellicis', the 'Codex Theodosianus' and 'A. Marcellinus', all from the same period. However, if the 'Augustan Histories' are what they claim to be – biographies of emperors by six authors writing early in the 4th century – the documents that they cite, usually taken to be one author's forgeries, would be authentic (at any rate before a later editor got to work on them). Inevitably the documents should possess a sentence length different from the main text of the 'Augustan Histories', and should therefore have been removed before the computer analysis.

Further, a correct control for the 'pure' text of each of the six authors of the 'Augustan Histories', i.e. neglecting the added documents, would be an early 4th-century manuscript as the average sentence length of Latin prose might have changed between the beginning and end of the 4th century. More appropriate controls might be found in the addresses to the early 4th-century emperors within the Panegyrici Latini, a collection of laudatory speeches addressed to contemporary emperors.

Sansone[2] also later queried the computer analysis, on the basis that later editors of the text could have interjected different punctuation from that of the original manuscript. The computer analysis had considered that sentences be terminated with a full-stop, a colon or a question mark, but these might not have been part of the source text, and there remained the problem of how to deal with clauses enclosed within hyphens.

The last problem may be described as a minor difficulty of technique. I have created a new computer program called 'Counter', which, like Marriott's, counts the number of words in a file, assesses mean sentence length and estimates the standard deviation (a measure of the range of mean values). It additionally tests whether there exists a significant statistical difference in mean sentence length between two files. I was surprised to discover that my mean sentence length per chapter measured over the eleven chapters of this book lay in the remarkably tight band of 22.1 +/− 2.5 words, while a book I wrote ten years ago (on a completely different subject) had a mean sentence length over seventeen chapters of 22.5 +/− 4.6 words. There was no statistical difference between the two sets of sentence lengths. We assume, then, that mean sentence lengths can be used to compare authorship.

I have used 'Counter' to explore the biography of Aurelian, the second longest in the 'Augustan Histories'. It was allegedly written by Vopiscus, and contains several cited documents as well as a curious discontinuity in the narrative about two-thirds of the way through the text. It is therefore of interest to compare the authorship of the two parts of the text before and after the discontinuity using Marriott's measure of sentence length, both including and omitting any documents cited in the text. My figures differ slightly from those given by Marriott. The explanation may lie in different source texts, different text accuracies or different programmatic assessments of what constitutes a word. The results are given in Table II:

Table II: Biography of Aurelian

Source	No. Words	No. Sentences	Mean sentence length	Std. Dev.
Aurelian biography (Marriott's original data)	7,740	482	16.1	10.3
Full text of Aurelian biography	7,775	454	17.1	11.6
Full – no documents	5,446	293	18.6	11.8
1st Part biography	5,828	331	17.6	12.5
1st Part – no documents	3,926	200	19.6	12.7
2nd Part biography	1,947	123	15.8	08.7
2nd Part – no documents	1,520	093	16.3	09.3

My data show, from comparison of SEDs by the procedure of Marriott, that there is a better than 98% probability that the differences between the mean sentence lengths of the first and second parts of Aurelian (in both cases after removal of cited documents) are real, rather than due to chance. This is a highly significant outcome, statistically. Does this provide evidence of tampering by late addition of material to the Aurelian biography in the 'Augustan Histories'? The grammatical structures of the two parts of the biography seem to be too similar to support such an explanation. The controversy therefore remains unresolved.

Next, I compared the two parts of the Aurelian biography, after removal of documents, with texts known to be contemporary with their claimed dates of writing. I chose two addresses to the emperor Maximian (AD 286–305) in the Panegyrici Latini, where they are labelled 'X' and 'XI' (Table III).

Table III: Aurelian Biography and Panegyrici Latini

Source	No. Words	No. Sentences	Mean sentence length	Std. Dev.
Aurelian I – no documents	3,926	200	19.6	12.7
Aurelian II – no documents	1,520	093	16.3	09.3
Maximian (X)	2,653	109	24.3	16.3
Maximian (XI)	2,925	134	21.8	15.2

There is not a statistically significant difference between the two Maximian texts, nor between Maximian XI and Aurelian I. However, Maximian X is significantly different (99%) from both parts of the Aurelian Biography. The panegyrics have average sentence lengths comparable with those of the De Rebus Bellicis and Codex Theodosianus, and thus provide no evidence that authors at the beginning of the 4th century AD wrote generally shorter sentences than those at the end of the 4th century.

In conclusion

The same computer technique that was used to verify whether the 'Augustan Histories' were written by one hand, rather than by six authors, can also be used to demonstrate that more than one hand was involved within a single biography by a single author. The two sections of the biography of Aurelian by 'Vopiscus' show signs of having been written by different hands. It is impossible to say whether this was due to one author copying uncritically two distinct sources, one after another, or if a later copyist appended further material to Vopiscus' original text. Analysis of the panegyrics provides no evidence that writers at the beginning of the

4th century used shorter sentences than those at the end of the same century. The theory that a single late 4th-century author wrote the entire 'Augustan Histories' remains unproven, so far as computer analysis is concerned.

NOTES

1   Marriott, I, 'The authorship of the Historia Augusta: Two computer studies', *Journal of Roman Studies*, 69:65–77 (1979).
2   Sansone, D, 'The computer and the Historia Augusta: A note on Marriott', *Journal of Roman Studies*, 80:174–7 (1990).

Index